Evangelistic Sermons at  *Aberavon*

Evangelistic Sermons at Aberavon

D. M. Lloyd-Jones

THE BANNER OF TRUTH TRUST

THE BANNER OF TRUTH TRUST
3 Murrayfield Road, Edinburgh EH12 6EL
P.O. Box 621, Carlisle, Pennsylvania 17013, USA

*

© Mrs D. M. Lloyd-Jones 1983
First published 1983
ISBN 0 85151 362 X

*

Set in 12 on 13 point VIP Garamond
and printed in Great Britain by
Hazell Watson & Viney Ltd,
Aylesbury, Bucks

Contents

[v]

Contents

Contents

Introduction

*

Dr Lloyd-Jones and his family moved from South Wales to London in 1938 but, with the intervention of World War II, it was not until 1944 that they were finally settled in the suburb of Ealing. Somewhere among their possessions was a large cardboard box, once holding clothes and now filled with Dr Lloyd-Jones' manuscript sermons from his first ministry at Bethlehem Forward Movement Church, at Sandfields, Aberavon (1927–38). Unknown to publishers, the box lay in the attic of their home until Mrs Lloyd-Jones recovered it in 1981.

The existence of those manuscripts explains why at this date the first volume actually to be written by Dr Lloyd-Jones can be published. All his major later work already in print, was taken down as he spoke and subsequently edited. For the first ten years of his ministry, however, it was his habit to write one sermon in full every week and for reasons which he explains in *Preaching and Preachers*:

'I felt that writing was good discipline, good for producing ordered thought and arrangement and sequence and development of the argument and so on ... If I am asked which sermons I wrote, I have already said that I used to divide my ministry, as I still do, into edification of the saints in the morning and a more evangelistic sermon in the evening. Well, my practice was to write my evangelistic sermon ... I believe that one should be unusually careful in evangelistic sermons. That is why the idea that a fellow who is merely gifted with a certain amount of glibness of speech and self-confidence, not to say cheek, can make an evangelist is all wrong. The greatest men should always be the evangelists, and generally have been.'[1]

From the large number of sermons which Dr Lloyd-Jones prepared in this way – writing every word from the introduction to the final 'Amen' – the following twenty-one, all based on texts from the Gospels, have been selected.[2] While his evangelistic preaching ranged through the whole Bible, many of his most influential sermons, preached in Sandfields and across Wales in the 1930's, were taken direct from the words and miracles of Christ.

Something of the spiritual effects of these sermons has been indicated in *D. Martyn Lloyd-Jones, The First Forty Years*[3], and the type of hearer who began to attend upon his ministry is vividly depicted in Mrs Lloyd-Jones' *Memories of Sandfields 1927–1938*[4]. For those who have read the history of this extraordinary period in his early ministry these sermons will be of great interest. Mrs Lloyd-Jones writes, 'It is an interesting fact that he was never in any sense tied to these manuscripts. I do not think that he ever took them with him into the pulpit and if they were ever preached in other places than Sandfields, the sermons would never be carbon copies of the original. Points would be emphasised, thoughts expanded and the whole often presented with a new introduction. In other words the writing of the complete sermon was a discipline, self-imposed and only discarded when growing calls on his time made it impossible to continue.'

[1]Hodder and Stoughton, 1971, pp. 215–16
[2]The exceptions to this are the sermons, 'True Christian Discipleship' and 'The Narrowness of the Gospel', taken from *The Christian World Pulpit*, Jan. 16, 1936, and *The Westminster Record*, April, 1936.
[3]Iain H. Murray, The Banner of Truth Trust, 1982
[4]Banner of Truth Trust, 1983

But there is a much more important reason why they should be printed. Dr Lloyd-Jones was called to the pulpit at a time when he was in a special degree filled with concern that no one should mistake, as he had done, nominal Christianity for the real experience of salvation. Too commonly the churches were simply assuming the Christianity of their hearers and as a result there was a general decline both in conviction of sin and in a consciousness of the wonder and power of the gospel. In respect to that situation, it was given to him – in a manner reminiscent of some of the famous younger preachers of other centuries – to proclaim the truth with unusual authority and with passion for the salvation of his hearers.

Those features still live in the words which he wrote. Undoubtedly had Dr Lloyd-Jones edited these early sermons there would have been sentences or phrases which he would have revised. Even at the time, he wrote exclusively for the pulpit, and without the slightest thought of publication. Apart, however, from the most minor revision, supervised by Mrs Lloyd-Jones, and the addition of titles to the sermons (which the preacher himself never used), these pages are as the author himself prepared them for the expectant and often subdued multitudes who heard them fifty years ago.

They are sent out now as examples of what gospel preaching ought to be and in the conviction that they will speak again to the hearts and consciences of other generations.

The Publishers
Edinburgh, January 1983

1: *Christianity – Impossible with Men*

*

And they were astonished out of measure, saying among themselves, Who then can be saved? And Jesus looking upon them said, With men it is impossible, but not with God: for with God all things are possible.   Mark 10 : 26, 27[1]

The more I think about it, the less surprised I am at the apparent and increasing failure of organised Christianity to appeal to the masses in these days; for the plain and obvious fact is that we, who still continue to attend our places of worship, have more or less 'sold the pass' and have neglected or given away that vital principle which ever was and always will be the true heritage of the church of Christ on earth. For it appears, on looking into it, that the church has always triumphed and had her greatest successes when she has preached the two-fold message of the depravity of human nature and the absolute necessity of the direct intervention of God for its final salvation, or, in the words of Peter, that 'there is none other name under heaven given among men, whereby we must be saved.'

A church which preaches that, either attracts or repels, you either join her or hate her and persecute her, – one thing is certain, you cannot ignore her, for her message will not ignore you; it hurts, it upbraids, it condemns, it infuriates, or else it draws and attracts you. You are either right in, or definitely outside. If you feel you can save yourself, then this message insults you and annoys you, you resent the impertinence and the interference with your life; but if you feel you are lost and helpless you run into her open arms for release and salvation.

But how many of us believe that message in these days?

[1]Preached at Aberavon, April 22, 1928, also at Porthcawl and Llandrindod in July and August respectively of the same year.

How many of us believe truly that but for the intervention of God in our lives we would be damned and lost? Does the Christian church in these days give the impression, this exclusive impression, that mankind is doomed apart from the grace of God in Christ Jesus? Are we as certain and as confident of this as the apostles were, as the saints always were, and as the church has always been during every period of religious awakening and revival? This to me is the acid test of church membership, for, after all, everyone must agree that this is the central truth of the Christian message. It was the central truth in the teaching of Christ and has ever been the central truth in the tenets of the church, whether Roman Catholic or Protestant, and that in spite of all the division into sects on other and smaller issues. Now there have been times when men have been concerned about the secondary and smaller issues, when they have divided and argued concerning the implications and the working out of this central truth. They all agreed that man was saved by the grace of God, but differed in the emphasis which they placed on the part of man and the part of God in this scheme, and the stress they laid on free will etc. But, as I see things in these days, the fight is not concerned with implications and corollaries, but rather with the central truth itself. It is no longer the case that any one sect or denomination is on trial, it is no longer a dispute between the various groups and divisions; the whole church, every church which claims the name of Christian, is on trial, ultimate issues are in the balance. That is why some of us so deplore the petty bickering concerning this or that minor matter, and the jealousies of the various sects towards each other – it is futile and childish to be arguing as to which is the best room in the house when the whole house is on fire! The flames are involving all the rooms, each is filled with smoke and our business is to quench the fire, not to save our own favourite bits of furniture.

What I mean is this, that the prevalent and favourite

view in the world, and also, to our shame, in the church in these days, is that every man has his own salvation within him, and that all he needs to do is to exercise this. Indeed it goes further and says that we are all gradually and surely working this process of salvation in ourselves by an evolutionary process which will eventually produce 'the perfect man'. You are all familiar with this view which states that mankind is gradually but surely evolving towards a higher type and how the people who hold it turn to history for material which they claim supports this view. Now it is not at all surprising that the world, that is to say the atheists and others, should hold that view. They must hold some view because, as someone has said, 'No age can live without an inspiration'. Finding things so hopeless at the present time, they quite naturally throw their imaginations into the future and console themselves with the thought that, although we are so bad, we are indeed improving. They point to the great advances that have been made, the hospitals and charitable institutions, the increase of comfort, the way in which pain can be avoided and relieved, the abolition of slavery and of various cruel sports, the abolition of woman and child labour in mines and factories, and the general improvement in the humanitarian instincts of the masses. 'Mankind is gradually evolving to a higher type', they say in view of these things.

Now there is no question but that these great improvements have occurred, but still I ask, do they prove that each one of us is a better man than our forefathers say of 500 years ago or even earlier than that? Does the fact that all these improvements have occurred mean of necessity that you and I obey with more and more facility the voice of our conscience within us? Are we more moral and better men merely because of these things? Is there less jealousy and envy and hatred in the human heart than there used to be? Is there less immorality and divorce in this country than there used to be? What is the difference between slavery and modern industrialism, between the old aristocracy which we have destroyed and the plutocracy which has risen on its ruins?

In the middle of the last century men boasted that their swords had been beaten into ploughshares, but we have seen these very ploughshares smelted into high explosives. There may be less open theft and robbery than there was once, but nothing is commoner in our society today than to have people boasting of how they avoided the customs officers! And on one could go. These charges are all eternal, you and I remain what we ever were. Temptation is as subtle today as it ever was and men are as weak as they were in the days of the Old Testament. 'How dreadful life must have been in those days,' we say. 'They had no comforts, no hospitals and all these other things, and how cruel they were. What a great advance mankind has made since then'. On that negative argument they base their whole case. Because there were no hospitals in the days of David, it is assumed that we are a higher type than the people of those days. But why not read the Bible and take it as it is? Consider the positive things that we read of the people of those times. What are they? We are told that they were tempted, were weak and fell. To what sins? To the very sins that are most rampant amongst us in these days. These facts contradict the modern view, and there are many more which we will leave for the time being.

I really was amazed the other day to find a man stating seriously in a newspaper that amidst the mud, the blood and the gore of the last war, that in that inferno he had almost become an atheist and said that there was no God. Finding men butchering each other in that way and in those terrible conditions, he felt that they were so dreadful that the only conclusion he could come to was that there was no God. Yet, this man, at the same time, believed that mankind is gradually evolving to a higher type! The supposed failure of God becomes the basis of his belief in the gradual success of man. They really cannot have it both ways. 'Mankind has been evolving for millions of years', they say, 'into a better type' and yet from 1914–18 they found men behaving in such a bestial manner as to make them doubt the very existence of God.

What I am concerned with is this, that this notion of gradual development and progress has taken a very firm root in our churches and is believed very extensively. And if this is so, it is then unnecessary to believe that God intervenes definitely in individual lives – it is a gradual process and we are all gradually improving. No wonder that the words 'conversion' and 're-birth' are being heard less and less frequently. No wonder also that men and women in increasing numbers are absenting themselves from places of worship. A Christian church is a place where it is preached that God does intervene and interfere, and that, apart from Him, souls are lost; in her history that intervention has often been seen and witnessed by hundreds and thousands. And as long as the church preached that, and for ever magnified the power of God unto individual salvation, men and women came, sometimes out of fear and for other reasons, but they came because they felt that their attendance might make an eternal difference to their lives.

When the church does not preach the intervention of God, and believes instead in the gradual evolution of men, why! there is no need to go to church or chapel, you can evolve at home or out in the field or on the beach, and that is a perfectly logical position for the world to take up. But it is not Christian and any man who believes and preaches that, according to the teaching of Jesus Christ, has no right to claim the name of Christian. For according to Him men are saved, not by gradual development over millions of years but by a change of life, at times sudden and dramatic, here and now in this present life. If He did not teach that, I ask you in all seriousness, what did He teach? The thrill and the ecstasy have gone out of our churches, we no longer expect conversions, and we no longer get them, for it was of the essence of Christ's teaching that you get from God precisely what you expect or pray for with your whole heart and soul believing. The churches are ineffective and sparsely attended today. Why? Because they no longer believe in the power of God to convert and change men, here and now, but believe instead that the world and mankind are slowly improving. And yet, they persist in calling themselves Christian, which forces one to the conclusion that there must be something amiss with the common idea of what constitutes a Christian, and of what salvation means. For the majority of people, it means that they should avoid sins and do as much good as they can do to one another, and that Christ has become a benevolent reformer who provides us with an example which we ought to imitate.

Well now, let us consider what Christ really did think and say about this question of salvation. Read the Gospels again and I am sure that you will agree with me that nothing is more obvious, nothing stands out more strongly than the truth stated in my text tonight, namely, 'that with men it is impossible' and that it is possible only with God, or, as Paul puts it, 'it is the gift of God'. Let us consider some of the things Christ says.

Take first 'the Sermon on the Mount', that statement which many pretend to believe and on which according to them they build their philosophy and view of life. In reality, however, when you come to examine what they say, they have only extracted certain things which they like and have ignored the rest. What does it ask of us? We must be 'poor in spirit', 'meek', 'merciful', 'pure in heart', 'peacemakers', we must suffer persecution and scorn, gladly and joyfully for His sake. Not only must we not commit lust but we must not even *look* with lust in our eyes, we must love our enemies and bless them that curse us, we must do good to them that hate us, we are asked to be perfect, 'even as your Father which is in heaven is perfect', and many other things of that nature. That was laid down, not as something which was to be expected from the perfect man who would evolve in millions of years, but expected there and then and ever since. Jesus Christ made it perfectly clear that He expected it from His followers at the time. Come now, let us face that challenge, we who are so much better than our forefathers were. What have you to say about it? For myself, with shame and with tears, I have to repeat the words of Jesus Christ, 'With men it is impossible'.

Take again that other statement which He makes in this 10th chapter of Mark to the effect that 'Whosoever shall not receive the kingdom of God as a little child, he shall not enter therein', for in many ways that, to me, is even more difficult than the Sermon on the Mount. What does it mean? It means that my mind and heart and soul, like that of a child, shall become a clean sheet, that I must abolish and blot out all my knowledge of sin and evil, that I must rid myself of all the imaginations, insinuations and innuendoes which have accumulated in my mind since I was a child, that all my worldly wisdom and cuteness and cleverness must go, that I must feel helpless and have implicit trust in Another; in other words, that I must realise my utter dependence, face to face with eternal life and salvation, upon Someone greater than myself. My own knowledge will not save me, my cleverness, my great efforts will be of no avail. I must *feel*, not pretend, that I am helpless and therefore give myself over entirely to God as a child gives itself to its father. I must feel as blank and as void, faced with God, as a child does. 'With men it is impossible'! The more I try to forget myself, and my knowledge and my cleverness, the more I remember them and the more they worry me. The more man 'evolves' the more mind and thought does he develop – will he ever develop the soul of a child?

Consider also the case of the rich young ruler, described in this chapter. 'Thou knowest the command-ment, says Christ to him. 'Do not commit adultery, do not kill, do not steal, do not bear false witness, defraud not, honour thy father and mother'. 'Master, all these have I observed from my youth, replies the young man, and we, who cannot repeat his statement feel that he at any rate is saved. 'No', replies Christ, 'One thing thou lackest – in spite of all this and in spite of the fact that I love you, you must sell your goods and give them to the poor and take up the cross, and follow me'. Keeping the commandments is not enough for this salvation. 'Who then can be saved?' 'With men it *is* impossible' – even with this excellent young man; even with Nicodemus; even with that scribe who later on came to Jesus and who agreed with Him that there is one God, and who agreed about the greatest commandment, concerning whom we are told that 'when Jesus saw that he answered discreetly, he said unto him, "Thou art not far from the kingdom of God"'. 'Not far from the kingdom'. Who then can be saved and enter in? 'With men it is impossible'. 'I believe', says the man, 'that Jesus of Nazareth is the greatest man who has ever lived and I propose to follow Him and to imitate His example because I believe it is the best'. My dear friend, before you set out and begin to strive night and day, and work and sweat and half kill yourself, let me remind you that He has told you Himself that the thing is impossible, for He teaches that 'the kingdom of God is within you', and therefore before you can be in it you must completely change yourself. 'Can the Ethiopian change his skin, or the leopard his spots?' Yes, as easily as you can love your enemies, and enter the kingdom as a child.

It is not difficult to be a good citizen of a kingdom which is external, which is outside you, it is really not very difficult not to steal, and not to commit the common crimes against the law of the land. We might with a great effort be able to be worthy of citizenship in an ideal state such as that conceived by Plato and others, because that would simply mean an avoidance of offences against

others, but this kingdom of God is within. A thought
here is as bad as an act in an external kingdom, a desire is
as evil as a deed, to covet is as damnable as to commit. It is
not very difficult to give up a career, to give up wealth, to
give up prospects, to give up luxury and comfort, to give
your intellect and intelligence and powers and energy to
some good cause – well, if 'not very difficult', it can at
least be done by anyone who has a will and who is
determined. But before one can enter this kingdom of
God, one is asked to give up oneself, pride, ambition, love
of applause, popularity, notoriety and all! Can it be done?
No wonder that the disciples turned to Christ and asked,
'Who then can be saved?' We, here tonight, realising what
it all means, ask the same question, 'O Lord, who then
can be saved?' To which He answers, 'With men it is
impossible' – a man can not save himself, neither can he
save others, it is impossible. We cannot change ourselves,
much as we would like to. We cannot control our lusts,
and passions, our cravings and desires, our tempers and
our jealousies – our natures are stronger than ourselves.
'With men it is impossible'. But by the grace of God that
is not all, that is not the end, for with God it is not
impossible. 'With God all things are possible'.

This to me is the whole of Christianity. The ablest and
the best man in the world cannot save himself, but God,
who can do everything, can save all – even the most
ignorant and the worst and vilest. Now we begin to see
why it was that the publicans and sinners, the outcasts
and the despised followed Jesus Christ. For Christ asks
you and me, not to do the impossible, but to allow God to
do it for us. The Pharisees and scribes objected because
He held the standard so high, and well they might,
because they attempted these things in their own
strength. They lived good lives and felt that He was
making things impossible for them, but at the same time
the drunkards and the fallen women began to see some
hope for themselves. They knew that they had failed and

[9]

had made shipwreck of their lives, and knew that neither they themselves nor any power of man could ever put them right, but when they heard Christ saying that God was concerned, and that He would change their natures and their lives for them, why, they saw hope after all. 'I cannot change myself', says the man. 'I cannot go straight, I cannot fight my temptations'. 'Of course you cannot', says Jesus Christ, 'no man ever can, but God can change you, God can give you power and give you strength. Submit yourselves to Him'. No wonder that Peter said that 'there is none other name under heaven given among men whereby we must be saved.'

Cannot you see it every day round and about you? See the poor drunkard and watch men trying to save him. 'In the name of decency', they say, 'change your mode of life'. No change! 'In the name of manhood and for the sake of your street and town and neighbourhood pull yourself together'. No change! 'In the name of your King and Country I appeal to you to be sober and to go straight'. They responded to that call a few years ago and were prepared to die for that name, but it is apparently easier to die for King and Country than to live for them. 'In the name of and for the sake of your dear old parents and home, do try to go straight'. No change! 'In the name of democracy'. No difference! 'In the name of your political party do go straight and return to your wife.' No change! He cannot do it. 'In the name of and for the sake of your dear little children whom you love, do give it up and change your way of living.' Still he is helpless. Well, is there no hope? Yes, my friends, eternal hope. Throughout the ages men and women as bad as, and worse than, ourselves have failed to respond to all these appeals, but in the name of Jesus Christ, in the name of God, their whole lives have been changed. The impossible has happened and God has done it. They have found themselves changed men.

What is your weakness, your sin? In the name of God

and Christ submit yourself to His power. It is active still, it operates now. Look at some of these men here. You know how they once were. See the change. What has done it? The power of God and nothing else. Ask them how it happened. They cannot tell you. They felt a power dealing with them and shaking them and changing them. You feel you are a desperate case. So were we all, but with God 'all things are possible.' He can change you and re-create you. There is no excuse. Submit yourselves. Think. Pray. For His Name's sake. Amen.

2: *The Saviour of the World*

*

*And many more believed because of his own word; and said
unto the woman, Now we believe, not because of thy saying:
for we have heard him ourselves, and know that this is
indeed the Christ, the Saviour of the world'.*

John 4 : 41–42[1]

There is very little doubt but that what stands between
many people and a full knowledge of Jesus Christ, and
between them therefore and the true joy of salvation, is
the fact that they harbour certain views and prejudices
which make it well-nigh impossible for them ever to
obtain that knowledge and that joy. Up to a certain point
all is well, but beyond that point they will not allow
themselves to go. They have their fixed ideas and their
fixed limits, within which everything else has to be fitted
or else to be left outside.

Now this is a charge which is very frequently brought
against religious people, they are charged with being
narrow-minded, and with having a fixed outlook and a
lack of elasticity. Unfortunately it is, no doubt, true that
there are such people, yet this fault is by no means confined
to them. It is also very prevalent amongst those who are
outside the religious fold. I say this, not because I am
anxious to defend narrow-minded religious people – far
be it from me to do so – but rather because I am anxious
to show the danger of being narrow-minded, whether as a
religious person or as a non-religious person. The man
who says that his religion and his alone is the only true one

[1]Aberavon, late 1920's.

– the man who claims that he has a full revelation, and that unless you agree with and accept all his doctrines and dogmas without any questions – such a man we all recognize to be narrow-minded. But do let us remember that the man who says that all forms of religion are wrong, and who denounces and dismisses all religion and worship as being futile and childish, is equally narrow-minded, is equally exclusive and is equally intolerant and harsh. For the thing that makes a man narrow-minded is that he should close his mind and, as it were, pull down the blinds and close the windows of his soul, and thereby prevent any further light from entering. And when you come to regard it and to think of it in this way, I think you will have to agree that not only does it apply to the scribes and Pharisees who are in the church in these days, but also to the vast majority of the people who are outside, who are glibly dismissing all religious observance and every act of worship.

Now there is a form of this which is widespread in these days and which is responsible, I am quite sure, for a great percentage of the irreligion of our time and of the disregard of the things of the soul. It is the belief which so many people hold, that religion is only meant to apply to a certain type of person, that it was never meant to apply to all. And, of course, I need scarcely add that the people who say and believe that, always believe that they themselves belong to the group to whom religion does not apply. This is a very old fallacy, which is as old as human nature itself, a fallacy which crept in the moment man fell from his state of perfection – the fallacy of creating divisions and distinctions and of dividing human nature into various compartments and groups. Yes, driven to its logical conclusion it is the fallacy of denying the very existence of God. It is not the case with many of these people that they deny the value of religion altogether but that they limit it. They recognize that it does a certain type of person some good. 'It's all right for him', they say,

[13]

'but I am not of that type'. They start out with the view that human nature in themselves is different from human nature in other people and that, therefore, what applies to others somehow does not apply to them. I need not pause to point out the conceit which is inherent in this view and how they patronize those of us who believe in religion. 'You are made like that', they say, 'and no doubt religion helps you tremendously, but we are of a different mould'. And, of course, of a very much finer mould and texture! They can live without religion! 'Religion does not appeal to me,' says this type of man, little realizing that that is so because he has never allowed it to appeal to him, has never given it a chance of appealing to him. He has started out with the idea that he is not of that type, that he belongs to the other group and, as long as he holds that view, religion most certainly never will appeal to him. Indeed nothing can possibly appeal to him except his own ideas. He is not open to any other influence unless it be one which he can fit into his own little scheme of things. I therefore maintain that such a man is narrow-minded, that his outlook is cramped and confined. His view of truth is that it is something which can be fitted into his mind, instead of being something into which his mind ought to be absorbed and fitted. Why! if I only believed and enjoyed the things that I can understand, how small my life would be! How petty and how narrow! The things that make life worth living are the things we cannot understand, the mysteries of life and death, of love and devotion and loyalty and friendship. What cramps a man's life and outlook is that he should believe in and recognize all the world's false divisions of rank and class and occupation and status. What liberates is that a man should believe and proclaim that all those things are artificial, that after all

> *The rank is but the guinea's stamp;*
> *A man's a man for a' that.*

As long as I believe that my nature is somehow different from yours, I cannot have true fellowship with you; as long as I believe that there is something inherently different about my very soul and being, how can I truly sympathize with you and understand; as long as I believe that I need something different to satisfy me from what you need, and that my demands are something special and peculiar to me, of necessity I shall be self-centred and shall feel that there is a barrier between us. But once I recognize that these distinctions are false; once I realize that what counts most is that I am a man; once I realize that my human nature is the same as all human nature; once I recognize in myself the same possibilities of evil and of good, recognize that my essential nature is the same as all others, that I have the same weaknesses and the same possibilities – then I can no longer regard myself as some special being. When I see that, in spite of surface differences and minor descrepancies, I am not essentially different but have the same needs, that mankind in its centre is one, that all men and women in spite of what they may appear to be today are nevertheless men and women with a soul – with a being within them which is eternal, with possibilities which are divine – I can no more be exclusive. And once I recognize that the mere fact that we all sin makes us all equal, quite apart from anything else, once I subscribe to the view that 'one touch of nature makes the whole world kin', then, immediately I know all these things I can feel a fellowship with all men and women, a sympathy and an understanding – a sympathy born of experience of sin, of suffering, of grief, of love, of loyalty, yea, of being fellow-pilgrims on this earth.

That is the view of life and of mankind which Jesus Christ came to teach. He came to banish and to break down all divisions and distinctions whether religious or irreligious, and to proclaim that all men and women are one in nature and that all have the one great need, namely, knowledge of God. He constantly referred to God as the

[15]

Father in order to stress this. Now it often seems to me that the very first thing which we all have to recognize, before we can ever hope to get peace and happiness in life, is that we are all one. In other words, we have to shed all our wonderful ideas about ourselves and recognize that we are but flesh and blood and human clay. The first move on the road to being a Christian is to cease to be a snob, whether social, intellectual or moral. The way to obtain salvation is to seek it and what makes one seek for it is that one realizes one's need of it. That is in reality the great theme of the New Testament, that is the lesson which is taught there, time and time again. The humble ever find salvation, the proud and the arrogant ever remain outside. The people who consider themselves to be in a special and peculiar position never find happiness, for God does not legislate for special cases but for mankind – He provided a Saviour for the world in His Son. It is, therefore, our own responsibility if we consider ourselves to be such exceptional people that a world-Saviour does not include us.

Now there is no finer illustration of these truths, no more apt instance of the working out of this idea, than in this episode here concerning the Samaritan woman and these Samaritans to whom she reported her conversation with Jesus Christ. It is one of those grand stories which reveal the power of God and the power of the gospel. The very casual element which seems to be in it all heightens this and yet shows us the great possibilities there are in life for all of us, if we but take advantage of them. Nothing could well be quite as casual as the chance meeting of Christ and this woman – so unprepared, so unrehearsed. They just happened to meet and to start an ordinary conversation about a drink of water, and from that came the salvation of the woman herself and a large number of people who belonged to her town! That is the very essence of the gospel, the infinite possibilities which are present in the most unlikely circumstances. That is how the gospel has spread, that is how souls have been saved, that is what makes preaching worthwhile and a joy, and that is what sustains us in moments of depression and lassitude.

I like to think of this woman going out of the town that morning to the well, a burdened sinner, and returning a short time afterwards a redeemed soul and a new woman. And life under the guidance of God is full of that – that is why every Christian must be an optimist. You never know when God is going to appear, you never know when the Holy Spirit is going to descend, you never know when Christ is going to deal with you and remove your burden and give your soul release. Just when you are about to convince yourself that the night is going to be endless – the dawn breaks; just when you feel sure that the struggle is all in vain and that your fighting is useless – just then, and when least expected, you are rewarded with victory. That is the Christian story, it is not fiction but fact. Not once but thousands upon thousands of times has that happened, and it is the belief of the Christian, who believes in the unity of the human race and who regards all men and women as being equal, it is his belief that what has happened once can always happen again, that if one man has been saved, all men can be saved. Start with that view of life, start with that view of yourself, namely, that you are like everyone else fundamentally, believe in the possibility of salvation and, sooner or later, you will get it yourself. He who does not expect is he who does not receive.

Now consider all this in the light of these Samaritans and you will see how an honest, open, unprejudiced mind is rewarded. And what I wish to emphasize throughout is the ease with which they might have ignored this woman and her story and, in a sense, how natural it would have been for them to have done so.

Here were these men in the city, following their usual

occupations, probably not thinking of anything in particular, some of them busy in their shops and offices, others doing manual labour, others perhaps walking along the streets, and others standing in the square discussing the affairs of the day, when suddenly this woman appears and begins to shout, 'Come, see a man which told me all things that ever I did: is not this the Christ?' Now they knew this woman well, she was unfortunately a notorious character. At the moment she was living with her sixth husband, or at least one who passed as her husband. That is what we are told of her. We are not told how she came into such a state, we are left to imagine that. We are left to imagine for ourselves the awful picture of that woman's life. Maybe she had started well, maybe she was driven on to the wrong road by her first husband or by someone else. We do not know, but we do know that she was one of those poor unfortunate people who had gone down and down and down, who had broken every moral law, and had desecrated everything that is regarded as being sacred. Her life was in a hopeless tangle, and she was well known as what is usually termed 'a bad character'. Such, of all people in the world, is the one who suddenly announces that she has seen the Christ and that He is just outside the town! – this sinful, forlorn, notorious character, who had fallen so low that she had even ceased to be a topic of conversation, who was so desperate in her sin that no-one was any longer shocked by what they might hear about her. Such was the messenger! Such was the one who called upon the townspeople to come out of the city to see Christ! Why! there's enough gospel in that fact alone to save the whole world, if we could but see it. And yet how slow we are to see these things. How easy to say, 'What is that dreadful woman talking about? What is this hysterical outburst on her part? Thank goodness she has at last found someone who can frighten her and bring her to her senses.' 'Yes,' we may add, 'religion is quite useful in slums and in pagan

countries – such people need something to change them'.
How easy it is to say that and to leave it at that. The
messengers of Christ are strange people, the very last that
you would expect. Ex-convicts, ex-drunkards, ex-wife-
beaters, ex-everything that is bad. Are you prepared to
listen to them? Are you prepared to see that a gospel
which is large enough to save them, is large and broad
enough to deal with you also?

But if the messenger was strange, the message, or the way
in which she put it, was even more remarkable. 'Come,'
she said, 'see a man which told me all things that ever I
did'. What an extraordinary message! Come, see a man',
not who told me all my good points, not who praised me
and told me what a fine woman I was, but one who told
me my faults, told me about my sins, revealed to me my
own past life with all its horror. In other words she said,
'Come, see a man who has told me the truth'. Probably in
those religious services which she seems to have attended
at that mount near the city, she was told everything
except the truth about herself. At last she had found one
whose religion was personal, one who in honesty stated
the bare facts. Are you surprised that this woman should
shout that out in the streets? Surprised that she should
proclaim her own faults? Ah! that is the very secret of the
gospel of Christ. It understands human nature. I am
prepared to listen to a man who is serious and in earnest; I
prefer to deal with one who, though he may lash out and
hurt me and come near to offending me, nevertheless
shows that he is out to help me. Christ exposes our sins
and weaknesses, but God be praised, He does not stop at that.
Why was this woman shouting this about the streets?
Simply because Christ had not only exposed them but had
removed them. Why are Christian converts less ashamed
than others to refer to their past? Why are they so free to
speak about it? Simply because they know it is gone and no
longer counts. It is their way of saying good-bye to it.

[19]

Well, here were these men, listening to this woman. How easy it would have been for them to say, 'There's something in religion after all', and do no more about it. She had definitely convinced them of that, for we are told 'they believed on him for the saying of the woman.' This, to me, is the crucial moment in the experience of most of us. We see others changed as these people saw this woman changed and there are but two ways in which we can react to it. We either say to ourselves, 'Well, we're glad it happened. Religion is obviously suited to that type'. We may even add a regret that we are not of that type, so that it might apply to us also. How many thousands of people there are in this country tonight in that position! Their religion is second-hand. It is only based on the testimony of others, and on accounts of conversions in the mission centres and on the foreign mission field. It has never dawned on them to seek it for themselves, indeed, they are convinced it can never happen to them and therefore never seek it, and on they go through life with heavy hearts and problems unsolved, never knowing the true joy of salvation. Believing, because they have not thought deeply, that what has happened to others somehow cannot happen to them, they never strive to get it and never do get it.

One either reacts in that way or else in the way that these Samaritans reacted. Seeing the change in the woman and hearing her story, they determine to try it for themselves. There is a danger of their sins also being exposed, but what does it matter so long as they get the happiness which she has? What does it matter though the whole world may know your past, and all the town laugh at you because of your penitential tears? What does it matter when you know that God has forgiven that past, and you are filled with the joy of salvation and are thrilled with a new life? And off they go with the woman to see Christ. They could not deny the fact of the change in her, and yet they were not sure about this religious question,

'There is something in it after all, or there may be'. Some of them, perhaps, on the way to the well, felt sorry that they had gone, but on they went, determined now to find out for themselves. In this critical mood they arrived and saw Christ face to face and asked Him to stay with them and talk to them. That is the way. Try Christ before you condemn Him. Give religion a chance in your life before you say it is useless.

Well, you remember the sequel. What had happened to the woman happened to them. Their lives were changed, they knew their sins forgiven, they also became filled with this joy and they turned to the woman and cried, 'Now we believe, not because of thy saying, for we have heard him ourselves, and know that this is indeed the Christ, the Saviour of the world'. In other words they said, 'You made us believe that there was *something* in it, but what you said was a very poor picture of it. Why! this is life and life eternal. This is joy unspeakable. This is release from hell to heaven. This is darkness turned into light. This is misery turned into joy'. It seems a little unkind of them to turn to her and say that, and yet it is not. No one would agree quite so readily with them as the woman herself. How can one describe the glory of the knowledge of the forgiveness of sins? Who can paint an adequate picture of what salvation means? How can one tell fully to others the difference that conversion makes?

These people had gone out of the city believing that Christ was a great prophet, believing that religion and Christianity could save some people, but, having been saved themselves, they immediately saw that He could save all people. 'We know that this is indeed the Christ, the Saviour of the world'! Can you see the barriers falling, can you see the old divisions and distinctions crashing to the ground, can you see the new and divine humility coming in? 'He who has saved me can save anyone, can save the whole world', says the Christian.

Men and women, try Him! Believe that it can happen to

you. Nay, not only believe that, strive for it, work for it, do your best, struggle on, 'wrestle, work, pray,' fight to your utmost – remember that you may be expected to go out to meet Christ. Do this by reading your Bibles, by praying to God for forgiveness and light through Jesus Christ, by fighting sins and temptations to your utmost capacity. Do all *you can* while you pray for God's grace, and may the time soon come when you will come here and say to me, 'Now we believe, not because of thy saying, for we have heard him ourselves, and know that this is indeed the Christ, the Saviour of the world'. Amen.

3: *The Strait Gate*

*

> *Then said one unto him, Lord, are there few that be saved?*
> *And he said unto them, Strive to enter in at the strait gate:*
> *for many, I say unto you, will seek to enter in, and shall not*
> *be able.* Luke 13: 23–24[1]

I imagine that I am stating an absolute truth when I say that there is probably no matter which is so frequently discussed by so many people as the question which forms a part of my text this evening. It is the time-honoured topic of the Sunday School, the Bible Class, the debating society, yes, the public house and every other place where religion comes up as a subject for discussion. There is probably no one here tonight who has not many and many a time taken part in such a discussion, no one who does not hold very definite and dogmatic views as to the true answer. For it is a matter of universal interest because of its universal application. We all hold our views on questions like this, and give our answers with much assurance and confidence – it is surprising to note how every person imagines himself or herself to be an infallible authority on this matter of salvation. 'I cannot believe that God would do so and so', says the person, and therefore would have us believe, quite definitely, that God does not do so and so. If we cannot believe it – well, it just does not happen! For we are all authorities on this matter, particularly those of us who most strongly object to the idea of a pope! Well, here we are confronted with this very question in the New Testament itself, and with

[1] Aberavon, undated.

[23]

our Lord's definite and final answer to it. Now there are one or two preliminary observations that I feel called upon to make before I actually come to deal with what we are told here.

The first thing that strikes us in view of the answer of our Lord is the terrible arrogance and impudence, not to say blasphemous impertinence, which we all display when we discuss this subject. How coolly and glibly do we ask these questions and argue about them! How heedless and thoughtless we really are! The idea of such a question being discussed in the smoke-room or the tap-room, or in the light and frivolous atmosphere of a debating society! This matter of salvation being made use of merely to interest and amuse a number of people for a few hours, or for the purpose of making clever jokes and remarks and scoring futile debating points! How lightly and thoughtlessly do we habitually face this question! We have argued about it and discussed it scores of times, but we have remained exactly as we were; we have expressed our views on salvation times without number but still we have not obtained it. If nothing else happens as the result of the preaching of this sermon, I hope and pray that it will teach us all to realize that this is a matter which must be approached in the spirit of 'reverence and godly fear', that it is the most serious and the most aweful subject with which we shall ever be confronted.

My second preliminary observation arises naturally out of that, and is simply a reminder of the great truth almost universally forgotten in these present days, that the gospel of Jesus Christ is not something which offers itself to us for debate or discussion, but for our definite acceptance and belief. It desires not our approval but demands our obedience. It does not court discussion but rather commands diligence. Our Lord, here, when asked this question, did what He invariably did and what He expects His servants and representatives always to do. He did not so much answer this man's question as tell him what to do. He did not lead discussions, He gave instructions. In other words, if we are really serious about this matter of salvation, and not simply out to be clever, our business is not to express our own opinions and thoughts but to discover the mind of God. That can alone be found in the Bible. There is no other book which is the voice of God, there is no other book which has the same inspiration and authority. Neither is there any other man, nor has there ever been any other person who had the same divine authority to speak on these matters as Jesus Christ our Lord and Saviour. You will find that many men have returned a very different answer to this question from the one we have here. The popular writers of today would, almost without exception, give a very different answer. It is for you to decide whether you prefer to believe the passing and ephemeral theory of some person who happens to be alive and popular today, as so many others, now long since forgotten, were popular in their day, or whether you are prepared to listen to this Book and to this Person who speaks in and through it. Here is something which has stood the test of twenty centuries, here is a view which has brought light and release to innumerable souls, many of them the greatest and noblest the world has ever seen. This alone remains. Other theories have come and have gone, have had their vogue but have soon ceased to satisfy. It is for you to decide. All I would do would be to warn you to be very careful, and to appeal to you with all my might to hearken unto the answer given by Jesus Christ our Lord. I do not know what view of salvation was held by the one who originally asked this question, and I do not know what view you may hold of it individually here tonight, but, whatever our view, the answer of Christ is still the same, 'Strive to enter in at the strait gate'.

Let us look for a while at this word 'Strive' and consider

exactly what it means, for I think that we shall be able to shew that much confusion exists as to its precise definition. 'The important thing for all of you who desire salvation and are concerned about it,' says our Lord, in effect, to this man and to those who were with him, 'the important thing for you is to realize exactly what salvation means, and with steadiness and constancy of application, and earnestness of endeavour and singleness of aim to strive after it.'

At some time or other the Spirit of God visits each one of us and moves us and disturbs us. It may be in a meeting such as this, or while singing some hymn, or perhaps at the death or funeral of someone who is very dear to us. Perhaps, again, in some accident face to face with our own death, or in one of many other possible circumstances and positions, the Spirit of God deals with us. We become conscious of a power and a presence that we have never felt before. We become melted and softened for the time being. It suddenly dawns upon us that we have not been what we ought to have been, that our lives have been sinful and selfish, that all along we have been worldly and have forgotten God and His eternal love in Jesus Christ. And while we thus feel sorrow and remorse about our past and our sins already committed, a feeling comes at exactly the same time, urging us to a better life in the future. In a kind of sudden glimpse, we see what a glorious and happy life the good and Christian life really is. We long to be better and purer and cleaner, we yearn for that straight and noble life which suddenly becomes revealed to us, and then and there we decide that we shall be better in the days that are to come. We see it all so clearly and we cry partly in sorrow, partly in joy. Now you all know what I mean by that, for you all have experienced it at some time or other, probably more times than you can well remember. What is the meaning of such an experience? It is the voice of God calling us from sin unto salvation. It is our heavenly Father sending us a message of pardon and forgiveness and calling us back to our home. It is the Spirit of God striving with our souls and urging us to quit our sin and seek after holiness. There is not one living but that, at some time or other, he or she has had some such experience.

Now the question that arises therefore is, What use have we made of it? What has been the result and sequel of these moments of tenderness and remorse? What has been the outcome of these occasions when we have been alarmed at our own sinfulness and coldness, and terrified at the thought of the doom that must inevitably await us, were we to cross over to eternity in such a state and condition? How have we improved these gracious occasions when God has spoken to us in spite of our sinfulness? Can we honestly claim, all of us, that we have taken full advantage of them and that, realizing their gracious and loving nature, we have striven with all our might after salvation and, forgetting all else, and allowing nothing else to interfere or side-track us, have concentrated the whole of our energy and attention upon this all-important matter? It is because I know full well that we have not, that I draw attention to this matter tonight, and propose to illustrate the various ways in which we tend to misuse and abuse these gracious times when God talks to our soul. I cannot hope, in one sermon, to deal with all the mistakes that men make in this respect; I shall choose some of the most obvious and most common errors.

(1) Nothing is more common than for men and women, when thus spoken to by God and thus convicted by His Spirit, to do all they can to rid themselves as soon as possible of the uncomfortable and painful feeling which it evokes. They get home from the service, or from the funeral, or from the hospital, or wherever they happen to be when God visits them, and, at once, they search for some means whereby to get rid of the feeling of unhappiness which they have. There is a voice within them telling them to keep quiet and to be alone and to

allow God to do His work, telling them to avoid company
and conversation and everything that will tend to distract
them from the contemplation of their own soul and their
God. But there is another voice telling them not to be
foolish and silly, not to allow themselves to be made
miserable and morbid, that brooding and thinking over
these things can never help them, that the sermon has done
its work, that they have felt what they were meant to feel,
and that the effect will continue again, and that therefore
in the meantime there is no point or purpose in their
remaining alone. And how this second voice appeals to us
and suits our mood! For we dislike being serious and
unhappy; we do not enjoy thinking of ourselves as sinners
and lost souls. It is upsetting and uncomfortable, and, to a
nature that desires nothing but happiness every moment,
most galling. It craves for quick and immediate release,
and falls back upon any expedient that promises to relieve
the misery and the strain. How well this is illustrated in
the Bible! Do you remember the story of Cain? God spoke
to him and warned him and threatened him. And Cain
winced and said, 'My punishment is greater than I can
bear'. He realized the full terror of the Lord, but instead
of improving this knowledge and doing his utmost to
please God and make atonement for his past, we are told
that he 'went out from the presence of the Lord, and
dwelt in the land of Nod' and 'he builded a city' and
became very rich. How natural it was! He had
committed that great sin and it was worrying him. God
was speaking to him and giving him no rest; but Cain was
not truly repentant. All he desired was immediate peace
of mind and God's method was such a prolonged and
laborious one. So he went into business and made
himself as busy as he could! 'I'll work as hard as I can', he
said. 'I'll plunge into business. I'll give myself no rest and
no time to think'. And he became rich and built a city.
Anything to have peace of mind, though it may mean
working like a slave. I need not apply the story. How

many poor souls are trying to do the very same thing today! Trying to forget and bury their past by an active busy life, foolishly imagining that sin can be crowded out by an active, strenuous, existence.

But take the case of Saul, first king of Israel, and observe another way of getting rid of the conviction of sin. Saul had gone wrong and had departed from the ways of the Lord. And he knew that he was wrong and was unhappy about himself. Moreover, from time to time, the Spirit of God would deal with him, would remind him of his own glorious beginning, of the way in which God had singled him out and called him to be king, and would then point out to him the shame and pity of his transgression. And Saul would be terribly miserable and unhappy. It is said that 'an evil spirit from the Lord troubled him'. Here was this great man wretched and miserable and casting a gloom over the entire court. But someone suggested to him one day that they should send for an expert player on the harp and get him to play to the king every time these evil fits came on. And Saul consented and said 'Provide me now a man that can play well and bring him to me' (1 Sam. 16:17) And they sent for David and he came and played. This is what we are told. 'And it came to pass, when the evil spirit from God was upon Saul, that David took an harp, and played with his hand: so Saul was refreshed, and was well, and the evil spirit departed from him' (1 Sam. 16:23). What a picture! This great soul which had gone wrong, gradually sinking to perdition. God in His infinite grace, trying to stop the rot and arrest his destruction, but the man, instead of thanking God and improving the occasions, doing everything he could to silence the voice divine. Saul goes to hell while David and his harp silence and drown the voice of God. Ah! I need not go on. We all know what I mean. You go home from chapel feeling serious and sad and unhappy. But instead of allowing the gracious work to go on, you pay a friendly call upon someone or other and you begin to talk and gossip, or you turn on your wireless set, or read a novel, or do one of the many hundred things that suggest themselves and which, though harmless perhaps in themselves, as David's playing upon the harp was, nevertheless at that particular moment are the tool and voice of the devil to frustrate the work of God in your soul.

(2) There are others who misuse these heaven-sent opportunities, not exactly in that way but in another way which is equally futile. These are guilty, not so much of quenching the spirit, as of allowing it to die gradually. They search after salvation by fits and starts. They make efforts, but they are spasmodic and temporary. Every time God deals with them, they recognize His voice and for a while try to improve and reform. They come to chapel and look serious and earnest. They attend regularly for a while and avoid this evil and that, but it only lasts for a short time. Soon, they begin to slacken off and to be less careful and eventually they cease to come at all and slide back into their old condition. But after a while they reappear once more and go again through exactly the same process. To all such, who definitely know that God has spoken to them and who from time to time have longed for salvation, the command of our Lord is, 'Strive!' Be steady, be constant, set your teeth and brace back your shoulders! Be diligent, be persistent, apply yourself whole-heartedly and with full determination! The man who succeeds in business and at his work is not the man who only works when he feels like it and irregularly, but the man of grit, the man of determination, the man who is there in spite of everything. '*Strive* to enter in at the strait gate'. For if you do not, you will end exactly where you started in spite of your occasional and spasmodic efforts.

(3) There is then the group which consists of those who may be described as the people who are always 'hanging round' near the gate, but who are very careful not to strive to enter and press through it. They know that that gate

leads to life and they hope to get through it at the end, but in the meantime there are many things that they are very fond of on the outside and they do not intend to relinquish them until the very last moment. They come to chapel regularly and very often are church members, they decide that they will lead a better life and try to perform good works in the future. Oh yes! they are very near the gate. They are just outside it, but they use their very proximity to the gate to silence the voice of God within their souls. They soothe themselves with the thought that they are church members, that they avoid certain sins and do good, and thus they silence that voice which urges them to go still further on, to be whole-hearted in their religion, to forsake the world entirely, to strive with all their might to enter through the strait gate. Their very nearness to the gate keeps them on the outside of it. If any such be here tonight, and I am sure that there are, the message of Christ to you is 'Strive!' Get on! Do not stop. Do not feel satisfied. Finish with that sin! Give up that worldly enjoyment, which though fairly innocent is nevertheless holding you back. If you desire full salvation you must give your entire heart to God. Attending chapel is not enough. Church membership in itself does not save. Strive! Wrestle and fight and pray!

(4) There is then that very large group which consists of people who silence the voice of conviction within themselves by quoting Scripture and discussing theological doctrines. Instead of making full use of the visitation of God's Spirit that they have had, instead of striving after salvation with all their might, instead of listening to that inward prompting which ever urges them to take the right steps, instead of believing what our Lord Himself laid down as a rule in this respect when He said, 'If any man will do his will he shall know of the doctrine, whether it be of God', they do nothing, but immediately proceed to discuss the doctrines. And the favourite doctrine in this connection is the doctrine of election and

[31]

predestination. Those interested in this, point to certain men and women who, in spite of making no effort whatsoever after holiness, and who, rather, led a thoroughly sinful and wicked life, were suddenly arrested and converted by the power of God. Then they quote scriptures to the effect that justification is by faith only and of grace, that all is a gift from God and that no man can possibly save himself. It all sounds so correct and so scriptural and yet it contains one of the most subtle errors imaginable. 'What is the use of striving', they ask, 'when no amount of striving can possibly save anyone?' Therefore they decide to continue as they are and to do nothing! What a terrible and blasphemous error, what perverted notions of the doctrines of Holy Scripture! How they give themselves away! They are quite right when they say that no man can save himself, that salvation is the gift of God. It is the conclusion they draw that is wrong. God *has already* dealt with them when He has disturbed them. The Spirit *has already* convicted them. And although they realize that they can never earn or deserve salvation, they surely ought to yearn and long for it. And the moment any person so desires salvation, and realizes what it means, and sees for the first time his desperate plight and condition, though he cannot achieve salvation, he can at least give up his sin, and mend his ways, and do his utmost to lead a new life. He cannot save himself it is true, but he can hate himself and his sin and do all he can to get as far away from that as is possible. No, my friend, there is no scriptural authority or sanction from church doctrine for you to remain in your gutter of sin, awaiting some heavenly visitation. Prove rather that you desire salvation by doing your utmost to get away from that which is the greatest enemy of salvation, namely, your sin. It is not for you to be concerned and to argue about the plan of salvation. It should make no difference whatsoever to you what has happened to someone else. Do you desire to be saved? Are you tired of sin and of yourself? Do you long for release and for a new life? If you do, prove that you do, prove that you are genuine, prove that you hate sin by getting up out of it and leaving it. 'Strive to enter in at the strait gate'. The Scripture does not say that your striving will get you through, what it tells you is to strive. And all who are seriously concerned about salvation do strive, of necessity.

(5) The last error with which we shall deal tonight is the error of relying in these matters upon what is thought to be the love of God. Men cannot believe that all this struggling and striving and self-denial and self-crucifixion is necessary, and that only some people are to be saved while others are damned. 'God is love', they say, fondly imagining that that is somehow going to save them. All I would ask such persons is this, On what do you base your belief in universal salvation in spite of what we do? What is your authority for believing it? What is the sanction behind it? Do you know of any greater authority than Jesus Christ and His recorded sayings in this Book? Have you any authority at all apart from what you feel, and what you would like to believe? Consider, my dear friend, and realize that because you like a thing it does not follow that it is true and right. For you know already that most of the things you like are wrong. Your feelings and mine are no standard, for we are changeable and sinful. See the folly of pitting your opinion against this Book and against the whole revelation of God to man. You quote the parable of the prodigal son and say that you think of God like that, like that father. But consider that parable. It is true that the father forgave all and received his prodigal son with open arms and with a very warm welcome. God will do the same to you on the same conditions. But consider what had happened before the father fell upon his son's neck and kissed him! The poor prodigal had had an awful fight and struggle. He had risen up out of his sin, had ignored all the taunts and jeers of his fellow sinners,

had turned a deaf ear to all their arguments, had decided and determined to leave that strange country once and for ever, and finally, taking his courage in both hands, and screwing up his will, he had striven against all the odds and arrived home. Oh yes! God, like that father, is waiting for you and is ready to pardon and receive you. But have you left the strange country yet? Have you quitted your sins? Have you parted with your sinful friends? Have you made any move at all towards home? The love of God will certainly receive you and forgive you, but not until you, like the prodigal, feel yourself utterly and entirely unworthy of it.

I had thought of dealing with the way in which we should strive, but I must leave it for tonight. I have, in fact, indicated clearly, by what I have already said, how this is to be done. It means application, constancy, steadiness, reading God's Word, prayer and the parting with all that we know is wrong and sinful. But let us just look at some of the reasons which should move us to this striving, and which make striving imperative and urgent. They are all suggested in this paragraph.

There is, first of all, that reason we have so often considered together before, namely, that there is a time coming when it will be too late, and striving will be impossible. There is a time coming when the master of the house will have 'risen up and will have shut to the door'. Oh! let this consideration have its full weight with you. People sometimes come to me and ask why I preach such long sermons. 'Why not end off where you were?' they say, 'It was an excellent sermon and quite complete in itself up to that point. Why not keep over these reasons for striving until the next time you preach, and make a separate sermon of them?' That is very nice and very complimentary. But, dear soul, there may be no next time in your history or mine. This may be the last. The matter is urgent. Strive! Do not lose a moment! 'The master of the house' will rise for certain, and you never know when that will be.

The second reason I find here for the urgency and the necessity for striving, is the 'straitness' or 'narrowness' of the gate. There are many, as I have already said, who take up their position near the gate, who are anxious to get through just before they die, who hope to get to heaven and to obtain salvation, but who desire to make the best of this world as well. They live a worldly life and will not part with certain things for the sake of Christ. They make certain reservations and cannot see why this and that is not consistent with a Christian and a saved life. Oh yes! they hope to get through at the end, at the last moment. So they keep near the gate all their lives. They regard the people who live a long way off from the gate as being fools and lunatics. 'How can they hope to get through', they say, 'living such a long way off?' As for themselves, they feel they are all right because they are so near the gate! How blind and tragic they are! For they forget two vital and all-important facts. The first is that the entry is 'strait', is narrow, indeed so narrow that it admits only one person at a time. It is a kind of turn-stile. The second is that there are so many people who are relying upon the same dodge, the same hope – 'many I say unto you, will seek to enter in'. Do you see the picture? There they all are near the gate, with one eye certainly on the gate, the other on the world and all it has to give. Suddenly, they realize that the master of the house is shutting the gate, so they all make a mad rush and a wild dive for the door. But alas! the way is so narrow, the entry is so confined and they are such a crowd, that all they succeed in doing is to block up the road, hinder one another, create a state of panic and produce a stampede. The more frantic and violent they become, the more impossible do they make it for one another to get in! There they are, struggling and cursing and fighting and groaning, blaming each other

[35]

and stamping upon each other. Each one out for himself or herself, and all in their madness trying at the same time to get through a gate which only admits one at a time. Do you now see the reason for striving while there is still time and before it is too late?

But after a while this mad struggling crowd comes partly to its senses and has a conference and appoints the foremost to knock upon the door and ask for admission. 'Lord, Lord', they say, 'open unto us'. But he will answer and say, 'I know you not whence ye are'. To which they reply cheerfully and full of hope 'We have eaten and drunk in thy presence, and thou hast taught in our streets'. But he will still say, 'I tell you, I know you not whence ye are; depart from me, all ye workers of iniquity'. The fact that you have been standing near the gate all your life makes no difference whatsoever, for the fact still remains that you are outside it. A nodding acquaintance with Christ and His teaching does not save. 'Yes,' says 'the master of the house', 'I know that you have been standing near the gate all your life. I know that you have gone to chapel. I know you have given money to good causes and deserving cases. I know you have often cried over your sins, and bemoaned your sinful life. But what did you do about it when I warned you that Sunday night in Aberavon? What effect have all my repeated pleadings with you had upon you? Did you give up your sin? Did you strive with all your might? I know you've kept near the gate all your life, but why did you persistently refuse to come in, when I begged of you to do so? Why did you keep on clinging to those worldly things? Ah! I may well have been in your street, as you say, but what I really desired and tried to do, was to get into your soul and heart'. My dear friend! that is the position. Interest in salvation is not enough. Have you got it? Have you striven for it? Where are you? Are you definitely on the inside of the gate? If not, begin to strive at once. Never rest until you *know* you are forgiven.

The terror and horror of the condition of those who

remain outside, we have already depicted – their useless remorse and eternal agony. Too late, they wake up to a realization of what they have missed and forfeited; too late, they realize that they have sold eternal bliss for a moment's pleasure. There, inside, they can see those who have come from 'the East and from the West, and from the North and from the South', men and women who had many handicaps as compared with themselves, but who believed the Word of God. How terrible is their state. An eternity of vain and useless regrets.

Consider, on the other hand, the happiness and joy of those who are inside. A knowledge of sins forgiven, a certainty of God's love, safe protection against the wiles and entanglements of the devil, a never-failing source of power to rely on, and an assurance of unclouded happiness and joy after death, and to all eternity. Consider it, my dear friends. Realize that it is possible for *you*. Strive for it and after it with all your might and main!

Lastly, and perhaps most important of all, strive with all your might, were it merely that you may realize how weak and helpless and hopeless you are, and how utterly impossible it is for you to win through in your own strength. The most humble people this world has ever seen have been the saints. It is the people who do little, that talk a lot about what they do, and pride themselves in it. The man who is really busy and who is striving for all he is worth, has no time to boast and talk. The more you do, the more you will realize and learn how little you have done and can do. The more you strive after salvation, the more will you discover the holiness and purity of God. The more you see that, the more hopeless will you see yourself. And, finally, you will so realize your utter hopelessness that, imagining that you are getting further from the gate each day, you will cry out in despair to Christ to have mercy upon you and to deliver you. And just there when you are about to fall and faint in sheer exhaustion and despair, a hand will suddenly appear and take hold of you and steady you and draw you in through the door. For when you give up and give in and realize your own strength is not enough, you are on the very threshold and will be taken in. In the Name of God, therefore, I beseech you, 'Strive to enter in at the strait gate'. Amen.

4: *Why Men Disbelieve*

٭

*How can ye believe, which receive honour one of another,
and seek not the honour that cometh from God only?*
John 5 : 44[1]

One of the most outstanding characteristics in the
ministry of our Lord was the wideness of His appeal, the
all-inclusiveness of His gospel. He broke down all the old
barriers and distinctions. He paid little attention to the
time-honoured class divisions and differences. His Spirit
was not partisan, and He was not the product of any
particular school, His appeal was never to any particular
group or to any particular something in certain people –
He had come to speak and to appeal to man, not to any
special group of men. That is clearly an outstanding fact
about His ministry. It was this very fact that brought
Him into such constant trouble with the religious and
political hierarchy of His own day, it was this which
eventually brought Him to the cross and that cruel death.
What annoyed the religious authorities most of all was
that He was 'a friend of publicans and sinners', that He
actually consorted with them and ate food with them.
They stood aghast and shocked when they found that He
'received sinners' and made friends of them. They felt
that no truly religious man could possibly do such a thing.
According to their conception of religion, no man who

[1]Aberavon, September 14, 1930.

truly worshipped God could conceivably find any pleasure or profit in the company of notorious and obvious sinners. The fact, therefore, that our Lord spent so much of His time in the company of such people, and seemed to regard them as being candidates for God's love and eternal life quite as much as the Pharisees and scribes, led the latter people to regard Him as an impostor and an enemy of God. 'No!' they said, 'this man is not the Messiah, this man is not the expected One of Israel; his life and teaching prove that he is an enemy of true religion. He calls himself the Son of God, but in reality he is "a gluttonous man and a winebibber, a friend of publicans and sinners".' He offended the Pharisees and scribes for that reason – that He held out a hope for all, even for the publicans and sinners, the most hopeless of sinners.

But this same characteristic of Christ's teaching is equally apparent when we compare it with every other form of teaching. The breadth of scope, the all-inclusiveness of the gospel, becomes very apparent when we compare it with every other teaching which has ever been held before mortal man. How exclusive and confined in their scope were the Stoics and the Epicureans, how confined is every human philosophy and theory of life! All demand intellectual power and learning, all have, of necessity, to postulate something which can be the possession of but a few. Take any teaching about life that you will, outside this gospel, and what has it to offer to the average, ordinary man and woman? Above all, what has it to offer to the lowest and most backward type of humanity? Herein the gospel differs from all else, herein the Christian way of life is unique. It recognizes no distinctions and no differences. Our Lord came to bring 'the common salvation' and 'the common people heard him gladly'. His gospel, He said, was not for Jews only, or for religious people only, or for any sect or any group or any particular people. His message was that 'God so loved *the world* that He gave His only begotten Son that *whosoever* believeth in him should not perish, but have everlasting life.' Nothing could be wider or more inclusive. Those were His constant words – 'the world', 'whosoever'! He seemed to see a hope for everyone and everybody!

But here in this passage with which we propose to deal this evening, we find a strange limitation. Here we find this Person – whose ministry was characterized above all else by the wideness of its scope and the hope He held out for all – here we find Him stating quite definitely that for a certain class of persons, there is no hope whatsoever! He utterly despairs about these and can see no way in which they can be saved and inherit eternal life. Listen to His words! 'How *can* ye believe?' Never did he say anything with greater emphasis or certainty! Never did He speak with such a note of despair in His voice! He has tried them along all the known and possible avenues of approach, He has exhausted all the possibilities. He has threatened them with thoughts of the last Judgment, He has reasoned with them on their own level and from their own particular standpoint and He has appealed to them. But all is in vain. 'How *can* ye believe?', He cries in despair. 'Your case is hopeless'. Such is His verdict. He saw infinite hope for the wretched publicans; the old feud and barrier between the Jews and Samaritans did not in any way hinder Him from pardoning the woman of Samaria and many of her friends; the woman actually caught in the very act of sin was by no means outside the pale and scope of His gospel; the miserable denial of Peter was easily forgiven; the thief on the cross presented no difficulty; why, even those who were possessed by and filled with devils and evil spirits, and who were beside themselves in sinfulness, were not without hope! But here are people who are definitely hopeless. In this case, there is an insuperable barrier. People who 'receive honour one of another, and seek not the honour that cometh from God

[41]

only' cannot possibly believe in our Lord and Saviour Jesus Christ, and therefore cannot possibly please God and have the reward of eternal life. There are many, many obstacles to faith, every sin indeed is an obstacle, but this is the only one for which there is no hope. This therefore is the greatest enemy of faith, the greatest enemy of the Christian truth and gospel. Of all the enemies that the church has to fight, sin and excess and vice and lust, the most deadly and most dangerous enemy is what is generally called humanism. The more we think of one another, the more we honour one another, the more we live for one another and for this world, the less do we think of God, the less do we honour God, the less do we live for God's glory. Never was there greater need for the proclamation of this truth than during these present years when we are witnessing the verification of our Lord's statement.

First, let us look for a moment at the fact which is contained in this statement that – People who receive honour from one another, and seek not the honour that cometh from God only, cannot believe in me and in my Name. Are we not witnessing that during these present years? What is the great claim and boast of the average man today? It is that we as a race have advanced and developed from our barbaric and primitive stage, and that in every conceivable way there has been a marked and notable progress in the humanitarian instincts of the race. It is claimed that we are more refined, more sensitive and more sympathetic. The old idea of each man for himself has gone. We are now considerate and kind. We hate hurting each other or in any way causing pain to each other; we dislike competition and rivalry and believe in co-operation and mutual aid. We criticize the old, blunt, unvarnished and direct forms of speech and business methods. We are out, first and foremost, to be honourable and gentlemanly! We are even prepared to sacrifice profit and money in order to attain that end! We pride ourselves on our honourable natures, our gentle-manliness, our kindness and our consideration of others. We respect one another and are proud of the way in which we have advanced, and we are always congratulating ourselves and one another upon this marked improve-ment. Look at any sphere of life that you like and you will find that this is the case. Our newspapers every morning are full of this mutual congratulation in the political world, in business and in the various professions. Our one object and ambition seems to be that we should live in such a way that everyone shall praise us and have a good word to say for us. As long as the people say of us that we are honourable and gentlemanly, or good at sports, we care little for anything else. Our 'good name' is definitely our god; our greatest ambition is to do and say things which shall be well-pleasing in the sight of our fellows. But I need not elaborate. You are all familiar with it. You read it in the papers every morning, you hear it without ceasing wherever men and women congregate together. That we receive honour of one another is beyond dispute.

What of the other side of the picture as painted by our Lord? This again is painfully and devastatingly true. Our age is characterized by its desecration of everything that is sacred and of God. The Lord's Day is broken defiantly, boastfully and with pride. The Lord's Name is taken in vain and blasphemed. His Word is laughed at, criticized, derided, and whenever it is quoted at all, it is generally made use of for the purpose of some blasphemous so-called joke. The sanctity of marriage, the glory of chastity and purity, the supreme virtue of humility, meekness and disinterested love and all the great principles of the Christian religion are not only being ignored, but are being spat upon and held up to ridicule. Everything that is of God is at a serious discount, the Christian church has scarcely ever, in her long history, fallen upon more evil days. Need I say any more? Is the case not clearly proven?

[43]

Never have men thought more of one another, never have they thought less of God. Never has the humanitarian instinct of the race been so highly developed, never has the divine instinct been so conspicuously absent. Never have we been so gentlemanly, never have we been less godly. Never have men been so honourable, never have they been less holy. As the world admires itself more and more, it adores God less and less. As its wonder at the advance of man increases, its worship of God decreases. 'How can ye believe, which receive honour one of another, and seek not the honour that cometh from God only?' That they cannot believe is made painfully and pathetically true and obvious during these present years. Do *you* believe in Christ? Is He to you, your Saviour and Redeemer? Is He to you the Son of God come down from heaven to live and die and rise again for your sake? Do you seek above all else the credit and the glory which come from Him? If not, is it for the reason given?

Lest it may be, let us look into this matter further and discover why it is that belief is impossible for such people.

It is made quite clear in the context that they cannot believe because they are *superficial* people. They skim and skip lightly over everything and never look deeply into anything. Our Lord says of these particular representatives of this group to whom He was speaking, that 'for a season' they were willing to rejoice in the light supplied by John the Baptist (John 5:35). Yes! 'for a season' only, as long as John was new and fresh and the appeal of the novel and unusual still continued. But they soon tired of him and turned back to their old ways. They went to listen to him for a few times, but as soon as their curiosity was satisfied, or as soon as John began to get down to the very vitals and main essentials of his teaching, they tired and went home. They never really listened attentively to John, they never put his teaching into practice, they never truly became his disciples. No! they were only interested in a

[44]

new point of view, the new idea or the new voice. Ah, but how many such people there are today! They follow religion 'for a season'; some of them come to the house of God almost as regularly as the seasons come year after year. You see them for a while, then they disappear again. They come and go and attend on the teaching of God's word spasmodically. No! my friend, you will never know the salvation of God in Christ Jesus as long as you are merely content to consider it 'for a season', now and again. You must *seek* the honour that cometh from God only, and not be content with something that you can receive easily and without effort! This superficial mind is fatal to true religion.

Our Lord was so anxious to impress this lesson upon these people that He refers to it a second time. 'Search the scriptures', He says, 'for in them ye *think* ye have eternal life' (verse 39). Their trouble was that they *'thought'* they had eternal life in them. Mere possession and reading of the Scriptures, they thought, was sufficient. They took that for granted. They assumed it and went along quite gaily and contentedly. They were always talking about their Scriptures and always reading them. But they were doing so in a superficial manner. They were not 'searching' them, not reading them intelligently and deeply, not thinking about what they read. Had they but done so, they would have discovered that the Scriptures and, in particular, Moses, testified of Christ. But they did not, and that because they were superficial in their outlook. Even reading the Scriptures could not save them; nay more, the words of Christ Himself could not affect them (verse 47). The men and women of today write in the newspapers about their religion, about God, about Jesus Christ; they are always talking about these things, but, as we have already seen, it all leaves them quite unaffected as regards their moral and spiritual nature. Superficial talk, glib phrases, ready arguments and an easy familiarity with certain facts, will avail you nothing. The question is, Are you truly searching the Scriptures, are you seeking with all your heart and soul for that 'honour that cometh from God only'?

Beware of being satisfied and satiated with the credit and honour and glory that so easily come to you from the lips of men, beware of getting your reward in this world and mortgaging your eternal future, 'Set your affections on things above'.

But it is impossible for such people to believe in Christ, not only because they are superficially-minded but also because they are *dishonest and deceitful*. They are never seriously and persistently concerned about the deeper things of life and religion, as I have showed already; but the reason for that we must now examine. And let us state it quite plainly and without any introduction. All this modern boasting of our sense of honour and gentleman-liness, etc is based upon a lie and upon a fraud. It is entirely a matter of appearances and externals, of make-believe and sham. That is ever true of any society which lives first and foremost for the sake of getting applause and admiration. It is true of necessity. If we live for the sake of obtaining the good opinion of others as our main object and ambition, we shall, of necessity, concentrate more upon outward appearances than upon the inward reality. Men, we know, however clever and astute they may be, cannot really fathom the depths which lie within us; they have to judge almost entirely by what we do and by what we say. If, therefore, we are to please them, we must concentrate all our efforts upon our outward appearances, keeping the inner secret of the state of our heart to ourselves. Thus it comes about that people who live mainly for the sake of receiving honour from others scarcely ever spend any time in meditation, self-examination and prayer. They are always facing others. The result is that they never face themselves. They are always calculating and trying to determine what effect they will have upon others. Other people therefore become their conscience. The result is that their own conscience atrophies and dies from disuse! The man who is concerned most of all about his public appearances before men is never much concerned about his private attitude before God.

But this is not only philosophically and psychologically true, it is much worse. It is, I say, almost invariably, deliberate deceit and dishonesty! The world thinks highly of you. Men honour you and praise you. And you are proud of what they say. You accept their honour and revel in it and live for it. You allow them to think, and to go on thinking, that you are exactly what you appear to be! Ah! the fraud and the dishonesty! What if they saw your heart? What if they knew the recesses of your mind and your imagination? What if they discovered all the details of your past record? What if they knew you as your family knows you? Above all, what if they knew you as you know yourself, really, in your heart of hearts? You have a great and a good name, bouquets are thrown at you during your life and wreaths innumerable will be placed upon your grave. You are proud of yourself and satisfied with yourself. Men and women think highly of you, you are praised as a 'good sort', as a 'good fellow'. Your good-nature is proverbial. What a farce! What deceit! What if you were only found out? What would they think of you if every act and every thought of yours were suddenly placed before them? What if they could but enter your heart and mind for just one day and find out truly what is taking place there? What if they could see you when you feel quite certain that no one is seeing you? What if they knew your secret life as well as your public life! But I need not go on. We all know enough about life to know that all I have said is the solemn truth. Our civilization, our commercial life is based upon this fraud and deceit. We live on and for appearances. My point is just this: as long as we continue to do so, so long shall we be ignorant of the grace of God and of His salvation. As long as you are

[47]

content to go on fooling others about yourself, you will never face yourself, and until you face yourself honestly you will never feel the need of Jesus Christ our Lord as your personal Saviour. While you regard men as your final judges and are concerned about pleasing them, you will never be able to believe in Jesus Christ. A man who is dishonest with others, and therefore with himself, can never know God. It is utterly impossible. Worldly honour leads to pride and self-satisfaction. And we are told that 'God resisteth the proud, but giveth grace unto the humble'. You will never be humble until you face yourself honestly. Oh! I beseech you, forget men and all this world's honour and glory, and 'seek', only and earnestly, 'that honour that cometh from God only'.

But I must say just one word about the most important reason of all as to why these people cannot possibly believe. It is not only because they are superficial and deceitful, but also because they are so blinded, misguided, foolish and ignorant as not to see that all they value is quite useless, and that the only honour that is of value is that which comes from God only. 'Ye will not come unto me that ye might have life,' says our Lord to these people. Precisely the same might be said of the men and women of today. They *will not* consider their lives in the light of God and eternity. Having determined to live for this world, they deliberately ignore the rest. There is a strange wilfulness in this perversity – the more one tries to help them, the more they object to and resent it. Let no one imagine that our Lord speaks harshly and scornfully about these people. He speaks rather with that note of despair in His voice. 'What can be done for them?', He seems to ask. 'They will not consider God and His claims, they are so thoroughly selfish and self-centred that they cannot understand, and refuse to believe, anyone who is thoroughly unselfish and honest'. 'I am come in my Father's name', He says, 'and ye receive me not; if another shall come in his own name, him ye will receive'.

Unselfishness always appears to be a lie to a selfish person, the self-centred man can never believe that anyone is thoroughly disinterested. The cross of Christ was foolishness to the proud Greeks; it is foolishness today to every proud self-reliant person. They will not believe that Christ has died for them, largely because they are anxious to save themselves and really believe that they can do so! 'What can be done for them?' asks our Lord, 'how can they possibly believe?' Ah! the poor misguided fools. They are praised by men for their honesty, their sincerity, their zeal and their good works. Anyone who denies and criticizes the central Christian truths will always get a following, and receive much honour from men who are as blind as he is himself. Any man who comes in his own name rather than in the Name of Christ will always be received by the crowd! Heretics are always popular with godless persons and always make good copy for the press. But ah! the tragedy of it all. 'Ye are they', said our Lord to these people on another occasion, 'which justify your-selves before men, but God knoweth your hearts'. 'You are content to go on fooling men and you try to persuade yourself that you can fool God. But you cannot! He knoweth your hearts. However much you may ignore and forget Him, however much you may blaspheme His Name and dismiss Him from your world, He remains, and knows all about you'. Examine yourself and ask yourself whether you have ever tried to please God truly. You may have attended chapel all your life, you may have done a lot of good, you may be highly honoured and respected, but has it been the main ambition of your life to please God? Is that ever your uppermost thought? Do you think you have pleased God? You will never believe in Christ until you have tried to please God, because you will never feel the need of Christ until you do.

What, then, have we to do? The answer is given: 'Seek the honour that cometh from God only'. What does that

mean? It means above all else that you forget everyone
except yourself in this matter of the soul. You must cease
to be guided by what other people think of you, indeed
you must not even guide yourself. You must seek first and
foremost to please God and to be guided by Him. He has
told you His will. It is here in the Bible, in the Ten
Commandments and the Sermon on the Mount and in
other places. He desires you to lead a perfect and sinless
life and to honour Him in all things. He does not say that
good acts cancel evil acts. He says that evil is evil and shall
be punished. He does not call you first and foremost to do
good works, but to honour His Name by honouring His
Son Jesus Christ our Lord. Here are His words: 'He that
honoureth not the Son honoureth not the Father which
hath sent him.' If you want to please God, do not start by
doing good works and drawing out a programme for your
future. You will not be able to keep it any more than you
have been able to keep your past programmes. By your
works and actions you can never please and honour God,
for your nature is sinful and your flesh is weak. You can
never meet the demands of the Old Testament or the
New, for you are 'born in sin and shapen in iniquity'. You
desire to please and honour God? Think what it means.
Oh, the utter impossibility of it all! How can a man
please and satisfy God? But praised be His Name, He has
made a way whereby this becomes possible. 'If you really
desire to honour and please me', says God in effect,
'honour my Son and please Him.' Accept Jesus Christ as
the Son of God, trust to His death for your pardon, rely
upon His merit and glorious Person for your justification
and righteousness, make it the business of your life to do
all you can by His strength and help to please Him and
obey His commands, and you shall receive that honour
and glory and credit that comes from the only true and
living God.

It is not at all surprising that Paul, in writing to the
Corinthians, should have said, 'But with me it is a very

small thing that I should be judged of you, or of man's judgment: yea, I judge not mine own self ... but he that judgeth me is the Lord'. 'Ah', says the apostle, 'I have seen through the old fallacy. I once used to try to please others and to please myself, but I have long since given up. I try only to please my Lord now, I seek only the glory that comes from Him now. All the world's glory and praise could not make me happy. I was outstanding as a Pharisee, yet miserable as a man.' The thoughts and actions of other men can, finally, not affect us at all. They cannot make us truly happy or unhappy. They can kill the body maybe, but never the soul. What does it matter what men think of us? They are only men themselves and will soon be dead with us. What is the value of all the honour and glory they give us? It is not satisfying, it is not lasting. Why go on receiving such passing honour? Why not start from tonight to seek the honour that cometh from God? Do so by accepting His Son as your Saviour, by trusting yourself to Him, praying to Him, relying upon Him for help, though unseen, and doing all you can to honour His Name. Seek thus the honour that cometh from God only and you shall have it. It will come to you as a sense of peace in your breast, the old stress and strain will go, happiness and joy will begin to flood your being, you will become victorious where you formerly fell and failed, and though men may deride you and laugh at you, you will know yourself to be the honoured and favoured of God. Oh, my friends, seek it, seek the honour, for the promise still remains true, 'Seek and ye *shall* find'. For His Name's sake. Amen.

5: *No Freedom Except in Christ*

✳

*And ye shall know the truth, and the truth shall make you
free.* John 8:32[1]

I sometimes think that one of the very best signs which a
man can ever have of the fact that he is preaching the
gospel of Christ and not merely indulging his own fancy,
is that certain people should take a violent objection to
what he is saying and should feel a sense of grudge and
annoyance with him for having said it. Not that I believe
it is the business of a man who preaches, deliberately to
attack and to attempt to annoy people – for that is simply
a display of personal animus and spite – but rather that it
seems obvious to me from reading the Gospels and from
observing incidents such as this which we are considering
tonight, that the gospel has a curious faculty of annoying
people of a certain type. Indeed, I am not at all sure but
that one of the very chief causes of the decline of church-
membership and church-going is the fact that the church,
in an attempt to conciliate and please the masses, has so
diluted and devitalised the gospel of Christ, and has
rendered it so innocuous that it is no longer even being
considered by a large number of people as a possible
theory of life. 'Present-day preaching', we are told, 'does
not save men, the churches are getting no converts.' But
there is something even worse than that about the
situation as I see it, and that is, that present-day preaching
does not even annoy men, but leaves them precisely where

[1]Undated, c. 1931.

[52]

they were, without a ruffle and without the slightest disturbance. Now in reading the Gospels there is nothing which is quite so clear as the fact that Jesus Christ in His preaching had one of two effects upon his congregations – He either saved men or else definitely antagonized them and caused them to object and persecute and threaten and taunt.

How different is the picture presented in the New Testament from the picture presented by, and the view held of, the church in these days! People today think of a church as a place which attracts a certain weak, emotional, flabby type of person, where addresses are delivered which are perfectly harmless and lifeless, where delicate discourses are delivered on 'love' and 'beauty', where 'fine thoughts' and 'fine ideas' are voiced, where quiet, comforting and cheering words are spoken, and where, above all else, nothing should be said or done which in any way would disturb anyone, not to say annoy or irritate anyone. The church is regarded as a sort of dispensary where drugs and soothing mixtures are distributed and in which everyone should be eased and comforted. And the one theme of the church must be 'the love of God.' Anyone who happens to break these rules and who produces a disturbing effect upon members of his congregation is regarded as an objectionable person, is disliked and is charged with voicing his own opinions and prejudices instead of preaching the gospel which is said to be nothing but a constant refrain concerning 'the love of God'. Now, as I have already indicated, that charge may be perfectly true, a man's ministry may be objectionable just because he is a mean, petty soul who makes the pulpit 'a coward's castle' and uses it simply that he may vent his spleen upon his own personal enemies. But that is not the only condition under which a ministry can make itself objectionable to certain people – there is another reason, and that the highest and best reason, namely that the man is simply and honestly preaching the gospel of Jesus Christ.

Look at the Gospels and the account we have of the preaching of the apostles in the Book of Acts! If ever anyone knew the love of God, if ever the love of God to men was preached and understood, if ever there was an authority on that love, that one was Jesus Christ. He said He had come to earth because of it, went about and did His work sustained by it, revealed it in His miracles and wondrous works, and was prepared to die for it, and yet what was the effect He produced upon His congregations? Did all go home from the services smiling and happy, and feeling very self-satisfied and complacent? Was His perfect ministry one in which no one was offended and at which no one took umbrage? Do His services suggest the type so popular today – the buildings with 'the dim religious light' where nice hymns are sung, nice prayers are offered and a fine and cultural 'short' address is delivered? Look in the pages of the New Testament and see the answer. Look especially in the pages of John's Gospel – John the beloved disciple, John the apostle of love, John who actually wrote that much quoted phrase 'God is love' – read his account of the ministry of Christ. In it you will find that on one occasion because of certain things said by Christ 'many of his disciples went back, and walked no more with him' (Jn 6 : 66–67). On that occasion, the effect of His preaching was to send a certain number of people home determined that they would never listen to Him again. And as they went 'Jesus said unto the twelve, Will ye also go away?' – it looked as if everyone was going to leave Him and for the moment He seemed even doubtful of His own twelve disciples. No phrase occurs quite so frequently at the close of the account of His discourses as this, 'then they sought to take him' and 'then took they up stones to cast at him'. Almost every time He preached there was a conference among certain people as to how they could catch Him or destroy Him.

I need not elaborate any further – in no sense of the

word can the gospel as preached by Christ be said to have been comfortable to listen to; it never left men as they were, it either thrilled them or else infuriated them. For it is a double-edged gospel which states that 'he that believeth on him is not condemned; but he that believeth not is condemned already, because he hath not believed in the name of the only begotten Son of God' (Jn 3 : 18). If you are not saved by it, you are of necessity condemned by it. One thing is certain, we cannot remain indifferent to it. It is not that Christ was out to condemn anyone – He came to save – or that those who preach the true gospel are out to condemn, but that the gospel itself, the very truth of God must of necessity either save a man or else condemn him. It is inconceivable that the very Word of God should have *no* effect, and that we can listen to it and be left precisely where we were before. There is an 'edge' to all His statements, a sense in which they must seem almost offensive to every natural man, for in saying that He had come to save men, Christ implied that men needed saving and that without Him they were lost. Now that is one of the very last things that we like to admit about ourselves – it touches our dignity and our self-respect and we object much as those Jews did then, when He said, 'and ye shall know the truth, and the truth shall make you free'.

Just follow the history of the Jews and observe how they had reacted to the gospel of Christ. He was speaking to them about Himself, His mission and His union with the Father. His words were tender and sublime, 'He that hath sent me is with me: the Father hath not left me alone, for I do always those things that please him' (Jn 8 : 29). And we are told that 'as he spake these words, many believed on him'. In other words they believed that what He was saying was true and that He was indeed the Messiah who had been expected. So far, He had been speaking about Himself and they accepted His testimony, but when He went on to say, 'If ye continue in my

[55]

word, then are ye my disciples indeed; and ye shall know the truth, and the truth shall make you free', the trouble began. These very people who had just believed that He was the Messiah and that He was in constant touch and communication with God – these very people turned to Him and said to Him with mingled astonishment and annoyance, 'We be *Abraham*'s seed and were never in bondage to any man: how sayest thou, Ye shall be made free?' How surprising their objection seems to us if we only consider this account superficially! 'What on earth could they have objected to in that fine statement about freedom?' we feel like asking. 'Surely they should have accepted it gladly and have rejoiced in it?' And yet they did not and that for a very obvious reason. Jesus Christ, in promising them that the truth which they would receive would make them 'free', implied that at the time they were in a state of bondage and of slavery. Although believing that He was the very Messiah of God, they objected to this statement of His which suggested that there was something wrong with them as they were. 'We be Abraham's seed, and were never in bondage to any man: how sayest thou, Ye shall be made free?'

Ah! the gospel of Christ is all right as long as it merely deals with Christ and His mission, as long as it is only concerned with generalities, but once it begins to apply itself to us it becomes personal and we object. It is one thing to shed tears at pathetic pictures and representations of Christ dying on the cross, but remember, if you believe that Christ had to die on the cross to save you, it means of necessity that you were in such a dreadful condition and plight that nothing but that death could possibly save you. There is nothing which condemns us quite to the same extent as that cross and that death which save us and redeem us. Have you ever seen yourself as one so hopelessly involved in sin and so helpless face to face with life and the power of evil that nothing but that death could save you? If not, then you are in the precise position of these Jews. You believe that Christ was the Son of God; you believe Him, but you do not believe *in* Him, and belief, unless it is belief *in* Him, is utterly useless; as he proceeds to shew these people here. Is not this the great stumbling-block in these days? We like to read and consider the teaching of Christ, we like to consider and reflect upon His noble life and example, we may even admit that He was the Son of God, but we dislike this talk about conversion and rebirth. Why? Because they imply that we need converting and that until we are born again we are lost and 'dead in sin'. However much life may change and ideas and views may come and go, there is one thing so deeply entrenched in human nature that it never varies and never wavers, and that is our own good opinion of ourselves. We like a gospel that interests us, that charms us, that appeals to our emotions and sentiments, we like it in so far as it presents ideas and the ideal of life, but when it promises to 'free' us and to give us liberty, we stumble at it and object, because in promising us freedom it implies our present bondage. Yet this is what Christ offers and what Christ says, and our whole difficulty concerning it centres round our false conception of freedom.

Now the first thing that is made clear here is that our false conception of what constitutes freedom makes us blind to our real bondage. Concentrating as we do upon the things that are around us and fighting for freedom in certain particular matters, we may well not realize that we are in the grip of a personal tyranny and bondage. These Jews here, because they were the descendants of Abraham and free men in a political sense, scouted this suggestion that they needed to be made free. 'Why', they said, 'we have never been in bondage to any man' (regarding the Egyptian and Babylonian captivities as mere incidents!); 'We *are* free already. We have never bowed the knee to any master or any foreign power, we never have been slaves. Our freedom has always been our proud boast.' In

[57]

this talk of theirs we can almost hear the refrain of:

Rule, Britannia, Britannia rule the waves!
Britons never, never, never shall be slaves.

The whole human race is instinct with this feeling and men have died to win freedom in this political sense. Now every man worthy of the name is in full sympathy with this. The man who is content to remain a slave and to lie down under a cruel tyranny and despotism is despicable, and yet, wonder of wonders, they who are loudest in their clamours for this kind of freedom are very often the slaves of their own evil natures. Some of the greatest reformers, men who have lived and died for the sake of the freedom of their country and their class have, in the meanwhile, been the slaves of their own tempers, lusts and ambitions. 'We are free' said the Jews, 'and always have been'. 'Jesus answered them and said, Verily, verily, I say unto you, Whosoever committeth sin is the servant of sin.' People in the world today who are oppressing others, are free in comparison with those whom they oppress, yet, in their personal lives they are slaves and hirelings – ruled by a lust for power, a lust for money, lust of pomp and extravagance and self-indulgence. Political freedom is the right of man. 'Liberty, equality and fraternity' is one of the noblest mottoes ever coined, yet, I tell you that, having attained full freedom in that respect, we may yet be miserable and unhappy because we are the slaves of our own natures. The people whom Christ pitied most of all were those who thought that their wealth and position made them free-agents. According to Him the tyrant to be most avoided and feared is Mammon. John Bunyan, lying in jail in Bedford, knew a liberty and a freedom which his accusers had never experienced. Christian martyrs going to the stake have always pitied and prayed for the miserable people who sent them there. Political freedom is a grand thing, but it is not enough and it is not all.

Consider again the number of people who claim that they have freedom of thought. 'I refuse to be bound', says a man, 'by anything that has gone before. I claim to be an independent and original thinker. I refuse to take my views from others and to be tyrannized into believing anything.' Now there is a sense in which these words may be perfectly true and indicate Christian liberty, as I shall show, but apart from the freedom which the truth in Christ gives, how shallow and hollow a boast it is. What is your opinion and view after all? To what extent are you truly responsible for it? Consider what goes to the making up and determining of it. Look around and you will see that all these views are determined by a number of accidents. The place where you were brought up makes a difference – there is such a thing as a racial genius. Celts and Saxons start with a different bias and prejudice. Your parents and your forefathers make a difference. The facts of life round and about you count and count tremendously. Your friends, your school and college, your teachers, masters and professors – all have to be considered in the making-up of man's opinions. Look at the violent clashes between rival groups and rival classes. Both sides claim that they are thinking in a free and unfettered way, yet that cannot possibly be true. See the violence with which they put forward their views and the hatred and spleen with which they propound them. Observe how they vilify and abuse their opponents. Why? Because they are not in control or in command of their views, but are, as we say, 'carried away' by them. Before a man has a right to claim that he thinks in freedom, he must be able to say that he has seen and considered the other side as carefully and as dispassionately as his own. The old philosophers recognized this, and the absence of passion and violence in thought and views was to them the true test of wisdom and freedom of thought. Have you observed also how men's opinions and views change as their circumstances change and yet they still boast that they are free,

[59]

independent and original thinkers? 'I have come to the conclusion', says the man, 'that there is no God and that religion is all a farce and a dope.' And he prides himself on what he regards as his free, independent opinion. Are you quite sure that you have a right to express such an opinion? Have you considered all the arguments and the evidence, and have you an infallible theory by which you can explain life in the absence of God? We must recognize that there is a difference between freedom of speech and freedom of thought. We can all say what we like, but we certainly cannot think what we like – we are a mass of prejudices and hereditary and environmental influences. We are bound hand and foot in thought by all those factors which have gone to make us what we are.

But again, even if, like the ancient philosophers, we contrived to overcome all these prejudices, still, in a moral sense, we might well be slaves. How sad and pathetic and ludicrous is all this clamour in these days for moral freedom, and this claim that we have a right to live our lives in our own way! Far be it from me to advocate a cold, heartless morality (I spend most of my time in denouncing anything of the sort) yet in this moral freedom of which we boast how obvious is the tyrannical hand of the devil and of sin. In the name of this freedom men and women break away today from the demands of their parents, their husbands and wives, their children and all else. 'Why should I be bound, why should I not have freedom to live my own life?' And on they go. And yet, do they get freedom? Are they free in the way they like to think of themselves as being free? Are they happy and contented, is there nothing worrying them and restraining them? Having left parents, husband, wife and children, having broken all rules and restrictions, are these people free, and free to do as they like? No! However much they may shake off others, there is a voice and a person within them of which they can never rid themselves. How happy they would be if they could! At each move, there is a voice within calling out, 'Cad, coward, you mean person!' They try to drown that voice with more pleasure and more breaking of the rules of convention, but still it is there and whenever there is a lull in the game, this voice within, this other person inside, whom we take within us everywhere, taunts and upbraids, challenges us and mocks us. Why is it that one who starts upon the road of licence and of sin invariably goes deeper and deeper into it? The answer is that he cannot find satisfaction, cannot find peace, cannot find happiness and on he goes plunging deeper and deeper in an attempt to quell that voice within and to forget his own past. What do remorse and the agony of the morning after the debauch mean? Simply that that voice, that person within you, who follows you everywhere you go, is objecting, demanding his rights. 'Be sure your sin will find you out', says a verse in Numbers. You observe the way that it is put. Not of necessity, that the world will find out about your sin, not that others will get to know about it but your sin will find *you* out. It will not leave you alone. All the foolish, sinful, selfish things you have done, all the acts of meanness and pettiness, all dishonesty, all trifling with the moral code, all the things you do that you know perfectly well that you ought not to do, all the things you try to excuse yourself for doing, all those things in which you have to try to justify yourself by asking, 'Why shouldn't I do them?' – all those will rise before you and shake their accusing fingers at you. You are lying alone in bed with no one near you and there you will be faced by a panorama, a nightmare, of all those things you have done or have neglected. They will taunt you, they will laugh at you, they will probe you, they will tease and torment you and you cannot avoid them – 'be sure your sin will find you out'! Moral freedom? Why, none of us has it. Within ourselves is our own opposition and we cannot evade it. This person that goes with us everywhere,

[61]

follows us into the secret places and registers our very thoughts and imaginations – he is our master and we cannot avoid him. He is relentless and cannot be put off by excuses.

Need I say any more about the bondage? Anyone who thinks must grant at once that we are slaves and bound in the bondage of our own unworthy natures. What is more, Christ makes it plain here that we cannot hope to free ourselves, for He says that 'the *truth* shall make you free'. We cannot free ourselves, as we have seen, or we would all have long since done so, but, God be praised, we can be freed, for 'the *truth* shall make you free'.

Now a religion or a belief which does not free men is of no value whatsoever, and we have to remember that there is a form of religion and chapel-going and church membership which is sheer slavery. There are people who are religious just because they are afraid not to be; they attend a place of worship because they were brought up to do so, because it is the custom and tradition to do so. They believe the Bible merely because they were taught to do so and accept doctrines and dogmas because they were taught them by their parents and forefathers. That is what Christ in the 35th verse in this chapter calls 'being a servant in the house'. To profess belief in God and His Word, to obey God's commands, to abstain from vices and sins, to lead a decorous and respectable outward life is, in a sense, to be in God's house, but such a man is only there as a slave, as a hireling, as a servant. He is not free. His position is precisely the same as the Hindu or the Mohammedan, or the Pagan who worships the sun and other things simply because his fathers did so. He is bound by custom and tradition and by fear. That is not the freedom which Christ promises. It is but a shallow and superficial belief which is based on what others have thought and said about it. The faith which is impregnable, the truth which frees, is that which flashes upon a man's soul in such a way as to make him say, 'I *know* this to be the truth of God. Its teaching has touched the deepest springs of thought and feeling within my breast, it has awakened my conscience, moved my heart, kindled my aspirations after a better, purer life, brought peace and rest to my spirit, and though all should deny it, I know it to be true because it has changed my life.' The truth which frees is that which Paul had and which prompted him in writing to the Galatians to say, 'But though we, or an angel from heaven, preach any other gospel unto you than that which we have preached unto you, let him be accursed' (Gal 1:8)

Well, what was that gospel? Just this, that Jesus Christ, is the Son of God, that in dying He fulfilled the Law and destroyed the power of death, and that by so doing He cancelled the power of sin and wiped out the sinful debt of humanity and that by the power of His Spirit a man can be created anew and start upon a new life which is an eternal life. How can I be happy and be free with the load of all my past sins upon me? How can I answer this voice within me that mocks and taunts me while I am still conscious of my guilt? But when I see and believe that Christ has taken it upon Himself to deal with my sins, when I know that I am forgiven by God through Christ, when I know my past sins are blotted out, – let all the devils mock and laugh, let all the voices within me and in hell jeer and attempt to enslave me – I know I am free and can turn upon them. I know their power, thousands of times have I experienced it, but God be praised, I now know a greater power. I know a power that can lead captivity captive, a power that has swallowed up death and the grave 'in victory'. My past is clear and I am free. 'But still you have to live', you say, 'and you will meet temptations which will tempt your passions and your lusts. Surely your cry of freedom is somewhat premature?' No, my friend, the power in which I believe is not merely a power that deals with the past. Jesus Christ is not merely a historical person – He lives, He reigns and in the Holy Spirit He operates in this world here and now. My passions are not destroyed, my powers are not cancelled, but by His power they are used in another direction. The very passions and powers with which I used to serve the devil are now being employed in the service of God. My very weaknesses are now turned to the glory of God. The passion with which I cursed and blasphemed is not the passion whereby I glorify God; the ingenuity I employed to serve my own selfish desires is now the ingenuity I employ in preaching and publishing the kingdom of God and salvation for sinners. For it is not my past, nor any one portion of myself that has been saved, but I myself! That is the Christian profession, that is what is meant by the truth making men free. It is not self-confidence but confidence in Christ who has mastered and controlled my self. Relying on Him and on His power what need I fear? He stands between me and my past, is ever present to help, and is ever leading me on to the future. Though still I am weak, He is strong; though my grasp may fail and I may falter, His can never do so. I need not fear, I need not worry, His power is eternal and in its strength I am free! Let life disappoint me, let all things go against me, let all the devils in hell assail me, as they will, still I shall say:

> *From Him who loves me now so well*
> *What power my soul shall sever?*
> *Shall life or death, shall earth or hell?*
> *No! I am His for ever!*

Men and women! believe in Christ and you shall be free! Amen.

6: *Man's Fundamental Trouble*

*

And this is the condemnation, that light is come into the world, and men loved darkness rather than light, because their deeds were evil.   John 3 : 19[1]

There is a proverbial statement to the effect that 'a half-truth is more dangerous than a lie'. And nowhere, perhaps, is that quite as true as in connection with religion and the things of the soul. It is the whole explanation of the tragedy of the blindness of the Pharisees and scribes, who crucified our Lord, the explanation still of the unbelief of a large number of intelligent men and women, whom one would expect to be Christians. It is one of those things which stand out so clearly in the Bible and in the entire history of the Christian church, that, almost invariably, the last man to be brought under the saving influence of Christ is not the thoughtless, heedless reprobate, but rather the thoughtful, intelligent, highly moral person who has been doing his utmost to lead a godly life. It appears to be always very much easier to convince a person who has been entirely wrong, than one who has only been partly wrong. The Gentiles, who were aliens and strangers from the commonwealth of Israel and without God in the world, come into the kingdom of God very much more readily than those chosen people, the Jews, to whom had been delivered the very 'oracles of God'.

All this but illustrates the truth of the proverb in the religious world, and it illustrates still more the subtlety of

[1]Undated, c. 1931.

[65]

the devil. He knows that a half-truth can so easily satisfy the natural mind, he knows also that a half-truth is in a sense further away from the whole truth than an absolute lie. A lie is a blank contradiction, it makes no pretence or show of truth, it is entirely the reverse of truth. The half-truth on the other hand suggests truth and appears to be entirely on the side of truth. It grants so much that the unwary may well imagine that it grants everything. 'A little learning is a dangerous thing'. Dangerous, because the one who possesses it always imagines that he knows a lot and therefore becomes unteachable. That was the great trouble which our Lord had in His own days on earth. It is astonishing to note how much of His time was spent in arguing with the Pharisees and scribes. You do not find that the publicans and sinners argued with Him, they just dropped at His feet and worshipped Him. It was the good and learned people who disagreed with Him and finally crucified Him. And that, not because they entirely disagreed with Him but because, rather, they agreed so wholeheartedly with Him up to a point. It was beyond that point that they considered He was going too far, indeed that He was guilty of blasphemy. In a sense it was because they were expecting the coming of the Messiah that they crucified the Christ. Had they not been expecting Him to come, they would never have been so infuriated by the claims of that Person who, to them, appeared to be an impostor and a fraud. You have to have ideas before you can hold the wrong ideas; the man who has no ideas at all about a given matter is at least free from the charge of holding wrong and false ideas! That was the trouble with the Jews in the days of our Lord, they were partly right! The tragedy and shame of the Cross provide us with the most perfect and terrible illustration of the truth of that proverb which emphasizes the danger of a half-truth.

But this, I say, is a universal principle and its effects are as obvious today as they have ever been. Look at the religious situation at the present time and what do you find? The Christian Faith is succeeding, spreading, and gaining ground in those countries and districts and places where it was formerly not known at all or where it was entirely ignored. The pagans and the godless are responding to it and being changed by it. On the other hand, you find that it is declining and losing ground in the Christian countries and among men and women who have been brought up in religious homes, who were christened in their youth and who have attended their places of worship fairly regularly ever since. And, with regard to active opposition and criticism, it comes not from the dissolute and immoral so much as from the good and moral, the idealists and philanthropists. What an exact reproduction of the conditions prevailing during the days of our Lord's earthly ministry! It is the initial agreement that causes all the subsequent trouble. Take all these modern idealists and philanthropists and compare them with a Christian. You will find that they start on common ground. Both parties recognize that there is something wrong with the world and with mankind, both parties agree that all the misery and suffering and ugliness which are so evident in this world are a disgrace to the human race and to civilization. They are united in their condemnation of the monstrous inequality that prevails as between class and class, the wasteful luxury and indulgence at one end, the poverty and privation at the other. They both agree that life was meant to be noble, happy and lofty, and that squalor and filth, sin and wretchedness are things that should shame and humble us. The greed and selfishness of men, their lust for place and power, all the petty intriguing and scheming, all the dishonesty and trickery in connection with public affairs, all these things serve to depress and grieve the idealist and the Christian alike. Both are horrified by war as a method of settling disputes, both are almost driven to despair of human nature by divorce and infidelity, and the passionate excesses of their fellows. Looking out upon the world as it is today, they are in absolute and entire agreement that there is *something* wrong and something terribly wrong. They are agreed further that unless something is done to prevent the rot, civilization will tend to crumble away. So far, then, there is no disagreement. Both are agreed that there is something wrong. But from this point onwards the agreement ceases. Superficially, they are identical, but like those two houses pictured by our Lord in His parable, the foundations are entirely different, as different as sand is from a rock. They are agreed in stating that there is something wrong, but they are fundamentally divided and different with regard to the question as to what exactly *is* wrong.

I need scarcely press the point that such a difference is indeed fundamental and vital. But in order to make it quite clear I may be allowed to use a medical illustration and comparison. Think of a person lying ill in bed with a pain in his right side. Two people come to see him, the one a layman, the other a doctor. They both agree that he is ill, that he is not himself, that he is feverish, that he looks flushed and is obviously in pain. The layman suggests that probably he has just eaten something which has upset him and that soon he will be all right. The doctor on the other hand, examining the case more carefully, can see almost at once that the man is suffering from an acute attack of appendicitis, and that unless a radical operation is performed without any delay he will probably lose his life. The two visitors were in absolute agreement up to a point, quite agreed that there was something wrong. Where they disagreed, fundamentally and vitally, was in their diagnosis as to what exactly *was* wrong. Such is the difference between all the modern idealists and moralists and the Christian. 'And *this* is the condemnation' says our text, as if to say 'not this or that or something else, but *this*!' It is not sufficient that we should recognize in general that there are certain ills that afflict mankind and that things are not as they ought to be. We must discover the root cause, we must get down to the actual origin of the trouble. The disease must be exposed and discovered before it can be properly treated.

Now, here, we have the very pith and core of the fight that the revelation of God has always had to wage against 'the wisdom of this world'. Here lies the explanation of the clash depicted so often in the Old Testament between the false prophets and the servants of God. For the false prophets have always admitted that there is something wrong. They have never been totally blind and foolish. The charge against them is, always, not that they have cried that there was nothing wrong, but that rather 'they have healed the hurt of my people slightly', that they have prophesied smooth and easy things and a painless recovery, instead of facing and dealing with the real problem in an honest and radical manner. In a sense it is no part of the business of our gospel just to announce that there is something wrong and that the world is sinful. Every thinking person must be aware of that, every man who is honest with himself and who pauses occasionally to listen to the voice of the conscience that is within him, must recognize it at once. There are moralists in all pagan countries. The ancient Greek philosophers, in a sense, exposed the ills and needs of mankind almost as perfectly as does the divine revelation itself. All the honest biographies of all thinking men invariably reveal the same thing – a sense of dissatisfaction with themselves and a longing for something which they lacked. No! there was no need for the incarnation and the death of our Lord just to tell mankind that it was not well, the prophets of old and many others had discovered and stated that. Our Lord came to reveal the exact cause of the trouble and its only cure. '*This* is the condemnation ...' The gospel is as definite and dogmatic as an announcement or a proclamation – it does not put forward a theory, but states a fact. In thus placing emphasis on the word 'this', the evangelist reminds us of all the confusion that prevails, and shews us how the devil attempts to delude us by suggesting to us other and futile explanations of our troubles and difficulties. And in this verse he deals with two of the main fallacies with regard to the disease of mankind, which were not only current in his own day but which have remained, ever since and until today, the two main obstacles standing between many a man and belief in Jesus Christ our Lord. ·

The first is what I may call *the fallacy about intellect and knowledge.* Take the case of the Jews at the time of our Lord's earthly ministry. They thought they knew what the Messiah would do, they considered that their knowledge of the Old Testament was sufficiently great and accurate for them to be able to predict exactly what He would do when He came. Jesus Christ did not correspond with this; there were indeed many things in Him which utterly contradicted all their ideas and notions. He did not conform to their thoughts and wishes, therefore they assumed that He was wrong and an impostor. They thought that they knew better than He did and therefore asked, 'Who is this fellow?' And then, because He did not conform to their ideas and tally exactly with their preconceived notions of what the Messiah would do, they completely ignored all the wonders and miracles which He performed, were quite impervious to His message, and finally killed Him. Thinking that they knew better, they regarded Christ as an impostor and still continued to look forward to the true Messiah who should come. 'Ah! what blindness and sin', says John here, 'what perversity! You Jews are still looking forward to the light which shall lighten Israel, when the startling fact is that "light *is come* into the world" already. There is no need for you to wait and look ahead, look at Him.'

Is it not exactly the same today and particularly with educated, thoughtful men and women in the mass? They recognize the ills and evils of life but for their solution they still look to the future and not to the past. How clearly is this revealed in all their talk and written words. They speak of themselves as people who are searching for the light and the truth. They imagine themselves to be like pioneers and explorers facing some territory hitherto uncharted and undiscovered. They regard the entire past of the human race as being in darkness and ignorance, with superstitions and fears mainly in control. They regard man as having painfully developed from lower species, and as having had a terrible struggle and conflict with his own animal past. Hitherto, the animal in us, they say, has been in control, but by now, man is beginning to achieve that freedom he so sorely desires. Light and knowledge are beginning to dawn upon the human race, the explorers have just sighted the Promised Land at last, and soon the entire human race will have landed there and, in that pure atmosphere, we shall leave behind us all the things that now shame us. By the gradual growth of knowledge, and by the increased light that research and discovery will be able to throw upon the problems of life, man will become perfect and all his difficulties will be removed. 'Look forward!' they say. 'Forget the past! The star of man's perfection is gradually rising in the heavens and soon will light up all our present darkness and gloom.'

But you are all familiar with the argument. Acknowledging that the present position of things is bad, the modern idealist and moralist looks forward to a time, perhaps millions of years hence, when the light will dawn and man will be perfect. Could there be a more perfect parallel to the case of the Jews? The past is ignored, the fact of Jesus Christ is completely overlooked. There is no light except in the future and this for the reason that they assume that each generation knows more and is better informed than its predecessors, that 'knowledge grows from age to age'. They refuse to look back to Jesus of Nazareth because they, like the Jews, think that they

[71]

know more than He did. They think that the mere fact
that He was on earth nearly two thousand years ago
automatically puts Him out of court; the light, of
necessity, must come in the future, not from the past.
They cannot see that the light is already 'come into the
world'. They refuse to believe it. How utterly unreasonable is their position, how blind. What additional light do
they think they need? What are they waiting for? Is not
the Sermon on the Mount good enough as a standard for
their life? Do they wait for something still higher and still
more difficult? Does not the life of Jesus Christ satisfy
their exalted demands and desiderata? Was not His life a
perfect and a model life? Could they, and do they, wish for
something better? Is it conceivable that the future, to all
eternity, can possibly hold a person more God-like and
divine? Is it imaginable that there will ever be a fuller and
more complete manifestation and exposition of the love
of God than that which has already appeared in the
teaching and death of our Lord? What could be fuller,
what could be freer?

And with regard to ourselves, what greater hope for
mankind can be conceived of than that we should be and
become as Jesus Christ was; that we, if we believe on Him,
shall be conformed 'into His likeness' and indeed possess
His very mind? What greater light and hope upon the
problem of sin, and how to overcome the temptations
that beset us from without and within, can be expected
than that contained in the New Testament, where we are
promised that if we only believe Christ and trust
ourselves to Him we shall be baptized with His Spirit and
clothed with His power? What greater hope, face to face
with death and an unknown eternity, than the certainty of
the resurrection and Christ's actual conquest of death
and the grave? What more light do they need? Jesus
Christ lights up the whole history of mankind, solves all
the mysteries, turns the darkness of the grave into the
light of the resurrection morning, and reveals unto us the

very 'brightness of God's face'. Oh! foolish, ignorant, conceited souls! Why do you wait? 'The light to lighten the Gentiles' has appeared, 'the day-star from on high' has arisen, the bright and morning star is already shining in the heavens, 'the light of the world' has already appeared and has led countless millions, even through the valley of the shadow of death, to that land of eternal light. Do you look for light to the years that are to come, for salvation to the gradual dawning of knowledge? It may take millions of years, you say. But what of you in the meantime? Soon, you will be gone, with the mystery still unsolved. How idle are your hopes! Look tonight, look now, to that light which has already appeared, and which has shined without a flicker for nearly two thousand years and has brought peace and rest and light to souls that were once as dark as yourself. Look to Him and cry unto Him to save you.

But if all that is true, the question naturally arises as to *what explains the fact that men and women deliberately ignore that light and follow their own ways?* Why is it that all men and women, and in particular thinking men and women, do not recognize all this and believe in Jesus Christ? The answer is given in the remainder of this verse where we are told clearly and plainly the true nature of sin. This is the second great fallacy current today, as in the time of our Lord, and it explains fully why men and women still ignore Jesus Christ, who is the light of the world, and look to some hypothetical developments which are supposed to take place in the future.

Our ideas of sin and evil are too superficial and unreal. We explain evil and wrong-doing as things which are just negative and passive, as it were, simply the absence of good and right. We do not believe that there is such a thing or a state as being *positively* evil. The bad man, we have come to regard as a man who is not good. We do not believe that he is actively bad, or bad in a positive sense. The trouble with him, we feel, is that the good and positive and beautiful parts of his nature have not yet begun to function and to play their part. Another way of stating the same thing is to explain every sin as simply being ignorance. The sinful man is an ignorant man who has not yet learned about the beautiful and pure and good. It is not, we are told, that he knows both good and evil and deliberately chooses evil and gloats over it, but that rather he needs to be educated and enlightened. It is not that the poor fellow likes or enjoys evil, but that he is not aware of the good and beautiful. Sin is ignorance. Therefore the whole problem is an intellectual one and not a moral one. And, according to the modern idea of sin, such it is. What people need, it is said, is to be educated, to be given knowledge, to be told of the pure, the good and the clean, to be brought into contact with the great minds of the ages and into an atmosphere where all is healthy and beautiful. Now it is not at all surprising that such a view of sin should prove to be acceptable to people and commend itself to them. For how nice and consoling it is! You and I are not really bad, we are simply not good. There is nothing vicious and vile about us, we simply are ignorant of what is good. It is not that our very natures are depraved and twisted and our very hearts filthy, but that we have not yet dwelt for a sufficient length of time in that cultured zone where beauty, goodness and truth are ever present. We do not need to be changed and to be born again, we only need to be improved somewhat. Ah! it is not surprising that we like all that, because it flatters us. How much nicer it is than a gospel which says the exact opposite, which tells us that we are vile and filthy and that we actually love the darkness and prefer it to the light, that our sins and evil are positive, deliberate and wilful! For that is what we are told about ourselves in the gospel of Christ; such is the picture we present in the focus of the eternal light.

Now let us be honest and compare these two ideas of sin in the light of our own experience and that of others.

[74]

Are our acts of sin simply the result of our ignorance and lack of culture? Do we not know that the life depicted in the New Testament is the only true kind of life? Must we not all confess that we know full well that a good, clean and pure life is the right life, and that certain actions are wrong and sinful, but that nevertheless we have constantly committed them? To believe this modern theory of sin is to deny the existence of a conscience, and to destroy any lingering conception we may have of human responsibility. How false and untrue it is! How superficial and childish! The drunkard, the adulterer, the wife-beater, the thief, the dishonest person, the malicious gossip simply the result of ignorance! What folly to be asked to believe that they are not positively evil, and that all they need is to be taught and enlightened! How monstrous it is to think of these things being stated seriously and believed by men and women who, if they but examined themselves honestly for a few seconds, must see the fallacy. Would to God that their explanation was right – that I am not really responsible for my past sins.

But, alas, such is not the case! We know it all. We knew it before we sinned. We did it deliberately, knowing exactly what we were doing. Why did we do so if we knew it was wrong? Why do we not try with all our might to lead the gospel life seeing that we recognise that it is right? Why be so bitter towards religion when we know that it has been the greatest power for good which this world has ever seen? Why curse chapel-going and stories of conversion, when we know full well that our own friends who have been converted are admittedly better men now than they were before, better to themselves, better to their wives and children and better citizens? Why laugh and mock and jeer at an institution which can produce such a change and has done so along the ages? Why is it that all men and women who are not Christians would be rather relieved and very glad tomorrow morning, if it could be definitely proved beyond any dispute that there is no God, and that the whole of

[75]

religion is pure invention? Why would many, some of whom are even church-members, be rather glad to hear that, and to know for certain that there is no hell? There is but one answer. In our natural unregenerate state we 'love the darkness' and therefore hate the light. In spite of knowing all we know, we are what we are. We enjoy sin, we are happy sinning, we relish its taste, we love it though we know it to be illicit and forbidden and stolen. There we find our pleasure and our happiness, the delight and joy of our lives. What do we hate? Oh! anybody or anything that tends to upset our pleasure, or makes us feel unhappy, and who suggests that we are wrong. Who more so than Jesus Christ and His heavenly Father? Of course the sinner hates the Christian and the Sabbath day and chapel-going! For they all condemn him and make him see himself.

How perfectly is all this presented in that story of King Ahab of Israel, as recorded in the Book of I Kings 22:8. Ahab desired to go up against his enemies, in order to recover a town they had taken from him, and he asks King Jehoshaphat of Judah to go with him and join with him. Jehoshaphat suggests that the prophets be consulted first, so Ahab gathers them all together and they all give a favourable report and tell them to go on. Then Jehoshaphat asks whether all the prophets had been asked and says, 'Is there not here a prophet of the Lord besides, that we might enquire of him?' To which King Ahab replies, 'There is yet one more, Micaiah the son of Imlah, by whom we may enquire of the Lord, but I hate him, for he doth not prophesy good concerning me, but evil'. How true that reaction is of all of us in our natural state! Yes! We know all about the truth, but we hate it, for it condemns us and makes us feel miserable.

Let us honestly face ourselves. Such are our natures. They love the darkness, they hate the light. They are twisted, they are perverted, they prefer the wrong to the right and enjoy evil rather than known good. What we need is not more light, but a nature which will be capable of loving the light instead of hating it. The light is there, we know it to be there but we dislike it. We hate it. What is the point of hoping vaguely and theoretically for some supposed additional light, when we cannot appreciate and enjoy the light we already have? What we need is not knowledge, but love. We know what is right and good but we fail to do it because our natures are such that we do not love it. All the knowledge, culture, and training of the whole world can never change the nature, can never teach us how to love God. Try your best and utmost to do so. In the name of this gospel I defy you to succeed. But do not be so foolish, do not be so blind, do not be so mad. Acknowledge and admit here and now that it is your nature that is wrong, your heart, your essential personality and being. See further that as the years tend to pass, you do not improve but tend to get worse. Has anyone ever succeeded in turning his own hatred of God into love? He may have given up this sin and that, but has he come to love God? Has anyone ever done so? Can a man entirely and completely change his own nature? Do you now love God? for if you do not, you hate Him! No! no one has ever succeeded in bringing this change about and yet it *has* happened. Paul and millions of others at one time hated Christ and persecuted His church, but afterwards came to say, 'For me to live is Christ'. What had happened? Oh, well, they had seen themselves as they really were in the light of Christ, they cried out to Him for mercy. And they obtained it, and a new nature also in addition. There it is. If you do not recognize it you are damned. But, see it and accept it, and you are safe to all eternity. Amen.

7: *The Thoroughness of the Gospel*

*

And now also the axe is laid unto the root of the trees.
Luke 3:9[1]

These are the words in which John the Baptist, that great
herald of the Messiah and His gospel, sums up the very
essence and pith of the Christian message and revelation.
He was anxious that the men and women of his day
should grasp and understand that the new order that was
coming was indeed going to be entirely new, and quite
different from anything which they had seen or
experienced hitherto. And *the* big point of difference was
to be this very characteristic – the thoroughness of the
gospel. 'Now also, the axe is laid unto the root of the
trees'. It was to be no mere stripping of the leaves and
branches henceforward, no mere superficial dealing with
the problem; the axe was to be laid to the *root* of the trees!
That was John's big point in his preaching, that was the
note which he considered should be emphasized and
stressed most strongly. And that not merely because it
was the point which the state of the people called for most
of all, but because it happens to be the most outstanding
and characteristic thing about the gospel of our Lord.
But, such is the perversion of the human mind as the
result of sin, there is nothing in connection with the
gospel which is so frequently forgotten, so frequently
ignored and indeed so frequently denied. It could be

[1] September 20, 1931, the year when the awakening at Sandfields was at its
height.

[78]

shown very easily that what has really occurred in every period of revival and re-awakening is that the church has again discovered this truth about the gospel – that it is something essentially practical and definite that the axe is indeed laid to the *root* of the trees. Never perhaps was there greater need of our being reminded of this than during these present days. Never perhaps was the gospel of Christ more grossly and hopelessly misrepresented than just at the present time. I am not exaggerating at all when I say that the chief characteristic of the religious outlook of today is vagueness. And what is still worse is that it is claimed that this very element of vagueness is that quality which is most peculiarly and characteristically Christian. Let me show you what I mean by referring to the belief of the moderns and also to their way of life.

There was a time when the landmarks of belief and unbelief were fairly clear and definite. It was agreed on all hands that no man was a Christian, or had received salvation and was accepted of God, save he who believed definitely in the existence of the one God and that Jesus Christ was His only begotten Son, and that He had come to earth and lived and died in order to save sinners. The man who believed that with regard to himself was a Christian. A man who denied these truths and who refused to accept them was regarded definitely as one who was not a Christian, however good his life might be and however noble and beautiful his views might be about everything else. The position was plain and clear and definite. But who can say that of the position today? Is it not characterized rather by the exact opposite? Today if a man talks beautiful generalities and idealism, if he appears to do a lot of good and shows himself to be keen and devoted in a religion, it is argued that he is all right and acceptable with God, even though he does not believe in that God and refuses to accept Jesus Christ as his only personal Saviour and Redeemer. 'Ah', say the moderns, 'you, with your rigid demands and definitions are much too hard and narrow to be truly Christian. What if the man does not believe in Christ, and does not accept your dogmas about the Trinity etc, his beautiful life and spirit surely prove him to be a Christian?' Thus, though they deny the very elements and foundation truths of Christianity, it is argued that the followers of Buddha, Mohammed, and Confucius are really brethren with Christians, and will ultimately arrive at the same goal though along different roads and ways. Vague general hopes and aspirations after a higher and better life are regarded as quite sufficient. There is no clarity of view, no definitions of position – everything is vague, fluid and constantly changing. And, as I have pointed out, they regard any attempt at definition or clarity as being peculiarly anti-Christian and lacking in charity. Any examination of the roots, any insistence upon certain fundamental principles as being absolutely vital and essential to true faith in God, is regarded as being wholly inconsistent with the gospel. Generalizations and nebulous phrases about beauty, truth and love are the order of the day; they find a little bit of good and of God in everybody and in everything, and therefore, whether you believe in Christ as the only begotten of God or not, really does not matter very much and Gandhi is spoken of with the same reverence as our Lord Himself. And yet we are told by the great forerunner, the great herald of the gospel – 'the axe is laid to the *root* of the trees' – no more mere generalities and indefinite statements, but 'his fan is in his hand and he will *thoroughly* purge his floor'.

The same trend exactly is visible also in the modern view of life and behaviour. Never was there such laxity and failure to recognize certain definite standards, never was the axe further away from the roots than today. And again, I observe that what is most pathetic of all is that they try to claim that this laxity is the outcome of a Christian spirit of liberty and of charity. Gross sins and crimes are explained away and excused in the name of

Christ; all manner of evil is condoned and almost defended for the same reason. The very sense of good and evil seems to have gone; the standards and moral sanctions are no longer regarded and recognized. Good is found in all evil, nothing is regarded as really black – all is in a state of mixture and flux. Any definite pronouncement or any attempt to recognize a clear standard is branded as being anti-Christian. In other words it is but a further proof of my general contention that somehow or other the impression has got abroad that the chief characteristic of the Christian religion is its all-inclusiveness, its absence of landmarks and definitions, and the premium which it places on general pious hopes and aspirations. Its glory apparently is in its vagueness, its preparedness to say well done to all and sundry in spite of everything, its readiness to forget all about the roots and origins and vitals as long as superficial appearances are fairly good. Yet still there sounds the voice of John the Baptist, repeated at all times throughout the ages in days of revival and reawakening: 'and now also the axe is laid to the root of the trees'. But without wasting any more time in considering the modern travesty of the gospel, let us look at the gospel itself, concentrating especially tonight on this very quality which most of all characterizes it, namely, its thoroughness.

We shall look at this first of all as it is displayed in *the gospel view of man.*

It is perhaps common ground as between the moderns and the gospel that things are not right with man as he is at present. It is granted that the world is full of things which are wrong and sinful, but the cleavage becomes evident at once when we compare the ways in which the moderns and the gospel face that situation. The essence of the present day belief is that conditions and surroundings, lack of education and things of that description, are really responsible for most of the ills of

[81]

mankind, and that if only those things were rectified then all would be well. There is a deep conviction (as far as they are capable of any depth) that man himself, as it were, is all right, but that he is the victim of his surroundings. The faith in mankind is endless and boundless. It is firmly believed that man can reform himself and put himself right, and that if he is given but a little encouragement along these lines, he will soon proceed to do so. Hence all the emphasis during the past fifty years on education and social reform and things of that description. My charge against all that is not so much that it is entirely wrong and that it has not been dealing with the problem which it recognizes. My charge rather is that it has been so superficial and so general as to miss entirely the real source of trouble which is deeper down. This is precisely what the gospel deals with in applying the axe to the root of the trees, in its view of man in general. It has known all along that mankind has tried to excuse itself by blaming such things as circumstances and surroundings. It knows that that was the favourite trick of the children of Israel of old – they were always blaming something or somebody else for all their troubles. Yet it also knows clearly and definitely that that is not the true answer and explanation. For nothing is more remarkable in the history of the children of Israel than the fact that they were more prone and given to sin when things were going well, and only turned to God when things were going against them. Time and time again did God give them ideal conditions, as He had done to Adam at the beginning, but each time the same thing took place. They became dissatisfied and lusted after something else. Ideal conditions did not produce ideal people and they have never done so throughout the ages. Prosperity and education and knowledge, far from solving the problem of sin and unhappiness, have, in a sense, but increased it. The real trouble with man is not that he is the unwilling victim of his circumstances and surroundings, not that he is an idealist ever craving for the best and highest, who is for ever being thwarted and hindered by the evil world; the real trouble with him is that he likes sin, enjoys iniquity, and craves for things which he knows to be illicit. It was in paradise that Adam fell; it was in Canaan, not in Egypt, that Israel sank to the deepest depths of idolatry and enmity against God; it was the Messiah, the Son of God, that the ancient world crucified. It is in spite of all the reforms and improvements of the last century, all the increase in knowledge and culture, that this present generation is one of the most godless and pagan that this world has ever seen. The tree must be judged by the fruit it has produced. This vagueness and indefiniteness in religion, the denial of the atonement and of the old evangelical doctrine of grace, have had a long and a fair trial. In a way, they have held supreme sway for the last thirty years at least. What has it led to? What have been the results? What has all the preaching of a vague idealism and this gospel of a little good in everything led to? Look around you. Empty chapels, Sabbath desecration and a moral standard which is as low as to be almost non-existent! That is what the superficial view of man and his problems has led to. Is it not time that the axe was laid to the root of the trees and we really began to face ourselves honestly?

But there is a better way in which we can state the same truth and it is, in a sense, the whole difference between Judaism and the gospel, the whole difference between the modern view of man and the Christian view of man and his sin. The non-Christian view just looks at the sins themselves and is anxious to try to put an end to the sins alone. It tries to put an end to wars for that reason, it tries to pass temperance legislation and things of that description. It cannot see, as the gospel would have us see, that the real trouble is not merely that we actually commit the sins, but that we should ever have desired to do so. The non-Christian view is content and happy and

[83]

pleased with itself as long as it does not commit the sin; what causes the Christian heart to bleed and to break is that he should even covet. It is not the mere act of sin, but that I should desire to do it, that I should want to do it, that I should derive some fiendish, devilish pleasure in doing it! That is the real trouble. Our very nature is wrong. It is not only that the outside world tempts me and attracts me. That I could understand and see without breaking my heart. What condemns me is that there is something within me that responds to it all, and indeed does so readily and gladly, something that says, 'Amen' -, so be it - something that lusts and craves and thirsts to go after it! That is our trouble and it is shewn us by the gospel alone, which probes us to the depths and examines and applies the axe to the very roots. It reveals us to ourselves as we really are; it shows our nature to be so rotten, so vile; it lays bare the roots and shows clearly that their state is so unhealthy and diseased that no mere clipping and dealing with the branches, no mere application of superficial remedies will avail; the change must be radical and fundamental. The only hope for mankind is actually to be born again and have a completely and entirely new start and beginning - a new nature, new roots. The men of today say that they are tired of sentiment and slop, that they believe in realism. They have given up religion because they regard it as a form of dope with its emotionalism. They want facts and reality. Yet they reject the only gospel which gives them facts, facts about themselves and their real state and nature.

But let us consider for a while *the thoroughness of the gospel as revealed in its view of worship and communion with God.*

The sermon preached by John the Baptist which is recorded in these verses in the third chapter of Luke is particularly insistent on this point, and I need scarcely remind you that it was one of the main themes in our Lord's preaching. Two aspects of this are particularly emphasized in this connection.

The first is emphasized in verse 5: 'Every valley shall be filled and every mountain and hill shall be brought low; and the crooked shall be made straight, and the rough ways shall be made smooth'. It is also brought out in that phrase in the eighth verse where John says, 'and begin not to say within yourselves, We have Abraham to our father'. And all this is greatly enhanced when we remember that the words were spoken to the Pharisees and scribes and Sadducees. It is just a reminder to us of the supremacy of God and that he does not judge by appearances. The great characteristic of the worldly judgment is that it goes almost entirely by superficial appearances, as indeed it must. Hence the world is full of divisions and distinctions, of mountains and valleys, of crooked and straight, of children of Abraham and those who are not. Some appear to be nice and good and moral and clean, others foul and vile and immoral and diseased. Some appear as if they had never done any wrong, as if they had no need to repent and had no need for Christ to die for them on Calvary. They see the need of conversion and rebirth in violent and terrible sinners, as they call them, but as for themselves they cannot see the need, neither can the world. Such is the superficial view. But how different is the appearance when the roots are examined! What a difference there is when you cease to compare them with each other, and place them all face to face with Jesus Christ and with God. Compared with the Himalayas our little mountains and valleys cease to be and are all one; compared with God's plummet our straight and crooked become indistinguishable; compared with the Son of God distinctions into Jew and Gentile cease to be relevant. God has revealed Himself in His Son and the revelation has condemned all. Degrees of imperfection no

[85]

longer count. 'There is none righteous' – no one without sin – 'no, not one'. The axe is indeed laid to the root of the trees and *all* have fallen.

But the Christian view of worship reminds us also of another truth which is sadly forgotten during these present days, and that is, that the gospel calls for a definite act of repentance and decision whatever our state or condition – we must 'bring forth fruits worthy of repentance'. Ah! how thorough is the gospel! It will take nothing for granted and it probes and examines to the very depths. A general agreement with certain propositions is not enough, a good disposition will not satisfy. That I say, I believe in God and Jesus Christ, and so on, is not accepted merely on my statement. What have I done about it? What proof have I got of my genuineness? That I have enjoyed sermons, that I hope to get to heaven, and talk about God, will not satisfy the gospel demands. Am I genuine? Have I produced fruit worthy of repentance? Have I left my sins? Have I turned my back upon iniquity? Has there been a definite decision in my life? Have I said farewell to all I know to be wrong? Have I prostrated myself before God and thrown myself on His mercy? Have I, forsaking all else, committed myself to Him and consecrated my life and all to Him? Idealism and nice and good talks and tears, and occasional spasms of being filled with true hopes, ideas and aspirations – all these things are not enough and avail me nothing. The question is, has my religion affected my life, changed my disposition, renovated my nature, affected all my actions and dealings? Religion and worship deal with God. Have I found God, and has my life become godly? Nothing else matters. All the good will and good intentions in the world are useless – the axe is now laid 'to the *root* of the trees'.

But, after all, the real thoroughness of the gospel is only to be seen fully when we consider the work of our blessed Lord and Saviour Jesus Christ. We have seen already the thoroughness with which the sin and need of man are exposed by the gospel and how, driving man from all his hiding places and excuses, it drives him to his knees and to an act of repentance; but nowhere is it more glorious than when it displays our Saviour as the Redeemer from sin. And as we consider this, no one, surely, can fail to rejoice with me in the thoroughness of the work, and in the fact that the axe was indeed laid to the root of the trees. Consider this as shown in His life, in His death, in His resurrection and in His endless glorified life in heaven. Oh! the thoroughness of it all, the finality, the radical nature of the divine scheme! Where can I begin? How can one hope to deal with it at all adequately?

First of all, *His life*. Let no one doubt His true humanity, let no one imagine that He was God with a mere cloak or clothing of flesh. 'He was made of a woman, made under the law'. He was born a babe in Bethlehem. Yea, though He was 'in the form of God, and thought it not robbery to be equal with God', He nevertheless 'made himself of no reputation, and took upon him the form of a servant, and was made in the likeness of men. And being found in fashion as a man, he humbled himself and became obedient unto death, even the death of the cross' (Phil. 2: 6-8). O yes! the incarnation is a real fact, it could not possibly be more thorough. And as He grew and lived He continued in the same way. He avoided nothing. He met all the difficulties and all the obligations. He shrank from nothing, but faced all. He even submitted to baptism without any real need, took the contradiction and abuse of sinners without complaint, and above all 'was in *all* points tempted like as we are, yet without sin' (Heb. 4 : 15). All the forces of the devil and hell were turned against Him, He was tested and tried to the uttermost, yet at the end He could turn to God and say 'Father, I have finished the work which thou gavest me to do' (Jn 17 : 4). There was nothing left undone.

But look at *His death* for a moment and consider it as an expiation for the sin of the whole world. What are we told about it? Well, those sufferings were enough, according to John, for all. Listen! 'He is the propitiation for our sins; and not for ours only, but also for the sins of the whole world' (1Jn 2:2). The whole world! The axe to the very root of the trees. Listen to the author of the Epistle to the Hebrews saying exactly the same thing. Referring to the sacrificial death of our Lord he says, 'But this man, after he had offered one sacrifice for sins for ever, sat down on the right hand of God' (Heb 10:12), and again, 'there remaineth no more sacrifice for sins' (Heb 10:26). But listen to the words of our Lord Himself as He calls from the cross, 'It is finished'. The sins of the whole world He had borne upon Himself, He had fulfilled the law, had silenced the jeers of all the devils, and had rendered satisfaction unto God. The sacrifice was completed. It was indeed finished, once and for all, world without end!

'But, ah' says someone, 'it cost Him His life and He was buried in the grave.' Wait! What of His dealing with death and the grave? There, too, you find the same thoroughness and completeness. This is the word, 'Death is swallowed up in victory'. Swallowed up! What could be more complete and entire? By the resurrection, by the rising from the dead, the very last enemy of all had been conquered for ever. 'Swallowed up', entirely consumed, thoroughly vanquished and destroyed!

But consider His sustaining power exercised from glory through the agency of the Holy Spirit. He not only saves from hell, He rescues from the power of sin, He preserves and keeps and sustains us all the way and to the very end. I have spoken of the thoroughness of the salvation. What could be more thorough or certain or secure than those words of Paul, 'For I am persuaded that neither death, nor life, nor angels, nor principalities, nor powers, nor things present, nor things to come, nor height, nor depth, nor any other creature, shall be able to separate us from the love of God which is in Christ Jesus our Lord' (Rom 8:38-39). Nothing more thorough? Yes, there is just one - a word spoken by our Lord Himself. Here it is, 'And I give unto them eternal lifee: and they shall never perish, neither shall any man pluck them out of my hand' (Jn 10:28). What could be more thorough or more satisfying? The gospel of Jesus Christ does not come to you with vague, useless idealisms and generalities, it is thorough-going and drastic. It lays its axe to the root of the trees. It convicts you of your sin and exposes your foulness. It lays bare your need, but, praise God, with equal thoroughness it deals with it. It convicts! Yes! But it also saves, and saves to all eternity. The work is done. It is already completed. You have nothing to do but to believe it, to accept, to act upon it by turning to God tonight, thanking Him for His Son and consecrating your life to Him for ever. 'Bring forth therefore fruits worthy of repentance' (Lk. 3:8). I urge it upon you, for thorough as His work as Redeemer is, His work as Judge is equally thorough. Listen to those ominous words, 'Therefore every tree which bringeth not forth good fruit is hewn down, and cast into the fire'. Not one will be missed. Every tree! None can escape judgment who do not believe in Him. Yes! His 'fan is in his hand and he will *thoroughly* purge his floor' 'The wheat' he 'will gather into his garner; but' and just as certainly, 'the chaff - he will burn with fire unquenchable' (Matt. 3:10, 12).

Oh! I beseech you, repent and believe, accept the gospel offer of salvation tonight and be made eternally safe. Amen.

8: *The Wedding Garment*

*

And he saith unto him, Friend, how camest thou in hither not having a wedding garment? And he was speechless.

Matthew 22:12[1]

One of the greatest dangers in connection with both the preaching and private reading of the Word of God is that they should simply produce some vague general effect upon us instead of that definite particular effect and result, which alone can benefit us. You must all have experienced this many a time. You sit and listen to the sermon or the address and something happens to you. You are moved and disturbed and perhaps carried away. It would be obviously wrong to say that nothing had happened to you, and yet if someone were to ask you at the end what exactly happened, what actually had occurred to you and in what respect or respects you had been affected, you would be unable to give an exact answer. There was an effect, but it was vague, general and indefinite. The result was that it passed off completely and left you precisely where you were at the beginning. The same thing can happen and will happen to us when we read the Scriptures privately for ourselves. The very cadence and music of the words, especially in our Authorised Version, affects and influences us and carries us away. We read one of the Psalms, or one of those mighty overwhelming periods of eloquence from the pen of Paul, such as the 8th of Romans or the 3rd of Ephesians, and we feel ourselves

[1]Preached at Aberavon, February 21, 1932.

being moved and stimulated. And yet, it may well be, unless we have been very careful and have been reading 'in the Spirit', that the whole effect has been purely general – poetic and aesthetic. We cannot describe exactly what has happened and in reality have nothing tangible left when the effect has passed away.

Now I believe we can lay it down as being axiomatic that God never intended that the reading or preaching of His Word should produce an effect like that. The Bible is not merely literature or poetry; it was never intended to produce merely an artistic or general effect. It is the Word of God to man, and what is intended is not so much that we should vaguely feel that God is speaking to us, but rather that we should know exactly what He is saying. Nor is it enough that we should have some sense and feeling of the holiness and awesomeness of it all. That is inevitable as a part of our experience, but my point is that we must not be content with that, nor even be carried away by that, for we must remember that God Himself is speaking to us. God's speaking in the Old Testament was direct and definite always. How much more so in the New Testament! Our business at all times therefore when studying the Scriptures is to guard ourselves against that mere general impression and to insist upon discovering what exactly it is that God is saying to us.

Now this is more necessary, perhaps, with this parable that we are considering tonight than with anything else that is to be found in the sacred records. It is such a perfect and, at the same time, such a terrible picture! We read it or hear it and we cannot but be affected by it. It may cause us to shudder, may stimulate our imagination and even alarm us by its horrifying figure of the end of this guest at the wedding feast, and yet the whole thing can be quite ephemeral and passing, and after a few hours we return to our normal state. I believe our Lord had this very thing in mind when in His story of the rich man and Lazarus He pictures the former in hell arguing and pleading with Abraham to send someone from the dead to plead with his brothers who were still alive. Abraham replies by saying, 'If they hear not Moses and the prophets, neither will they be persuaded, though one rose from the dead'. 'I have no doubt,' He seems to say, 'that they would be moved and alarmed for a while, but they would soon forget again.' We must not be content, therefore, with just feeling that this is a terrifying, horrifying picture. We must discover what exactly it is that it has to say to us. What is its message? Our Lord was not just painting a dramatic picture, not out merely to produce some histrionic effect. He was out to preach and inculcate a vital truth. What was that?

To my mind there is only one great principle taught in this parable. There are many minor and subsidiary truths but there is one that stands out above all the others. And that is, that ultimately and finally, there is but one test that God applies to us – whether we have given our wills, our very selves to Him or not. I say 'ultimately and finally' because that is the exact point which is made here, for we are shown with awful, terrifying clearness that unless we have actually done this, all else is of no value whatsoever. Here is a man actually in the banquet hall, seated at the table with the food placed before him and ready to eat, who, suddenly, at the critical, all-important moment is condemned, bound hand and foot and cast into outer darkness! And all because of just one thing. Everything right, except that he had no wedding garment on – that he had disobeyed the king in that vitally important respect! How frequently our Lord pressed this point. With what terrible clearness is it to be seen in the New Testament by those who have eyes to see! There it is, plain and clear, and yet men and women will not see it, and so go to perdition. Look at the parable about the two houses at the close of the Sermon on the Mount. Those houses were apparently identical in every respect, except in just one thing and that so vital that it made all the difference, that terrible difference! The similarity in all other respects could not compensate for that one difference. 'Listening to my words', says our Lord, 'is right and good. But it is not enough. They must be done, be carried out. That you have heard and enjoyed and praised will not save you. Have you *done* them? To call me "Lord, Lord" is good in its way but it is quite meaningless unless you do those things that I tell you.' Then again we see precisely the same truth brought out in the well-known incident of our Lord's meeting with the rich young ruler. After the young man had pointed out all he had done and how he had kept the commandments, our Lord turns to him and says, 'Yet one thing thou lackest. Go ...' Just *one* thing. Was the young man prepared to give himself, to give his will, entirely to Christ? Just that one thing! That one failure cancelled all else and the young man went away sorrowful.

Nothing matters except this one thing of giving our wills to God. It determines whether we are destined for heaven or hell. How vitally, how terribly important it is! And yet, how sadly ignored, and especially today! Is it not our one difficulty with the question of religion? We are prepared to do anything and everything else. But not this. And it applies not only to those who are outside the Christian church, but also, alas! to many who are inside. Those outside are often willing to give up this and that sin, are prepared to do a certain amount of good and help others, ready even to read their Bibles and attend a place of worship on Sunday, but they cannot see why they must stay behind in the aftermeeting and acknowledge Christ to be their Saviour and Lord and align themselves with others who make the same profession. They are prepared to give well toward the funds and so on, but they are not prepared to give themselves. They say they believe the gospel and that they propose to be, as it were, unofficial Christians outside the church. They cannot see that they must be known and recognized as Christians and as active church members helping to bear a common witness and testimony to the saving power of our Lord. Yes! everything except the wedding garment!

But I say that it applies also to many who are members of churches. Their name is on the church roll, they attend regularly on Sundays, they give generously towards the cause, they desire to go to heaven. But they cannot see that all this necessitates their forsaking worldly, fleshly pleasures, their giving up of everything that their conscience tells them is wrong and all the things that are so frequently condemned in the New Testament – lusts, passions, envyings, greed, avarice etc. They cannot see that they ought to enjoy the prayer meetings and the fellowship meetings and throw themselves wholeheartedly and entirely on God's side. They desire to be Christians, but in their own way and on their own terms, and not as laid down once and for ever in the New Testament, and as confirmed ever since in the lives of the saints. Yes, there it is again! Everything! except the wedding garment! Everything, except giving up our wills, our very selves to God, everything except the one thing which is essential, namely, that we should cast ourselves entirely on His mercy and place ourselves wholeheartedly and without reservation in His hands! Do we realize what such a resistance means and implies? Have we ever contemplated the dreadful consequences in which it will involve us? It is because I am anxious that all our eyes may be opened to this terrible sin of refusing to give ourselves to God, and that thereby we may come to hate and abominate it and, forsaking it, give ourselves to God, that I ask you to consider with me some of the principles involved in this matter. They are all shown clearly in this parable.

Consider, in the first place, *the arrogance* and *the enmity towards God* which this attitude displays. One does not need to be a very profound psychologist in order to see that that was the fundamental trouble with this man to whom our Lord refers here. Neither does one need much insight into oneself to see that there is that sort of person in each and everyone of us who is born into this world. Shall we listen to him as he soliloquises seated there at the table. He has heard the invitation and has accepted it and has entered the banqueting hall. He is anxious to be there and to have all that he can get, but he objects to this need and necessity of wearing the wedding-garment. He looks round and sees all the others properly and appropriately clad and in his heart he despises them. 'Ah, the miserable worms,' he says, 'all bowing and scraping to the king, all afraid to maintain their own individuality and independence. All like sheep obeying this king. Who is this king? What right has he to dictate to me or to anyone else as to what we should do? I am prepared to come to his banquet in honour of his son, but why cannot I come in my own way? I prefer to come dressed as I am, why must I be forced to put on a certain type of garment? I won't do it! This king has no right to expect it either. Who is *he*! I come to this banquet in my own way and refuse to be dictated to by anyone!'

How natural his thinking is, but how terrible! Prepared to eat of the king's banquet and to get all the pleasure at it, and yet insulting the king and dishonouring him. Taking the gift and yet feeling a sense of grudge and enmity towards the giver. Accepting of the king's bounty, and yet questioning the king's greatness and dignity! Nay more, feeling a real sense of grievance against the king. Look at the wretch as he sits there at the table! He is the one exception, the one odd person at the feast, the only one who, in the smallness of his heart and soul, causes a discord on this joyous, happy occasion. And all because of his own little self-importance! All because he refuses to be like everybody else. All because he still keeps on thinking about his own little rights and big ideas even in the presence of the magnificence and kindness of the king. There he sits in the bitterness and misery of his soul, a perfect picture of hopeless self-contradiction, muttering to himself and trying to preserve his own dignity even in the presence of his king. That is the picture. His object was, as we say today, 'to stand up to the king', to 'assert himself', even while he was accepting a gift. How ungracious, how arrogant!

But all that is a perfect picture of sin. That is indeed of the very essence of sin. Do you remember the account of the first sin which is given in the Book of Genesis? It is precisely the same thing that is said here. The serpent approaches Eve and says, 'Yea, hath God said, Ye shall not eat of every tree of the garden?' In other words, 'What right has God to say that?' Then when Eve proceeds to repeat the commandment he replies: 'Don't believe Him. Ye shall not surely die.' And again, 'For God doth know that in the day ye eat thereof, then your eyes shall be opened, and ye shall be as gods, knowing good and evil.' 'Who is God?' says Satan in effect, 'what right has He to speak like that and to rule you in this way? Don't listen to Him. Live your own life in your own way. What right has God to upset your life and stand between you and your pleasure? Why will He not allow you to do as you like and worship Him in your own way?'

Yes, there it was at the beginning and it has remained the same ever since. Have we not all known these questions within our own hearts? Are not men and women voicing them constantly during these present days? 'Why should God do this or that?' or 'I do not see that God should do this or that.' 'What right has God to dictate?' 'What right has God to send anyone to hell?' 'What right has God or anyone else to ask me to give up my will to Him?' Or as someone actually put it to me last summer, 'I would prefer to remain a failure using my own will than to be a success and find happiness by giving my will to God.' In our pride and self-will we try to stand up to God. We put our little opinions against His! We desire to get to heaven but, we say, we 'cannot see' this and that.

We cannot see why God insists upon our believing that Christ died for us and that that is the only way to His heart. We cannot see why we must give up our sins and give our very lives to Him. We feel it is unfair, that it is wrong, that God is a tyrant and, forsaking this sacred writ which is the only authoritative statement on the subject, we are trying to construct a new God who is all-loving but devoid of righteousness and truth. God must be as we think! And if there is anything that does not tally with our view it is a blemish in God!

Oh! the arrogance and enmity of sin. Do you realize that you are guilty of it? Do you know that every time you query or question or debate with the voice of God as it speaks within you and urges you to give up all else and give yourself entirely to Him, that you are in that precise position? The creature arguing with the Creator! The clay reasoning with the potter. The subject insulting the king! The wedding garment in itself matters very little. The point is that the wearing of it is the king's wish. The actual little things concerning which you are quibbling with God, in themselves are hardly worthy of our consideration. The terrible thing is that we are questioning the whole authority of God – putting our opinions and ideas against His! Oh! let me make this quite plain. We are to submit not because we agree but because it is God's will. By nature, we will always disagree. We like sin and enjoy evil and if we are to wait until we no longer do so we shall have to wait for ever. The first reason for leaving sin is that God commands me to do so. He is perfect. He is pure. He is just and righteous. He made me. He loves me. He knows what is best for me. Though I do not fully understand or know the reasons why, I do it because He tells me. He knows better than I do. I trust Him more than I trust myself because He is who and what He is. Beloved friends! see the arrogance and enmity and spitefulness of your refusal to bow the knee to God's will! That is exactly what sin and disobedience means. You are questioning and querying Almighty God! The only reason He gives when He asks us to be holy is that He is holy Himself!

But when we consider the *base ingratitude which this attitude reveals*, its arrogance becomes still more obvious. I have already described this man as being mean-souled. How obvious that is when we consider the facts. To start with it is made clear that he had no claim whatsoever upon the king. There are certain people who by birth, as it were, have the right to be present on state occasions. There are certain people who are entitled to expect an invitation and feel aggrieved and slighted if they do not receive one. And such people had been invited by this particular king but had all failed to be present. This particular man of whom we read in our text did not belong to that group. He had no right, no real claim whatsoever. It was nothing but the graciousness of the king that had invited him at all. In a sense he was quite unfitted and quite unsuited for such an occasion. He was not of the royal blood, nor even of the aristocratic or noble blood. He was just an ordinary man who by a very gracious act of his sovereign was invited to the feast. What an honour! What a great privilege! Suddenly in the midst of your duties and perhaps in the midst of doing something even against the king – for we read that some were 'bad' – to be invited into the palace! There he was in the palace with a glorious feast before him, with the lights and the gaiety, the pleasure and all that resulted from the munificence of the king who was anxious to honour his son. All, everything, for nothing and without his being consulted at all. All free! He had nothing to do but to show his gratitude and thoroughly enjoy himself. All he had to do was to show his appreciation and to do everything he could to be worthy of the great occasion, and in no way to disappoint his gracious benefactor! But as we see here, he failed to do so and allowed his pride to upset everything. Was there ever such ingratitude, such baseness! What a cad he appears to have been! What a vile creature! What a miserable worm!

And yet, what is all that in comparison with what is true of each one of us who refuses to bow the knee willingly and readily to God? Do you realize what that refusal really means? Let me tell you. I have told you often before, but may the Holy Spirit so strengthen me tonight that you may so see it as to hate yourself for your ingratitude, and put yourself right with God at once! I have pointed out that this man had no claim whatsoever upon the king's munificence. How much more so is that true of us with respect to God? We have no claim upon Him and no right to His gifts. Worse, by our sinfulness and disobedience, by our flouting of His laws and our spurning of His voice, we have not only forfeited any claim to His love, but have actually invited His wrath and condemnation. We have sinned deliberately against Him, deliberately turned our backs upon Him, and have done everything which is insulting to His holy Name. Though men may have been outwardly respectable and free from certain sins, can they claim that they have obeyed God and that they have been what they have been in order to glorify and magnify His holy Name? Not to think of God is grievously to offend Him. Not to praise Him day by day for all He is and has done is in itself terrible sin. The *angels* adore and worship Him, why, even the Son bows down before Him! And you and I have gone for days, weeks, months, years without ever thinking of Him at all, and even when He has disturbed us and tried to speak to us we have asked Him to wait until we have more time! No! we have not a single claim on His love and we richly merit His eternal wrath. But, so wonderful and amazing is His love, that, in spite of it all, He sent His only begotten Son to live, die and rise again for us. In Christ He offers us complete pardon and forgiveness, reinstatement in His family as sons, power to overcome the devil and all evil, all

[99]

the fruits and graces of the Holy Spirit in this world and, in the world to come, everlasting bliss and eternal life. In spite of all our sins, *that* is what He has done. He has done much more than to invite us to the banquet in honour of His Son. He gave His Son to death and the cross for our sake. Oh! what a gift! What amazing love! What mercy and generosity! It is so great as to be beyond our comprehension. The greatest gift possible. An infinite and eternal gift. The king not only giving a feast, but giving Himself! But because He insists on one simple little condition, in a sense a mere trifle, simply that we should honour Him and show our gratitude to Him who so richly deserves it, we object and grumble and complain and regard Him almost as an enemy. Could anything be so terrible! Could anything be more ungrateful! Simply because He asks you to be holy and to be adorned with His righteousness, simply because He asks you to take off those filthy rags of your sinful life or your self-righteous attitude, you spurn His love and reject His amazing gift. Have you seen that? Have you realized it? Oh! see it tonight! Behold God's love pouring itself out for you on Calvary's hill. It is bad enough, as we have seen, to question His law, but oh! the enormity of the sin that rejects His love. Can you not see that

> *Love so amazing, so divine*
> *Demands my soul, my life, my all?*

Ah! the ingratitude of it all.

But I must say a word about *the folly and the tragedy of this attitude.* Surely the man depicted in this parable is the most wretched person mentioned in the New Testament. For sheer misery and wretchedness there is nothing that even approaches this. There he sits, thinking himself to be so clever, nursing his self-esteem and despising his fellow-guests who appear to him to be slavish and frightened.

How proud of himself he must feel! What a wonderful man he is to get what he wants in his own way! But suddenly the king appears and, beholding this man and observing him to be without the wedding garment, approaches him and says to him gently, 'Friend, how camest thou in hither not having a wedding garment?' And he is speechless! What can he say? That word 'Friend' has done it. It has made him see himself and his utterly despicable nature. 'Friend'! But it is too late. The opportunity has gone. When an offer of love is rejected there is nothing left. He is bound hand and foot and cast into outer darkness where there is nothing but weeping and gnashing of teeth and all the agony of useless remorse. Oh! what a fool! what madness! There in the outer darkness, cursing and kicking himself, tormenting himself because of his folly – when he might have been with the others in the banqueting chamber, enjoying the feast and the music and the good cheer and all the happiness and joy of the gorgeous palace! All because of just that one act of disobedience.

Oh! the tragedy of it all! What a fool we see him to be. How obvious is his error! But have you realized that your position is even worse if you have not submitted yourself unreservedly to God in Jesus Christ our Lord? As certain as you are alive now, all this will happen to you one day. You will see Him and all He has done for you. You will see how you might have conquered your sins and temptations in this world and how you might have inherited heaven, like so many others that lived at the same time as yourself in Aberavon and who had precisely the same difficulties. Ah yes! you *will* see it. But it will be too late then. And you will begin an eternity of useless remorse, of hell! All because you would not submit. All because you ignored God's voice within. All because you held on to some useless worldly pleasure or some sin, all because you feared the opinion of men more than that of God. Oh! I plead with you, see the madness, the folly, the tragedy of it all. It is not yet too late. There is still time. You can do it now. God's majesty dictates it, His love demands it, your own eternal soul cries out for it and deserves it. Give in! Give yourself to God tonight! Do it now! Submit and be saved. Thank God now for His amazing gift of love. Show your genuineness and appreciation by standing for Him tonight, by letting others know that you have given yourself to Him and by pledging yourself that as His Holy Spirit strengthens you, and at whatever cost and sacrifice, your one ambition for life and for ever will be to glorify and magnify His Holy Name. Put on the wedding garment now and enjoy the heavenly feast for ever! For His Name's sake. Amen.

9: *Away from Jesus or With Him*

And they began to pray him to depart out of their coasts.
And when he was come into the ship, he that had been
possessed with the devil prayed him that he might be with
him.   Mark 5:17–18[1]

I call your attention to these two verses this evening
because, between them, they seem to me to sum up the
whole of mankind, and indicate the only two possible
divisions or categories into which mankind can be
divided. We all, finally, belong to the one or the other of
these groups. We desire either to get rid of Christ or else
to be with Him and give ourselves entirely to Him. There
is in reality no other possibility. We are either for or
against. But, such is the deceitfulness of our human
nature, we are always trying to avoid that fundamental
division, and ever trying to persuade ourselves that there
are other innumerable and closely related categories. We
have a feeling that this clear-cut cleavage here revealed,
between the attitude of the Gadarene people in general
and this man in particular, is extreme and therefore does
not fit the average case. We read that these people 'prayed
him to depart' or, as Luke puts it, 'besought him' to
depart and we tend to take shelter behind these strong
terms. They almost suggest violence to us and we feel that
whatever else our attitude may or may not be, we have at
very worst never 'prayed or besought' Christ to depart
from us. And yet, the whole teaching of the gospel is that
eventually we are in one or the other of the two groups.

[1]Aberavon, February 28, 1932.

[103]

What matters, ultimately, is not the means or methods which we adopt, not whether we are violent or not, but the state of our hearts. Passive resistance is as much resistance as that which is active. A refusal to honour is definitely to dishonour. One man attacks with vehemence and vituperation, but he who merely curls his lip and sneers disdainfully is often a much more dangerous enemy. It is not the form or the particular mode of expression that matters, but the state of the heart, the motive. And my contention is that finally there are but two motives, but two attitudes towards Christ and salvation. We either pray him to depart or else we pray to be allowed to go with Him.

It is because we fail to recognize this today that there is all this present confusion both within and without the church. We will insist upon judging ourselves and one another by almost every other standard – sins, good works, talk, etc., etc. These are our categories. We speak of people as being respectable or not respectable, or we speak of them in terms of certain particular sins and their precise way of committing them, thereby confusing the issue and forming but a superficial judgment. That has always been the tendency of mankind, that has always been the greatest enemy which the gospel has had to fight. The whole essence of the gospel teaching is that, finally, nothing matters save our attitude towards Christ and the salvation which He brings us from God. That is why it is really the gospel of the grace of God. That is why all who truly believe it must for ever and to all eternity be so thankful for it. What saves me is that I am now judged by that standard. Were I judged by my own standard of morality and behaviour, I should of necessity be condemned, for I fail to satisfy my own demands. Were I to be judged by the standard of the Jewish moral law, I am hopelessly condemned and without a standing. Were I to be judged by the lives of the saints, my chances of salvation would be practically nil. Were I to be judged by the perfect life revealed and lived by Jesus Christ of Nazareth, then I am utterly undone. But by the eternal grace of God that is no longer the test. The question now is, What do I make of Him? What is my disposition towards Him? What is my attitude towards His salvation? By the grace of God I am not simply asked, 'Are you perfect?', and condemned at sight because of my imperfection. In Christ the new question is, 'Would you like to be perfect?' 'Do you long to be good and pure and noble?'

That is where so many good people go astray and that is why I call attention to this well-known incident here tonight. It brings out the new test or differentiation introduced by the gospel. The man from whom the devils had been driven did not immediately become absolutely perfect. We are actually told that Christ had in a sense to correct this and to show what was right. Oh no! he was not perfect. It was not that which differentiated him from his fellows. What was it then? Just this, that he desired to be with Christ, whereas they desired to get rid of Him! A Christian is nowhere depicted in the New Testament as one who is absolutely sinless and perfect – that is the false charge brought against us by the world. The Christian is one who longs, who desires, to be perfect and sinless and who is striving so to be. Often failing and falling, sometimes discouraged and almost dismayed, but still hoping, still fighting, still pressing towards the mark. As I say, by the grace of God we are judged, not so much by what we are, as by what we hope to be – what we would like to be! It is all a matter of motive, of fundamental disposition. And at that level, as I have already said several times, there are but two possible positions. And we must insist upon keeping this perfectly clear and distinct. Respectability or not makes no difference here, culture or its lack cannot count at this point, open or hidden sins are identical at this level, indifference and

[105]

active hostility appear as twins from the same parent here. The question is, What is your ambition? Are you out to be holy? Do you long to know God and to be reconciled to Him? Whatever else you may do or not do matters not at all. The only thing that matters is, What do you feel about Christ? Do you desire to get rid of Him? Or do you desire to be with Him? For, as certainly as we are in this chapel at this present moment, it is either one or the other. Which is it? Be honest! Examine yourself! Make quite sure tonight with the aid of the Holy Spirit who is here to help us. Your eternal destiny may well depend upon it.

Shall I try to aid you by indicating some of the ways in which men show plainly that their real desire is that Christ should depart - that they may get rid of Him? That He is present with us here tonight in this building and on all such occasions, His own promises during His earthly life and ministry prove abundantly. More than that, how frequently have they been verified in the subsequent history of the Christian church! I need not stay with that - we are all well aware of it. His presence also during illness, bereavement, and trials, we all must recognize. No one can protest for a moment that he or she has never had even the opportunity of accepting or rejecting Him. We no longer see Him with the eyes of flesh as those people did long ago, but though 'unseen He is for ever at hand'. He makes his proposals to us one by one. The invitation is to 'whosoever will'. Oh! yes, we have all known and felt His presence. What have we done with Him? I fear that many have done their very best to get rid of Him like these people here and have prayed Him to depart. How have they done that? Here are some of the ways.

They may have deliberately held themselves back and quenched the Spirit in chapel or church. One Sunday, while sitting in the chapel and listening to the sermon, or perhaps at some point during the service, they felt themselves being moved and disturbed. Something was leading them on and dealing with them. They felt 'a presence' and knew that God was dealing with them. They realized they were being softened and melted and on the point of losing themselves and giving in. They already felt a partial sense of release and joy, but, fearing that they might make a scene or that they would be laughed at, they deliberately resisted and tried to shake off the influence. And they succeeded! In what? In driving Christ away!

Or perhaps it was that they did not experience quite as much as that, but they experienced a good deal of it and knew that God had been dealing with them. And yet, instead of longing and waiting for the next Sunday and going with all speed to God's house, they have deliberately stayed away and remained at home. 'Ah', they have said, 'if I go there again I shall almost certainly get converted.' And they have stayed away. Why? Because they do not want to be converted. In other words, they have done their best to get rid of Christ.

Another way of doing the same thing is to ignore the voice of conscience and to continue deliberately with those things against which God's voice within you warns you. This may be a form of pleasure or amusement, or it may be a book, the deliberate object of which is to try to ridicule the Bible and undermine its influence. Or it may be done by continuing to associate yourself with people whom you know to be bad and harmful in their influence upon you. In any way whatsoever that we disobey the voice of our conscience we are simply trying to get rid of Christ.

Another favourite way is so to busy ourselves with other things that we shall have no time for thought or contemplation. We try to crowd Christ out of our lives by means of other things – work, business, family, friends, anything and everything except Christ. But I need not elaborate. We are all, alas, familiar with these things. The poor Gadarenes did it with Christ in the days of His humiliation. We do it with Christ in His most exalted

[107]

state. They prayed Jesus of Nazareth to depart from them; we shut out of our lives the Lord of glory! What can account for such madness? In considering what accounted for it in their case, we shall discover the causes in our own case. Then, having dealt with that, we shall proceed to the more pleasant and happy business of showing what exactly it was that made this demoniac man who had been healed so anxious to go with Christ.

What was the matter with these Gadarenes?

The first thing that is brought out very plainly and clearly in all the accounts of this incident is that they were filled with a *spirit of fear*. This miracle seems to have alarmed them and more or less terrorized them. And it was as the result of this fear and terror that they pray Christ to depart from them. What are the causes of this fear, what are the elements that together produce this anxiety in the presence of Christ? Let us just look at some of them.

There is no doubt but that the miracle itself and the extraordinary results which it produced, in itself partly gave rise to this fear. We must not be too hard on these Gadarenes. There is something in the very nature of miraculous events which is awe-inspiring. At the close of the preceding chapter we read an account of our Lord's performing that miracle at sea and quieting the storm. And we are told that the disciples 'feared exceedingly'. That, as a matter of fact, was their common and most frequent reaction to every exhibition of miraculous power on the part of our Lord. We find it again on the Mount of Transfiguration. The disciples were 'sore afraid'. To a lesser extent we have all noticed it at certain times. Is there not something awe-inspiring about birth and especially about death? The stoutest hearts are always shaken in the presence of death. Here is a mystery – a sense of power which we cannot fathom or understand. And these Gadarenes felt that about Christ and the miracle He had just performed. In a sense it was the fear of the eternal and the almighty – the fear of the power of Christ. It is mainly superstitious and yet there is that in it which belongs essentially to true religion. But I have referred to it this evening because I know that sometimes it can be a very important factor in this question of conversion. A man is being dealt with and is in the actual process. But he holds back because of this sense of fear. He does not know exactly what it is. But there is a vague sense of fear of the infinite and of the unknown. And the devil is well aware of this and encourages it and tries to persuade his innocent victim that this power is harmful, that he is losing himself and may well lose control of his reason and of his senses. So he advises the would-be convert to hold back and hold out and not give himself up in this way to another power. And in sheer terror and fright, without knowing or understanding exactly what they are doing, many do hold back. It is a new experience and they do not quite understand it. What have I to say to all this? Simply this. Do not listen to the devil! The power, though great and eternal and beyond your understanding, is nevertheless the power of God, the manifestation of eternal love. Unfathomable power! Yes! But the power that quells the storm and restores order out of chaos. It *is* almighty. But it is also good. Let not the power frighten you. It is the power of God!

But that alone does not explain the fear of these Gadarenes. There is little doubt but that what frightened them most of all was their own sense of guilt. And the presence of Jesus Christ always produces that! You remember how Peter felt it when he first knew the Lord? What were his words? 'Depart from me; for I am a sinful man, O Lord' (Luke 5:8). In Peter's case it was a noble feeling of unworthiness in addition to the sense of guilt, but the main point is nevertheless the same. Beauty always exposes ugliness, spotless perfection unmasks a sham; nothing reveals to us our emptiness and woe so much as the lives of the saints, and above all, the life of our blessed Lord Himself. Standing in the presence of this amazing Person who had just performed such a wonderful deed, seeing and observing His meekness and His calmness, His unaffected manner and His quiet confidence, catching perhaps a glimpse of something super-human in His eyes, they just felt themselves to be vile and contemptible. He seemed to be opening up the very recesses of their hearts. He seemed to read them as an open book. As He had cast the devils out of that man and into the swine, so He seemed to be able to look through them and to devine their deepest thoughts. What might He do or not do? They just felt themselves withering in His presence. If He did not go soon they might all be unmasked in the presence of everyone and all their sins revealed. And they were afraid of it. Afraid of themselves, afraid of their own guilt and afraid of the judgment that was to come! It was intolerable, so they begged and implored of Christ to go. He convicted them of their sin and made them see themselves as they really were.

Men and women still try to shake off Christ today, by the various methods we have noticed, for this very reason. Listening to the sermon they begin to see that the gospel is right and that they are wrong. Their sins are brought out before them one by one. They feel ashamed and horrified. And as they sit and listen and hear that there can be only one end to such a life they are filled with terror and horror. They know the gospel is right and they have a glimpse of their own awful state. It is not surprising that they are filled with fear and terror. In a sense, it is not surprising also that they imitate these Gadarenes and try to get rid of Christ. The state of being under conviction is not only uncomfortable but alarming and awe-inspiring. One feels wretched and miserable. And the impulse always is to avoid that which so disturbs us. 'Keep away from chapel, stop reading the Bible and singing hymns. Cease doing everything that tends to remind you of your

sinfulness and of the retribution that is to come.' That is
what a voice within us whispers to us. Keep away from it
all! We all hate to be made miserable and unhappy and, at
first, that is precisely the effect which the presence of
Christ produces. He unmasks us and searches us to the
depths. Yes!' conviction is hateful and alarming and
human nature does its best to wriggle out of it and avoid it
and to get rid of it. But oh! the mistake, the tragedy! If we
only realized that Christ was doing it for our good. If we
but realized that it was the first essential stage in putting
us right! If we but grasped that it was nothing but the
prelude to conversion – that He who makes us feel the
guilt can also remove it if we only allow Him to do so.
Instead of running away or keeping away because of the
painfulness of conviction, thank God for it and ask Him
to complete the work!

I must just note the other element in this fear. That
was, I am sure, a feeling that He who had done so much to
this demoniac and also to the swine, not only had
sufficient power to do the same to them, but probably
would insist upon doing so. He seemed to be able to do
anything He liked and no one could stop Him. It has
been suggested that the loss of the swine accounted for
this feeling. It may have done so up to a point, but there
was a still greater loss. He would change their entire lives,
He would rule and govern them. That would mean an end
to everything they liked and enjoyed. All their sins would
have to go. It would be the end of all their 'good times',
they would lose their 'freedom' – they would just be His
slaves! It was a last desperate struggle for 'liberty'. Have
we not all known that feeling at one time or another – that
terror, that fear? We see ourselves being changed, having
to give up certain things for ever, our lives being entirely
revolutionized, parting with life-long friends, everything
we like having to go and much we dislike coming in. Ah!
there is probably many a person here tonight who in a
sense is prepared to accept the gospel in general, but

[111]

when he sees that it means and implies certain things, he holds back. Absolute surrender to Christ! There it is, he is almost doing it. But to say 'farewell' for ever to certain things? No! he cannot do it. Yes! following Christ may mean financial loss, loss of livelihood, friends and many other things for the time being. These people saw that and were alarmed. But they only saw one half of the Gospel!

Such is the explanation of the madness of these Gardarenes. They were blind to the fact that Christ could do for them what He had already done for the demoniac man. They just saw the first work, the first half of the gospel. And before our Lord had been given an opportunity to show them the other half they had asked Him to go. Like many today they had realized that there was a power in the gospel, but they had not realized that it was 'the power of God unto salvation'. Those are the things that explain why these people asked Christ to depart, the reasons why so many try to shake off Christ today.

But let us look at the other picture and try to discover *what it was exactly that made this man who had been healed so anxious to go with our Lord.* What explains the contrast? Such a marked contrast! There are some people today who, imagining themselves to be very clever, think that this desire is always a sign of madness and religious mania. But that is obviously wrong, for this man had just been made sane! While mad, he disliked Christ and tried to get rid of Him; it is only after the miracle that he desires to be with our Lord. Ah! it is always madness that rejects Christ. Why does this man 'pray' to be allowed to accompany Christ? Why is he ready to leave all and everything to follow Him? And why is that always the truest test and indication of a solid work of grace in the human heart? The reasons are obvious and self-evident but they are so glorious that I cannot forego the pleasure of stating them once again.

The first thing was, obviously, *his sense of gratitude to Christ* and his desire and anxiety to shew it. What could have been more natural! Read again the description we are given of this man's life before he met Christ. A wild, a dangerous demoniac; living amongst the tombs; tearing and mutilating himself; having no rest nor peace; ostracised, feared and hated by all, and indeed tremblingly afraid of himself. His misery must have been great and terrible! All sorts of efforts had been made to control, to heal and cure him (see verses 3 - 4). Fetters and chains, the efforts of family and friends, had all been tried many and many a time and were all useless. The man himself could not find peace, neither could all who were round and about him. But here comes Jesus of Nazareth and, in only a few minutes, what all else had absolutely failed to do, is accomplished and the man finds himself 'sitting and clothed and in his right mind.' Need I make any comment? What no-one else, even his nearest and dearest, had been able to do for him, Christ does. Oh! the blessed release! oh! the happiness, the joy! 'What shall I render unto thee?' 'What can I do?' Nothing is too much to do for such a benefactor. He deserves all, He deserves our very selves. Do you hear that other madman, who had set out for Damascus 'breathing out threatenings and slaughter', crying out of a heart full of thanksgiving and praise when he had only seen Christ for a moment, 'Lord, what wilt Thou have me to do?' He insulted and hated Him before, but once Paul saw Him and realized who He was and what He had done for him and for the whole world, he just cried out in effect, 'O Lord, what can I do for you? Make me your slave. I care not how humble the task as long as I am near you.' And so it has ever been. No one has ever truly realized what Christ has done without loving Him and adoring Him and feeling anxious to be ever, always near Him. What can I feel but gratitude and love towards Him and His gospel? He has purchased my freedom, removed the load of my sinful past from off my shoulders, taken away from me a terrifying sense of guilt, removed for ever the fear of death and the grave and assured me of my acceptance with God. Can I now hear too much about Him? Can I ever tire of such a Person? Can anything ever be so wonderful and so glorious as to feel His presence nigh? Anxious to get rid of Him? Why, my only worry and sorrow is that my faithlessness keeps Him away. Do I fear and hate Him and try to get rid of Him? No!

> *I hate the sins that made Thee mourn*
> *And drove Thee from my breast.*

and now pray

> *More of Thyself O grant me hour by hour.*

Have you ever felt that? Let me remind you tonight, He died for you, He gave Himself for you and, if you but believe it, He will do for you all that He has ever done for all the saints. What knowledge and culture and business and pleasure and family and friends can never do, Christ will do tonight if you but allow Him. Give in to Him! Allow Him to do it! Then you will understand this man's desire to be with Him.

But that was not all. The man was anxious that his present blessed state should continue and persist. It was so wonderful. It was so glorious. And just at this point there was a bit of a fear. Here was this wonderful Jesus, who had just performed this miracle and brought this great happiness into his life, on the point of leaving and departing. Christ alone had been able to heal him and conquer the devils. He himself had failed and so had all others – Christ alone had succeeded. And now, He was going! 'Ah!' cried the man to Christ, 'do let me come with you. I am afraid to trust myself and my own powers. I am afraid lest those devils will return and enslave me again. I cannot trust myself and I fear them. I know I am all right now. But what of tomorrow? Oh! let me go with you!' Every Christian knows exactly what that means. A man is not a Christian until he realizes how weak he is and how strong the enemy is. The Christian does not rely upon himself and his own strength. It is his knowledge of his own weakness that drives him to Christ continually, and his knowledge of the strength of the enemy also. That is why I stand here Sunday after Sunday inviting you to come to Christ and to give yourselves to Him. The contest with the devil is unequal. Greater men than ourselves have already been conquered. You go down day by day and hour by hour. What hope have you of conquering 'principalities and powers ... the rulers of the darkness of this world ... spiritual wickedness in high places'? (Ephesians 6:12) It cannot be done. Realize that you are defeated. Confess your failures. Acknowledge your sin. Yes, the power of the enemy and our own weakness are always good reasons for being with Christ.

But I must not end on that negative note. The man wanted to be with Christ, not only because he knew his own weakness and the power of the enemy, but because he realized that the power of Christ which had set him free could also keep him free. What if the devils returned? With Christ he was safe. Christ had already mastered and conquered them. Whatever happened, with Christ he was always safe, for He is not only mighty to save, but also to keep, and that to the end! Yes! this man wanted to go with Christ in order that he might be *kept* free and safe.

But he made one mistake. He thought the physical presence of Christ was essential. Our Lord, by sending him home, on his own, proves that it was not. A new convert sent straight back to his old haunts alone? Yes, it is quite safe! It was Christ that sent him. And when Christ so sends, He accompanies! That was true in the days of His flesh, it is still more so now and since He sent the Holy Spirit. Trust Him! Obey Him! Do all He tells you.

And He will be with you. 'He will never leave you nor forsake you!'

You will still be tempted and tried, at times even fiercely, but like all the saints you will be able to say

> *Temptations lose their power*
> *When Thou art nigh.*

You may fall, but you will never be 'utterly cast down' (Ps. 37:24). There will be trials and tribulations, but He will bring you through all 'more than conqueror.' Believe on Him tonight and give yourself to His keeping. For His Name's sake. Amen.

10: *Repentance: The Gate to the Kingdom*

*

> *But what think ye? A certain man had two sons; and he came to the first, and said, Son, go work today in my vineyard. He answered and said, I will not: but afterward he repented, and went. And he came to the second, and said likewise. And he answered and said, I go, sir: and went not. Whether of them twain did the will of his father? They say unto him, The first. Jesus saith unto them, Verily I say unto you, That the publicans and the harlots go into the kingdom of God before you. For John came unto you in the way of righteousness, and ye believed him not: but the publicans and the harlots believed him: and ye, when ye had seen it, repented not afterward, that ye might believe him.'*
>
> Matthew 21 : 28–32[1]

An equally good name for this 'Parable of the Two Sons' could be 'the parable on repentance' for in it our Lord most clearly records and teaches His view of that all-important subject. Repentance comes into many of His other parables and lessons, but sometimes it is more or less incidental. Here, He definitely and specifically speaks this parable in order to illustrate His view of repentance and that alone. Reading the parable again and pondering it and meditating over it, I have been deeply impressed once more by the all-importance of this subject. Indeed, it seems to me that what accounts for the fact that so many people today are outside the gospel and the kingdom is just the fact that they have never truly appreciated the place and significance of repentance in the New

[1]Aberavon, October 16, 1932.

Testament teaching. The more I look at it, and the more I consider it, the more deeply impressed I am with the all-importance and the centrality of this aspect of the truth. The moment we stop to consider it, this becomes self-evident to anyone who is at all familiar with the New Testament. Let me show you what I mean.

To start with, repentance is actually the first and most important truth in the New Testament if we consider the teaching mainly from the point of view of chronological order. The first preacher that appears in the Gospels is John the Baptist. I need scarcely remind you that he preached 'the baptism of repentance for the remission of sins' (Mark 1:4). It was the first statement of the first preacher of the New Testament. The next in order is our Lord Himself. What did He preach? Here is the answer: 'Now after that John was put in prison, Jesus came into Galilee, preaching the gospel of the kingdom of God, and saying, The time is fulfilled, and the kingdom of God is at hand; repent ye, and believe the gospel' (Mark 1 : 15) – the same message and the same emphasis. Then we find our Lord sending out the twelve apostles to preach and to heal and this is how Mark describes their going, 'And they went out, and preached that men should repent' (6 : 12). The message is still the same. That is the position in the Gospels. But turn on to the Book of Acts and see there the formation and beginning of the Christian church as we see it today. There, specifically Christian preaching begins and the first recorded sermon is that preached by Peter on the day of Pentecost. What do we find? The people who had listened turned to Peter and the rest and asked, 'Men and brethren, what shall we do?' To which Peter replied, 'Repent, and be baptized every one of you in the name of Jesus Christ ....' (Acts 2 : 38). Still the same! Then consider the preaching of that other great preacher that appears in the Book of Acts – Paul – and you will find that the message is, 'And the times of this ignorance God winked at; but now commandeth all men everywhere to repent' (Acts 17:30). There are many other statements along the same lines. So that merely from the point of chronological order, repentance is first and supreme. How tremendously important it must be therefore.

But we are reminded in this parable of another reason for regarding it as such a vitally important truth, and that is that it is clearly the gate through which all must come who desire to enter into the kingdom of God. *All* must come through this. Our Lord makes it plain and clear here that the Pharisees and the chief priests and elders were expected to repent quite as much as the publicans and harlots whom He also mentions. *All* have to repent. It is therefore a fundamental and vital truth. It is not one of those secondary and less important matters. It is not one of those points on which there can be legitimate variations and differences of opinion; it is pivotal, it is central. Precisely the same point is made frequently by the Apostle Paul in his addresses and in his letters. The message he preaches is such that it is clearly proved that 'there is none righteous, no, not one' and 'that every mouth may be stopped, and all the world may become guilty before God' (Rom 3:10, 19). It is *the* starting point therefore, the point to which all must come. Profession of religion and a religious upbringing make no difference. The fact that the second son had said 'Yes' to his father makes no difference. He had not gone. Whatever our past, if we have not at some time or another come into this attitude of repentance, we are outside the kingdom. But if, on the other hand, we have refused like the first son and have sunk deep down in sin, still it is to this same point of repentance that we have to come. We can say, therefore, quite definitely that Christianity starts with repentance.

But perhaps we can put this still more strongly by saying that our Lord makes it very plain and clear, repeatedly, that the one thing which damns and condemns people and keeps them outside the kingdom is that they have refused to repent. That is the charge here against the chief priests and elders. 'For John came unto you in the way of rightousness, and ye believed him not: but the publicans and the harlots believed him: and ye, when ye had seen it, repented not afterward, that ye might believe him'. In the same way, you remember, He condemns and pronounces his curse upon Chorazin, Bethsaida and Capernaum for this same reason, that they had not 'repented in sackcloth and ashes.'

Well, there we see some of the reasons given in the New Testament for the all-importance of repentance. It is the first truth that is preached and is impressed upon the people; it is the gate through which all must go who enter the kingdom of God; and refusal to go through it, damns and condemns, whatever else may be true or untrue about us. It is central and vital in the Christian truth.

Is it not surprising, therefore, that there should be such little emphasis placed upon it today in teaching and preaching and in the general outlook? Does it not account for the present state of affairs – the numerical weakness of the churches, the lack of a strong and bold Christian testimony and witness, and the bewilderment of the masses who scarcely know even what Christianity means? For if we are uncertain about the origin, how can we proceed? If we are utterly wrong about the foundation and the first principles, how can we hope to erect a durable edifice? If we have not even mastered the alphabet, how can we grasp the teaching? But that is the position today. There is much talk about the kingdom of God but little, if any, about repentance. They want to get into the kingdom, they say, and work in it, but they will not come to this only gate of entrance – repentance. There is a real difficulty about the subject today.

Some actively dislike repentance and refuse to have anything to do with it. The very word repentance, they say, savours of the police courts and introduces ideas of justice and righteousness which seem to them to be an utter contradiction of the love of God, and which seem therefore to reduce God to the level of some irate and almost furious earthly potentate. They feel that this insistence upon repentance, this demand that man should take up that one and only appropriate attitude before God, somehow or other limits God's love and mercy if indeed it does not actually contradict it. Those two things are regarded as being almost antithetical, repentance and love. God, they argue, would not be a God of love if He refused to forgive people simply because they refused to bow the knee to Him. 'That is not the picture of God that Jesus gave', they say. And then they proceed to expunge and expurgate from the Gospels every statement of our Lord's which emphasizes the righteousness and holiness of God and to quote only those passages which seem to suit their case.

But what is really pathetic is that even in their own very favourite passages this doctrine of repentance is taught in as clear and as definite a manner as anywhere else. You cannot drive repentance out of the teaching of Christ without destroying His teaching utterly and entirely. Let me give you an instance of what I mean. How frequently is the parable of the prodigal son quoted in order to show the so-called love of God in contradistinction to the so-called Pauline theology and the legalistic view of the atonement. 'Ah', they say, 'that is Jesus' view of God and forgiveness. The father waits for the son etc.' Yet there is nothing so tremendous and in a sense so dramatic in the parable as the words, 'And when he came to himself', in other words, when he came to true repentance. You find precisely the same thing in connection with the parable of the Pharisee and the publican. How often is the love of God emphasized here, to the exclusion of the penitence of the publican! And so on, not only with our Lord's parables and sermons but also with His actions, His miracles and His acts of mercy. 'Ah', it is argued, 'you never find Him insisting upon this repentance and

[121]

making a kind of *sine qua non* of it. He just forgave.' What they actually fail to observe about all this is that all these people were already penitent. There is no need to *preach* repentance to those who are already on the ground and licking the dust. They have fulfilled the one condition already and can therefore be forgiven directly and immediately. And thus it is true to say that in all these glorious instances of the free love of God in the New Testament, repentance is always present and always presupposed. But, where there is no repentance there is no love from God and no forgiveness. We must be careful therefore lest we damn ourselves in our apparent cleverness and wrest the Scriptures to our own destruction. There is no 'love of God' for you unless you have repented or unless you do repent. Make no mistake about this. Do not rely or bank on God's love. It is only given to the penitent; there is no entry into the kingdom of God except by repentance. That makes it doubly important therefore that we should all be quite clear about it. There is no excuse and there will be no excuse at the end! As we have seen quite clearly, it is emphasized in the New Testament teaching more than anything else.

Well then, we must ask ourselves, What is repentance? How many stumble at this point! Alas! what tragedies have happened because of people's failure to understand the meaning of this term. What countless thousands, not to say millions, must be in perdition tonight because they did not grasp this truth. How many, I wonder, in this congregation and in the world tonight are not true Christians simply because they have failed to realize exactly what repentance means. And the errors, as always, are to be found on the one side and on the other. There are some who read too little into the meaning of repentance. For them, it is just a superficial kind of sorrow and regret on account of something they have done. As long as they feel sorry after sinning, they imagine that all is well, that God has forgiven them and that they will go to heaven. And so they go on sinning, and then again feel sorry before sinning again. We shall see how hopelessly inadequate that view is in a moment.

But there are others who read too much into the meaning of repentance, by which I mean they read much that is never found nor mentioned at all in the New Testament. These are the people who tend to confuse the actual thing itself and its occasional concomitants. They have read John Bunyan's account of himself during his period of repentance, or some similar account. They find that for eighteen months and more he was in a terrible, awful agony, having the feeling of being as it were suspended over hell and almost smelling the brimstone and seeing the fire. Or they have met others who gave a graphic description of how they could not sleep for months, how they felt utterly and absolutely deserted and how they had become almost frantic with grief and sorrow because of the depth of their sin and their failure to find God, and so on. Now, because they have never felt or experienced this kind of thing themselves, they assume that they have never truly repented and that therefore they are not saved. Because they have not agonized or seen terrible visions, they suppose that all is wrong. And there they are, waiting for these things to happen, or perhaps actually trying to induce or create within themselves these terrible feelings. They read their Bible with that intent, they analyze themselves to others and try to get others to condemn them, they almost wish they had committed some so-called terrible sin in order that they might have the true view of themselves. There is no length to which they would not go. Ah! the terrible miseries which many have caused themselves needlessly, simply because they have not realized the New Testament teaching on repentance.

Well, what is it? We are told here in a very simple and a very direct manner. Let us analyze the parable and discover the principles. They are all here. And after that we shall shew how this doctrine, far from contradicting that of the love of God, is but a further great and glorious proof of it.

What is repentance? What does it imply?

It is plain and clear, in the first place, that it means a change of mind and a confession that you were wrong. The father said to the first son, 'Son, go work today in my vineyard. He answered and said, I will not: but afterward he repented and went.' Now it is obvious that this son must have changed his mind. At first, he resented his father's order and command. 'What right has he to command me?', he said to himself, and much else along the same lines. And the result was that he turned to his father and said, 'I will not go.' And there he remained. The first step in this son's repentance was that he thought again about the matter. He might very well not have done so. He might have dismissed the matter entirely from his mind and gone on to something else. But for some reason or other he returned to the question. Why? Oh! it doesn't really matter why, but we can be quite sure that the main reason was that there was something gnawing away in his breast, condemning him and urging him to reconsider the whole matter. It wouldn't leave him alone. And then he sat down and really considered the matter once more. He faced it again. He thought about it again. Instead of brushing it aside and ignoring it or doing his best to forget it by plunging into business or pleasure or some such thing, he just sat down and thought about it and reconsidered it. That is always the first step. Look at it in the case of the prodigal son and in the case of all others. The tragedy with so many truly is that they will not even consider the matter again, they will not think about it. With a wave of the hand they dismiss religion, encrusted in their prejudices they will not even think about it again. Once a man begins to face these questions, there is hope for him. Once a man begins to attend a place of worship and to listen to the gospel case he is on the way. In a sense the first great effect of the gospel is just to ask men to think again.

But that, in itself, is not enough. The man in this parable did not merely think about the question, he thought deeply and thoroughly, he genuinely weighed up and considered the case and having done so he saw quite clearly that he had been wrong. And without the slightest hesitation, and in honesty to his mind and to himself, he at once confessed to himself that he had been wrong and changed his mind about the whole matter. Merely to think again is not repentance. It is of the very essence of repentance that there should be a change of mind and a confession of former error. This again is the central point in the story of the prodigal son. You remember how he came to himself and began to think. Then he realized what a fool he had been and how wrong his actions had been. He faced himself honestly and no longer tried to make excuses. 'There is no excuse', he seems to say, 'there can be no excuse for such madness. I have just been a real fool and there is no more to be said.' The same is true also of the publican in the parable of the publican and the Pharisee. He confesses his wrongs and his mistakes. He changes his mind about himself and everything he has ever done. That is always the first move in repentance. Have you really faced yourself and your life? Look at it now. Consider it honestly. Face it again. Can it really be defended? And those particular things in it that you are always arguing about? You have not started to repent until you have faced them honestly, until you have admitted that they are wrong and have ceased to argue about them. Are you still defending yourself and your sins? Are you still trying to justify yourself? Are you still trying to persuade yourself and others that there is no harm in those things? If so, you are certainly different from the prodigal, the publican, and the first son in this parable. These people were first honest enough to face the truth and to give in. As certainly as I preach to you, you know that those things are wrong. Very well, stop arguing about them. Just admit and confess to *yourself* that they are wrong. You need not say a word to anyone else for the time being. Just admit it to yourself. That is the first step in repentance.

But that is only the first step. Having admitted to himself that he was wrong, this first son then proceeds to admit it to his father and to the whole world by changing his mind, by doing what he had refused to do. In other words, the second principle in repentance is that we acknowledge our sinfulness before God and feel regret for having offended Him. This first son, when he had seen that the thing was really wrong, must have spoken to himself like this: 'After all, this is not the way to treat my father. He has been good and kind to me, and in any case he is my father and has a right to command me. I should not have spoken to him like that. It was not only undutiful, but unkind, and it must have hurt him. Such conduct is really inexcusable.' This again appears as a principle in all the classic cases of repentance in the New Testament. Do you remember the prodigal addressing his father? 'I am no more worthy to be called thy son. Make me as one of thy hired servants.' In other words, he feels a sense of shame. He is conscious of having been a cad and he admits readily and freely that he has no claim whatsoever upon his father's love. He has forfeited all. The same is true of the publican. He falls to the ground, beats his breast and, feeling so unworthy that he cannot even look up, he cries, 'God be merciful to me a sinner.'

Need I apply what I am saying? Well might this son here be grieved with himself at the way he had treated his father. Well might the prodigal have well-nigh broken his heart in that strange land when he actually realized how he had wronged his father and besmirched the family name. But what of you, my friend? And your relationship to your heavenly Father? If your life is wrong to you, how much more so to Him? If our earthly father feels it much, how much more so God, the heavenly Father? Can you still go on ignoring Him and criticizing Him and regarding Him more as an enemy than as a Father? Can you still go on asking in anger, 'Why does God do this?' and 'Why should God do that?' Do you still feel that punishment is unjust and that God deals with you unfairly? He it was that made you. He it is that has been sustaining you. Every good you have ever known comes from God. How often has he spared you when He might have destroyed you? How often has He restrained you when you least knew it? Yes! consider how He sent His only begotten Son to live and die for you, how He gave His all for you, and you laughed at it all and ridiculed it and threw it back into His face, saying like this man, 'I will not.' Surely you can see the enormity of it all now. Surely you must feel that you are a cad and worse. Surely you must agree with the publican and with all other sinners that you really have no claim at all upon the love of God and that you are entirely without excuse. Are you ready to admit it, now? And to Him? Are you ready to tell Him, to confess before Him and to cast yourself entirely on His mercy, without any plea, and without any further argument? That is the second stage in repentance – seeing not only that you are wrong, but that you have wronged God and regretting that you have done so.

But the genuineness of that regret is measured by the third principle that our Lord enunciates in this parable. This first son not only sees that he has wronged his father and feels sorry for having done so. He proves and clinches it all by actually going and doing what he had formerly refused to do! And this in a sense is the acid test. This is the most important point of all. For we do not really acknowledge God and truly acknowledge our sorrow and regret for having sinned against Him, until we place ourselves entirely in His hands and do exactly what He tells us. But this is the most difficult point of all. This is

[127]

where we are tried most of all. It is one thing to see that you are wrong, and even to see that you have wronged God and even to regret having done so. But it is another and a very much more difficult thing to renounce yourself and acknowledge Him utterly. This is where the rich young ruler failed. He was quite all right up to this point. But when Christ asked him to give a practical proof of his real desire to get eternal life at all costs, by asking him to go and sell all that he had and give to the poor, he failed, and went away sorrowful (Mark 10 : 22). To say that you are sorry that you have disobeyed God in the past is not enough. You must give a tangible proof of that by obeying Him in the present, and by committing yourself to obedience as long as you live. For that is what God really desires - to have our will. So He places this test at the very beginning. And how perfectly is it illustrated in the case of this first son! There is no further argument or hesitation. He just goes and does what he knows to be his father's will, without any reason at all except that his father had asked him. God the heavenly Father is waiting for all of us to come just to that.

What, then, is that? What is God's will for us? What does He desire us to do? This is what our Lord says in reply, 'This is the work of God, that ye believe on him whom he hath sent' (John 6 : 29). That is what God wants us to do. That is the way to please Him - just to believe in the Lord Jesus Christ, to acknowledge that He is the Son of God, that He came on earth and lived and died and rose again in order to save you; to admit and confess that apart from what He has done for you, you are entirely hopeless; that you are trusting solely and only to His merit, and that you resolve here and now to show your appreciation of what He has done for you by pledging yourself to a life of obedience to Him, and that by His grace and strength and help you will forsake all known sin. That is God's command to us. That is what God wants us to do - to believe that He forgives us all because Christ died for us, to believe that He of His love sent Christ specifically for that end and, believing that, to give up our life of sin, trusting to Him to keep and sustain us. God the Father asks you to do just that and to do it because He asks you. It is the final stage of repentance. Sorrow for sin and all the good actions in the world will not do instead. His will is 'that you should believe on him whom he hath sent'. He does not ask for various feelings, He does not ask for understanding or learning, He asks for nothing but just a simple belief in the Lord Jesus Christ and a giving of yourself to Him in obedience and a turning away from your sin. To stop and ask various questions and to raise various difficulties is to be in the position of this first son before he repented. He then stopped and hesitated, thought this and that, argued, and refused to go. But after repenting, without any further hesitation or argument he just got up and went. Are you ready to do likewise, or are you waiting for various feelings, or waiting until you feel yourself a great sinner, or waiting until you feel you are better and stronger and more fit to be a Christian, or waiting until you understand how Christ saves you, or waiting to understand miracles? All that just means disobedience and a turning to God and saying, 'I will not.' God asks you now, where you are and exactly as you are, to believe this gospel and act on it. He asks you to take Him at His word without any signs or feelings. He has sent His Son and He asks you to accept Him, without understanding and to believe the record and act on it. He asks you to become as a little child and say, 'I believe Jesus Christ died for me, I believe God forgives me for that reason only, and because of that I turn my back on sin and evil from tonight, trusting Jesus Christ to keep me and protect me'. That is it! Are you ready to do it? You have not repented until you have done that, and without repentance, let me remind you again, there is no entry into the kingdom of God, no love of God for you, no salvation, and therefore nothing awaits you but disaster

and doom. Be wise, imitate this first son. Get up and do it
now!

But I cannot close without a further appeal to you, and
that by means of showing you how this teaching on
repentance, far from contradicting that on the love of
God, really displays it in a most glorious manner.

In the first place, how great and infinite is the love of
God, that He should be satisfied just with our repentance
alone. What would be our position were He also to ask us
to make full restitution for all that we have done against
Him? What if He asked us to undo all the wrong we have
done in the past to Him and to others? He would be
perfectly entitled to do so. Or what if He turned to us and
said, 'Well, I will not punish you and destroy you now,
but, after all, you cannot expect to be reinstated in my
love and affection. I will take you back, but as a servant or
a slave and you shall pay off for the rest of your life the
damage you have done in your past!' Again we would have
no grounds for complaint. But oh! how wondrous is
God's love. He demands nothing except a contrite,
humble, penitent heart. All He asks of us is that we
should realize our sin, confess and acknowledge it, leave
it, and accept His pardon and forgiveness and only in His
strength. In other words, all He demands of us is that we
accept His offer. And think of it! Once you repent you
stand before Him as if you had never sinned at all! All
your past sins and transgressions are blotted out. He
regards you as a son and showers His gifts upon you. All,
simply on the condition of our repentance. What a
bargain! What amazing love! Heaven, without money and
without price, but simply on the condition that I
acknowledge my sin and confess my need of Him.
Everything, simply on the condition that I confess and
realize my nothingness! Mercy and forgiveness for my
every sin on the simple condition that I see my need of it!

But observe further with whom this bargain is made.

That is the most astonishing thing of all. We would not be greatly surprised were God prepared to do this with those who had sinned but a little and whose transgressions were but few. But we are told here that it applies to the publicans and harlots, to those who in the heat and passion of the flesh had sunk to the lowest depths of degradation and iniquity. 'Do you see them?' He says of these people. 'Behold them marching through the gate of the kingdom and entering upon everlasting life. Who are they? Ah! the publicans and the harlots, the very refuse of society, the most despised and scorned classes of society. There they go. Heaven is before them and eternal bliss.' How have they managed it? What is the secret? What have they done? Oh! they have simply repented. They have just believed the preaching of John the Baptist and Jesus Christ Himself. What amazing, wondrous love! 'All the fitness He requireth is to feel your need of Him'! But He hints that the love is even greater than that. He suggests in the 32nd verse that even the Pharisees and the chief priests might have been forgiven and might have entered the kingdom at this same price, if only they had repented. Even the Pharisees! Even the self-righteous. Even those who had called Him a blasphemer and who had persecuted Him. Even the hard-hearted and the self-contented. There is truly no limit to the love of God.

But perhaps the love of God is seen most clearly in this parable in that word 'afterward' – 'but *afterward* he repented, and went' – 'afterward'. What a blessed word! It is the word that has saved us all. Were it not for this we should all be damned. For we have all refused at some time or another and up to a certain point. We have all turned to God and have said, 'I will not.' Perhaps it was even with oaths and cursing. What if God left it at that? But ah! He doesn't. He gives us another chance! 'Afterward he repented and went.' And once he had done that, the former refusal and all else were completely forgotten. That thief dying on the cross had often refused Him and had often said, 'I will not.' But 'afterward', ah, yes, almost with his last breath, he repented and believed and all was well. What amazing love! And God is still the same! You have refused Him times without number. You have spurned the voice divine. You have rejected His offers. But it is not too late. Think again now. Change your mind now. Confess and acknowledge your sinfulness before God now. Accept the gospel now. Change your mind and do it now. The gateway into the kingdom is still open. God in Christ is still ready to receive you. Former sins and refusals will all be forgotten, indeed, all things will become new. What an offer! What love! You have but to do this and then one day it will be said of you, 'Yes, for many years they refused and refused, and said to all God's offers in the gospel "I will not" but afterward, indeed it was on October 16th 1932, they repented and went into the Kingdom.'

God grant that that may be the history of many who hear these words. For Christ's sake, Amen.

> *'Come unto Me, ye weary,*
> *And I will give you rest.'*
> *O blessed voice of Jesus,*
> *Which comes to hearts oppressed!*
> *It tells of benediction,*
> *Of pardon, grace, and peace,*
> *Of joy that hath no ending,*
> *Of love which cannot cease.*
>
> *'Come unto Me, ye wanderers,*
> *And I will give you light.'*
> *O loving voice of Jesus,*
> *Which comes to cheer the night!*
> *Our hearts were filled with sadness,*
> *And we had lost our way;*
> *But morning brings us gladness,*
> *And songs the break of day.*

[132]

'Come unto Me, ye fainting,
And I will give you life.'
O peaceful voice of Jesus,
Which comes to end our strife!
The foe is stern and eager,
The fight is fierce and long;
But Thou hast made us mighty,
And stronger than the strong.

'And whosoever cometh,
I will not cast him out.'
O patient voice of Jesus,
Which drives away our doubt,
Which calls us – very sinners,
Unworthy though we be
Of love so free and boundless –
To come, dear Lord, to Thee!

William Chatterton Dix, 1837–98

11: *Why Hopes of Heaven Fail*

✱

*Then said he unto him, A certain man made a great supper
and bade many ...*   Luke 14 : 16–24[1]

There is nothing so amazing in connection with the
gospel as the way in which, in addition to pointing us to
the general offer of salvation in Jesus Christ our Lord, it
also applies that same offer to the particular needs and
necessities of each individual case and position. This to
me will always be one of those final and absolute proofs of
the divine inspiration of the Bible. It seems to know us all
so thoroughly. The whole of mankind seems to be divided
up into groups and there is something special and peculiar
for each group somewhere or other. It applies its general
message to suit the individual case. And where the work
of the Holy Spirit in us becomes necessary is that we
should see into what group exactly we fall, and what
exactly therefore we need most of all.

What started this train of thought is that I observe that
this parable was spoken to one man and not in general to a
multitude of people. Our Lord had been bidden as a guest
to a feast. He had taken advantage of the opportunity to
address certain remarks to the people in general and also
to the one who had bidden him to the feast in particular.
And as He finished speaking, we read, 'And when one of
them that sat at meat with him heard these things, he said
unto him, "Blessed is he that shall eat bread in the
kingdom of God".' Immediately our Lord turns to him
and gives to him, in particular, this well-known parable of

[1]Aberavon, January 8, 1933.

[134]

the great supper. And in it, obviously, He has a special truth to teach to this man, something that he needed in particular as distinct from all the others. That, I say, is a principle which we do well to observe, and the neglecting of which may well mean the damnation of our souls.

It is interesting to note how this principle is applied by our Lord in His preaching and teaching. He does not speak in exactly the same way to all people. His essential message is always one and the same, but its application is quite different when he addresses publicans and sinners from what it is when He addresses the scribes and Pharisees. The remarks are pointed and applied in quite a different way. Likewise, we find Paul and the other apostles varying their methods in order to suit the particular case of different people. Paul does not preach to the Gentiles in exactly the same way as he does to the Jews. The central message is, of course, the same, but the exact way of presentation is different. In other words, all unbelievers, while being unbelievers, are not unbelievers for precisely the same reason. The things that stand between people and Christ are not always and inevitably the same things. There are some who doubt the very being of God Himself, and clearly they have to be dealt with along that particular line. Others, perhaps, believe in God but cannot believe in and accept Jesus of Nazareth as the only begotten Son of God. Here the case is obviously different and must be approached in a different way. Others again cannot bring themselves to believe the doctrine of the death of Christ – the atonement – or the resurrection. Thus it is seen that there are an innumerable number of forms which the one great central difficulty may take, and which have to be dealt with severally. At root they are all the same, they are all the work of the evil one and he cares little which it is as long as he can stand between the soul and Christ. But what is pathetic is that we all tend to assume that unbelief has but one form – open, blank, utter denial. And as long as we

[135]

can say that we are not guilty of this, we imagine that all is well and lull ourselves to sleep, fondly imagining that we are therefore quite safe. Nothing so displays an utter ignorance of the wiles and the subtlety of the devil as an attitude such as that.

How careful our Lord was to test His followers and disciples, how He feared a superficial grasp of religion on the part of those who went after Him. Indeed there is nothing, in a sense, that so characterizes His ministry as the way in which He seems to take nothing and no one for granted but makes sure of them. He does this at times in an almost surprising manner, yea, if we may say so with reverence, in a manner which is almost harsh in its severity. Do you remember the case of the young man described in Luke 9 who came to Him saying, 'Lord, I will follow thee whithersoever thou goest'? What a fine, an excellent, a noble young man! Surely the very type that our Lord was waiting for and expecting and we might imagine that He would give him a great welcome and reception. Yet, to our astonishment, it is to this very young man that Jesus turned and said, 'Foxes have holes, and the birds of the air have nests; but the Son of man hath not where to lay his head'. In other words, He turns to him and says, 'Do you really mean what you say? Are you really ready? Have you thought it out right through?' How unnecessarily sharp and severe it seems to us to be. Yet he spoke like that then, and here in this parable of the great supper we find Him doing precisely the same thing. As He finished speaking this man sitting near Him turned to Him and said piously, 'Blessed is he that shall eat bread in the kingdom of God'. But – instead of turning to the man with tears in His eyes and saying, 'Amen! Friend, you have said a great word and no doubt in view of your piety and your understanding you are destined to be so blessed and to receive that great honour' – instead of any such remarks or praise or commendation or expression of approval, our Lord turns to Him and speaks this parable.

What adjective can be used to describe this parable? It is severe, it is terrible. It is one of the hardest words our blessed Lord ever uttered. It is filled with indignation, judgment and doom. Do you remember that last verse, 'For I say unto you, That none of those men which were bidden shall taste of my supper'. The anger in verse 21 was terrible, but there is a finality of judgment and doom in that last statement which makes it stand out as one of the strongest statements ever made by our Lord. And what I am anxious to indicate and to emphasize above all else is the occasion which produced the parable and these statements. Had it been uttered to a blasphemer or to some violent sinner or bitter opponent of Christ and His gospel, in a sense we should not have been surprised at all. What amazes and almost dumbfounds is that it was spoken to this nice, fine man who had just shaken his head reverently and had said, 'Blessed is he that shall eat bread in the kingdom of God'. Why did our Lord behave in this manner? Why was it to that man in particular that He uttered these words? What is the explanation of this unusual severity in the presence of what appears to be unusual piety? The parable itself answers these questions and solves the difficulty, and, if we but look at it closely and analyze it, we shall see exactly what our Lord intended.

It is clear, in the first place, that our Lord was anxious to expose and castigate a certain type and view of religion and therefore a certain type of religious person. Incidentally also, He was obviously testing and trying this man to whom He addressed the parable. Well, what is the type of religion and religious person which He denounces? That is made quite plain in what He has to say about the people He mentions in His parable. These are the facts. A certain man, and obviously he was a very important man, made a great supper and invited certain people to it. There was no need for him to do so, there was nothing to compel him to do so. Out of the sheer goodness of his heart he does this and sends invitations to these particular people. And they, receiving the invitations, write back at once thanking him for this kindness and telling him that they hope to be there, and that they are looking forward to the great day. And yet, when the actual time arrives, when the supper is now ready and the great man sends out his servants to bring in the already invited guests, 'they all with one consent began to make excuse'. The first thing that is really clear, therefore, about these people is that their first, original acceptance of the invitation was something general and airy which they had never considered properly and truly. The invitation had come. They had seen it and had looked at it and without any further thought or hesitation, and because they felt that it would be rather nice, they had accepted it and had indicated their intention of being present on the great day.

It is not at all difficult, alas, to recognize the type of religious person that our Lord depicts here. It is the type that accepts God's invitation 'in general' and accepts the whole of the Christian religion in the same way. It is probably one of the most remarkable types that exists. It is exactly as our Lord says in this parable. They conform perfectly to His description. These are people who have never disputed nor denied nor queried any of the great facts or truths of the Christian religion. They have accepted all readily and gladly. Never have they been known to deny the being of God, never have they questioned the fact of Jesus Christ, His birth, death and resurrection, nor the truth about the Holy Ghost. Nay more, not only have they not denied these things, but when they are told that Jesus Christ came to die for sinners and therefore, for them, they say that they accept and believe it as a fact. They like to hear about the forgiveness of God, and when they are told that Jesus Christ came from heaven and suffered all the shame and

[138]

penalty of sin in order that they might be forgiven and go to heaven, they express their satisfaction and delight. For they want to go to heaven and they desire to enjoy all that God has got to give them. So when the invitation comes in the gospel, they accept it. Do you recognize the type? These are the people who say that they have always believed in God, and have always believed the gospel, and have always believed in Jesus Christ. They speak with an apparent piety and reverence, they attend religious services and bow their heads in agreement with the gospel message. How different they are from the sceptic and infidel, how different from the person who denies the very being of God, or who ridicules the whole gospel scheme of salvation! They are never to be found saying a word against it. Indeed, all they say is in its favour. Far from ever having denied or queried it, they have accepted it in all its entirety and have never thought of doing anything else. They have been brought up to believe it and have never doubted it at all. Like this man to whom our Lord spoke this parable, when they are in a religious atmosphere they seem to feel things very deeply and they bow their heads and say, 'Blessed is he that shall eat bread in the kingdom of God'. In other words, that seems to be their main idea and desire – to eat bread in the kingdom of God, to get to heaven and to be with God.

Well, who would imagine that there is anything wrong with such a person! Surely that is just what we would have expected our Lord to commend! Nice, good people who speak thus in pious terms in contradistinction to profligate sinners and arrogant infidels. But as I have already reminded you, our Lord seems to doubt such people. Or at the very least, He seems to feel that it is necessary that He should test and examine them. As this man sitting by Him utters these words, our Lord turns to Him and says in effect, 'Do you really mean what you say? Do you really envy those who shall eat bread in the kingdom of God? Would you really like to belong to that company? Do you thoroughly understand what you are saying? Are you genuinely anxious to please God and to get to heaven? Do you sincerely believe that Jesus Christ the Son of God came to rescue and to ransom you from your sin, and to reconcile you to God? You say you have always believed in these things and that you have never so much as even begun to deny or query them. Do you really believe it? You say you have accepted the gospel and its wondrous message. Is that truly the case?

What then is the matter with such a person? Our Lord proceeds to show us as He brings out the various points in His parable.

The first thing that is clear about such people is that they have never realized that Christianity is not something vague and general, but essentially something definite and specific. Indeed, Christianity is so definite and so specific that it invariably applies a test to our general beliefs or profession and insists upon knowing whether we really mean what we say. That comes out very clearly in the parable. These people had accepted the original invitation at once and without any hesitation. And if the master had left the matter at that point and had done nothing further about it, he might have thought of these people always as thoroughly nice, friendly people who at all costs were ready and waiting to be honoured by him at the great supper. But such was not the case. The time came when, the supper being ready, the master sent out his servants again and called upon these people to come at once. Then, and only then, their true nature appears. This second invitation therefore is the real test. The first was purely formal and general and implied no definite action on the part of the invited guests. But the second invitation is quite different. They are now compelled and forced to do something definite one way or the other. They must either go or not.

Now we have not even begun to understand the gospel

of our Lord and Saviour Jesus Christ until we realize that truth. The gospel is not only a great offer of salvation, it is not merely a glorious invitation from God Himself, it is a test and a discipline also. Alas! how many have been guilty of wresting the great scripture doctrine of justification by faith only, to their own destruction. How many have fondly thought and imagined that all we have to do is to say that we believe certain things and that then we are automatically and inevitably bound and destined for heaven. And how subtle is the error! As far as they go they are all right. But they do not go the whole way. Justification is by faith only. But let us also remember that it is equally true that 'Faith without works is dead', and that true faith always shows itself by certain definite actions. It is not only James who says these things, Paul speaks of 'the works of faith' and of 'working out your salvation with fear and trembling'. John speaks of those who, while they say that they believe and that they belong to the church, clearly show by their lives that they are liars. But nowhere is it more clearly taught than by our Lord Himself in parables such as this and in many other pronouncements where He says clearly and definitely that to call Him 'Lord, Lord' is not enough in itself, and that pious hopes and aspirations unaccompanied by works are valueless and useless.

But let us put all this in the form of three simple propositions which we can all, and must all, apply to ourselves. You say that you believe in God, that you hope to go to heaven and that you believe that God forgives you in and through Jesus Christ. Very well, apply these three questions and test your profession. First, does this belief make any demands upon you and test you? Are you conscious of the fact that it influences your life and makes a difference to it? To what extent do your belief and your religion make a difference to your life? How often are you activated by them, how frequently are they the motive in your words and in your deeds? Such,

inevitably are the first questions. The master sent out the
servants the second time with the definite final invitation.
Jesus Christ always does that. He came not merely to deal
with the guilt of our sin, but also 'that he might redeem us
from all iniquity, and purify unto himself a peculiar
people, zealous of good works'. Have you realized that?
Have you felt its demands? Yea, more, have you yielded in
willing obedience or have you, like these people, made
some excuse?

But the second question is based on the truth that this
final invitation of necessity originates a struggle within us.
When it came to these people, they wanted to do,
something else. An inevitable conflict ensued. There was
a struggle and an argument. Something within them told
them to go to the feast, to the supper, but the other
something urged them to stay away. Where there is no
conflict or struggle there is no life. Paul describes the
sinner as being *dead* in trespasses and sins – lifeless. There
is no real struggle in his life, no real fight. But of the
Christian he says, 'the flesh lusteth against the Spirit, and
the Spirit against the flesh, and these are contrary the one
to the other'. As soon as the life of the Spirit, the life of
Christ, enters our being there is inevitable conflict and
struggle. The two eternally opposed forces are set against
each other. Are you conscious of this? Is there a real
struggle going on within you because of the claim of God
and the claim of the devil? Are you at all disturbed? You
say you desire to go to heaven, but have you realized that
one only gets there as the result of the *fight* of faith? Turn
to the New Testament again and read it carefully. Its
picture of the Christian everywhere is of one who is
fighting a great battle, with Jesus Christ as his leader and
as his captain. He is out in a great crusade, a great war
against sin and all iniquity. Are you in the fight, in the
conflict? Christ calls upon all His true followers to enter
the fray. The second invitation always comes. What have
you done about it? A general belief in God, Christ and

heaven means nothing in itself. Are you definitely on their side? Have you turned up to the great supper when the call comes?

The third obvious truth is that Christ and His gospel claim first place in our lives and demand that everything else should be placed in a subordinate position. That is so obvious in the parable and elsewhere in this chapter that I need not elaborate my point. All I need do is to ask solemnly whether Jesus Christ is the Lord of your life, whether He reigns in your heart? When He sends the invitation, He expects you to come. As He speaks to you, in your conscience, in the Bible and in many other ways what do you do about it?

But let me try to show you how insulting to God is this merely general belief in the gospel which leads to no change in the life. And this, of course, is one of the most terrible things about this particular attitude. If only such people could be given to see how they insult the Almighty God, they surely could not persist in such an attitude. Look at it as it is exemplified in our Lord's portrayal of these people in His parable. They accepted the first invitation, they allowed the man to go forward with his preparations, but at the critical, crucial moment did not turn up. They allowed him to go to all the expense, etc. and yet left him with no one to partake of the food. Just picture it. This man's servants had known about the invited guests and had seen all the preparations. And now they see their master fooled and humiliated and ignored. Could anything be more insulting to him? But let us analyze it and we shall see that the insult becomes evident in two main ways.

We see first of all that they were guilty of accepting the invitation conditionally, the condition being that it should fit in with and suit their convenience. The fact that they accepted the first invitation proves clearly that, in a sense, they wanted to attend the great supper.

They realized that it was an honour, and, had nothing else intervened they would most certainly have been present. As long as it involved no sacrifice on their part, all would have been well. But as it happened, other things did intervene, and they found it to be a little bit inconvenient. So they argued it out thus: that probably their friend would make another dinner sometime at which they could attend, and that in any case he would not mind it very much if they did not turn up this time. They placed their own convenience before everything else. How terrible does this become when we apply it, as our Lord meant us to apply it, to God. And yet how true it is. We have seen God's command in Jesus Christ. We know His will concerning us, which is that we should be sanctified. But what is the response? We say we want to get to heaven and to enjoy eternal bliss. But what do we do about it? Do we begin to prepare for it at once? Do we show our appreciation of His eternal and amazing love by forsaking sin and all its ways at once, and giving ourselves wholeheartedly to Him? Let every man examine himself. Alas! how many do what these people here did. Oh! yes, they purpose to be better men and women but not just yet. They must do something else first. They want to go right through this life sinning and pleasing themselves and living to this world, and then, just at the end when it suits them, to turn to God and tell Him they are sorry and then go on to enter heaven. Could anything be more directly insulting? Asking God to wait! Accepting His offer of salvation on our terms and in our time! Saying we believe in Him and that we hope to go to Him, and yet giving ourselves to everything that He hates. My friend, God does not want your agreement and your mere fine phrases and your nice talk about Him, He wants you to forsake your sins and give yourself utterly to Him *now*. Do not make the mistake of thinking that you can use God at your own convenience. Do you really want to go to heaven? Prove it by showing at once that you prefer heavenly things, which just means forsaking worldly pleasures and carnal delights.

But then we see the insult still more when we consider the nature of the excuses, the nature of the things which are preferred to God. Our Lord gives three instances here. How indefinitely, almost, we could add to the list. And when you look at them quietly and dispassionately, how flimsy and foolish are the excuses. The land, the oxen, yea, and the wife. As if the land would suddenly move and vanish. As if the oxen could not wait even for a few hours. As if the whole of life could not be spent with the wife. How insulting! But apply it all to our treatment of God. We know His will. We know that He hates sin and evil. We know that He abhors all wrong. He has called us to be pure. He sent His only begotten Son to suffer and die in order to bring this about. We say we believe all this and hope to go to heaven. Yet how do we show this? By giving more time to the world than we do to God. By giving more money to mere pleasure, yes, and to things definitely sinful, than we do to God and His work. By showing more enthusiasm over games and politics, and mere men and women, than we do about Jesus Christ and God Himself. Could anything be more insulting, more terrible? If you desire these things of the world, if you really want them, it were better for you not to mention the Name of God at all. There is nothing which is more insulting to the holy Name of God than to profess Him with your lips and deny Him in your life. Oh! think of it, I plead with you. Look at the things you put before God. Look at them. Money, success, popularity, lust, passion, the good opinion of other men and women. Oh! see the enormity of it all, and here and now tonight, without any delay, repent, give up your all, your everything, and turn to God with a whole heart. If you really believe in God and in Jesus Christ, if you really hope to get to heaven, if you have accepted the first general invitation, prove your genuineness, *at once*, by responding to the further call.

[145]

But, lastly, it is clear that these people, who only believe in religion 'in general', have never realized exactly what they are doing and have above all else not realized that God is a Sovereign Lord. The people pictured in the parable no doubt thought that all would be well and that further opportunities would come. But listen to the words of our Lord: 'For I say unto you, That none of those men which were bidden shall taste of my supper'. Listen to those words and repeat them to yourself. Try to whittle or to water them down. Do so if you like. It is your own responsibility. Talk, if you please, about the love of God, but nevertheless I tell you on the authority of the Scripture, there is no love of God to the man who trades on the blood of the cross and who tramples Jesus Christ underfoot. The love of God is manifested in the fact that we have ever been invited at all to the supper. There was no need for Him to do so. He did it of His own free will. There is the offer, the free offer of pardon and forgiveness to all who believe in, and trust to, Jesus Christ as their Saviour and Redeemer from sin and from hell. We have seen what that means. You have but to accept the full invitation and do what He tells you, and in spite of all that has happened to you, in spite of all your sinfulness and denial, in spite of all that has ever been wrong in your life and in your nature, you are pardoned, restored and made children of God.

But if you reject God's offer, if you put anything else before it, if you begin to make excuses and to insult God and to insist upon your own terms, then there is but one alternative – hell. Meditate on these dread alternatives. If you say that you do not believe there is such a being as God, and that you do not desire to get to heaven, why then, you are quite logical and consistent if you live for this world and for all that it has to offer. But what is utterly ridiculous and sheer madness is for men and women who say they believe in these things, yet to put other things before them. End such madness tonight,

[146]

here and now. Having already accepted the first invitation, accept the second this evening. Show your faith in Jesus Christ by works worthy of His Name. Show you have a hope of heaven by beginning to prepare for it now! Show that you are beginning to love God by beginning to obey Him. The supper is ready, is waiting. Be wise. Come in and enjoy the feast. The wrath of the Master is terrible. But let us not think of that. Let us think rather of the glory and the wonder of the feast! For His Name's sake. Amen.

12: *Missing the Mark*

*

For Herod feared John, knowing that he was a just man and an holy, and observed him; and when he heard him, he did many things, and heard him gladly.   Mark 6:20[1]

*

I never read this verse and this entire paragraph about king Herod without feeling that it is one of the saddest and at the same time one of the most terrible passages in the New Testament. As I read it my feelings are mixed and are constantly changing. At one time, my heart seems to go out to Herod and I like him and feel sorry for him in his difficulties; the next moment he irritates and annoys me and I feel that he is beyond dispute the greatest fool and the most hopeless person that figures in Holy Writ. But there is always one dominant feeling which I never fail to experience whenever I read this account, and that is a sense of wonder and amazement that it is at all possible for anyone to come so near to being right and yet finally to miss the mark. For that beyond doubt is the main lesson of this well-known incident full as it is of dramatic power and intensity. And it is to that very matter that I would draw your attention tonight. Let me do so, without any further introduction, by putting to you certain general propositions which seem to me inevitably true in view of what we read here.

The first is that the gospel calls for a decision, and asks

[1]March 5, 1933.

us definitely to make up our minds and take a definite stand with regard to certain matters. That stands out on the very surface of the record as being the key to this whole sad and sorry story of Herod. He wavered and wobbled and never really arrived at a decision. But his association with John the Baptist also reminds us that the most characteristic thing about the preaching of the Baptist was the fact that he invariably challenged his congregations and tried to bring them to a decision. John did not indulge in trivialities, his purpose was not simply to regale his audiences with rhetoric and eloquence. He had a definite message and he called for a definite response. Indeed we read that his preaching was so searching and so compelling that the people actually cried out, 'What shall we do then?' That was the characteristic of the preaching of the herald of the gospel. And when our Lord came, you find that He did precisely the same thing. He faced the people with the only two possible alternatives: He pictured to them the broad and the narrow way, the wide and the strait gates, the house on the sand and the one on the rock, God and Mammon, and He called upon them to follow Him and to risk their all upon Him. And as you follow His ministry it is interesting to observe the way in which the people are compelled to take sides, either for or against. You can almost see it happening, you can almost watch the man who came to oppose and jeer, changing over and coming on to the Lord's side. His preaching led to decisions. As you go on to the Book of Acts you find the same thing. Do you remember how the 3,000 changed sides on the day of Pentecost, and how from saying, 'What meaneth this?' or, mockingly, 'These men are full of new wine', they said unto Peter and the rest of the apostles, 'Men and brethren, what shall we do?' Yes! right through the Book of Acts you find that, and it is difficult to know which instances to select. But in the last chapter we find that the effect of Paul's preaching in Rome, as everywhere else, was to divide the people into those who believed and those who did not. And as you follow the history of the church throughout the centuries, you will find that, during every period of power and strength, the preaching of the church has driven people to decision. I emphasize this point because, without being at all unduly critical, I fear it must be confessed and admitted that this is an aspect of the gospel and its preaching which is being sadly forgotten and neglected just at the present time. Indeed it is actually resented by many who become infuriated if personal pressure is brought to bear upon them, and if the preaching tries to move them to a definite decision. The idea seems to be current that religion is to be something purely general, something which we can sit and listen to and enjoy as we do so, something which comforts and consoles us when we are in trouble; in a word, something which does things for us without our doing anything at all, something which gives all and demands nothing in return. But this story of Herod and John the Baptist shews us the utter fallacy of all that and reminds us once more that the gospel calls for a decision. Shall I ask a simple question before we go any further? Have you made the decision? Has the gospel led to a change in your life? Has it affected you and moved you to definite action?

The question becomes of vital importance in view of the second general proposition which I desire to put to you, namely, that nothing short of a definite decision is of the slightest value. How evident and clear is that in this particular case of Herod. Here is a man who enjoyed the preaching and who liked the preacher, and who felt something very definite under the influence of the preaching. And yet the whole point of the story is that all that was valueless and useless, and that eventually he was more or less in precisely the same position as one of the greatest and most bitter opponents of John the Baptist and his preaching. How difficult it is for us to grasp that point, and yet how abundantly it is proved to be true, not only in innumerable cases in the Bible but also in the subsequent history of the Christian church. I always feel that it has been particularly true of the history of the church during the past fifty years or so. In a sense, the preaching has never been greater. Everything that learning and oratory and artistry can contribute has been present. Not only that, one has only to attend large preaching meetings, or to read the accounts of them, in order to discover that the meetings have apparently produced a tremendous affect. Men and women have been visibly moved, many melted to tears and the fervour in the singing has borne eloquent witness to the fact that great power has been present. Yet, it is actually during that time, and in spite of all that is true about such meetings, that the moral tone of our country has descended to its present level, and organized Christianity has become one of the least instead of being one of the greatest factors in the life of the community. Why is this? Surely there is but one answer. The effect has been purely general and has led to no real decision, to no true conversion and change of life. And therefore it has all been quite useless and ineffectual, if indeed it has not been positively harmful. Here, then, is a real snare of which we need to be particularly wary and which we must watch. There is only one true test which we can apply to ourselves with regard to meetings, or with regard to Bible reading, or with regard to our whole attitude to the question of Christianity. It is not whether I enjoy it, nor whether I have been moved and disturbed by it, nor whether I like it and agree with it, but simply this: Has it led me to a decision? Have I taken a definite stand about it? Has it led to action which has affected the whole of my life? In the absence of that, all else is quite useless and futile.

My third observation is that, in spite of the fact that ultimately they are in precisely the same position as all other unbelievers, there is, speaking in a natural sense, something unusually sad and pathetic about the case of these people like Herod who are 'almost decided' and actually on the verge of becoming Christian in the true sense. I say that it would be unnatural for us not to feel that. We are of necessity more interested in those who appear to give signs of being on the way. Their case is not identical with those who are without giving any sign whatsoever of being on the way. There are some who not only deny the truth but actually oppose it actively. There are those who never feel anything when they hear it, and who indeed seem, if anything, to be hardened by it. And we feel about such people that they are about as far away from the truth as a man can possibly be. But how different is the case of these people who are like Herod. And how many such there are today! Every time they hear the gospel they are moved and affected. They feel they ought to give in to it and are almost on the point of doing so. And yet they never quite get there. They always seem to be wavering and on the verge. Just a little more and all would be well. Just one further step and they would be in. But it never happens. What a strange type of person this is, and how pathetic! I sometimes feel that it is the most miserable type of all. For that reason, and for the further reason that there are probably many such people present here tonight I would ask you to accompany me as I try to analyze this strange position and show its terrible fallacies and its hopeless unreasonableness.

Let us consider first of all what it was that brought Herod so near to being right. Precisely the same reasons account for the fact that so many today are 'almost' Christians. What are they?

Well, it is very plain and clear that the life and personality of John the Baptist had made a great impression on Herod. We read that Herod 'feared John, knowing that he was a just man and an holy'. Whatever we may say or feel about Herod we must give him full credit for that fact. He had recognized that John the Baptist was a just and holy man. Many had failed to recognize that, but Herod had seen it. And that had greatly influenced him. He felt that a man like this could not be brushed aside and ignored. Herodias had not realized that, and she had frequently pleaded with Herod to destroy him and put him to death. Indeed I think it is plain and clear that she had often tried to bring that to pass in spite of Herod and without his knowledge. For we read that Herod 'observed him' which means 'kept him safely' or 'looked after him'. However difficult John might have made things for him, Herod saw clearly that John was a man of God; and he respected him and periodically went to visit him even in prison. Something exactly like that accounts for the fact that so many today are 'almost' Christians. In spite of their being what they are, they are charmed by the Christian character. They behold certain Christian people alive now, and they not only readily admit that they are the finest people they know, they are actually charmed by them. And when they read the lives of the saints and the heroes of the Faith, when they study the biographies of people like Hudson Taylor, Wesley and Whitefield, the Methodist Fathers in Wales, Bunyan, John Knox, Luther and Calvin, Augustine and others, why, they feel at once that they are the greatest people the world has ever known. And as they read about them they feel they would like to be like that. Their hearts are warmed and moved, a thrill passes through their body and they feel that that is the kind of life they also should lead. And when they come to the New Testament and confront the heroic figures of Peter and Paul they are simply overwhelmed. And when, behind and above all these, they look at Jesus Christ of Nazareth, and as they watch Him from His birth onwards, as they observe His kindness and gentleness, His power and His might, His perfect walk and His utter obedience to God, and when they see Him dying on that cross, without a murmur, for

[153]

a world of sinners who had betrayed Him and abused
Him, why, they simply cannot help being moved to the
depths. The record of Christianity alone makes the
position of the unbeliever utterly ridiculous. To deny the
gospel is automatically to disagree with the noblest souls
this world has ever seen. It is indeed to deny the Son of
God Himself. Let that, at any rate, be said to Herod's
credit – he had realized the greatness of John the Baptist
and that fact alone had affected and influenced him.

But, further, we see clearly that Herod also knew that
what John said was right and true, and that he even liked
it. Here is the phrase, 'and when he heard him, he did
many things'. Every time he sat there and listened to
John, he felt that everything that was said was right and
true. Who could gainsay what the Baptist said? Who
could reply to his devastating logic as he moved on from
step to step and point to point? Every time he heard him,
Herod felt that John was absolutely right and that his
arguments were irrefutable. There was no excuse to plead
and there was no real answer to the various charges which
were made. Obviously what the man said was absolutely
right, and having heard him, Herod 'did many things'.
Have you not experienced something like that? While at
home in his palace and listening to Herodias and her
counsellors and friends, Herod had often been almost
persuaded that John was wrong, and that he had a devil or
was some sort of a maniac. But every time he saw him and
heard his words, he just knew for certain that the truth
was entirely on John's side. And he had to admit it. No
one who is at all alive, or who thinks at all, can possibly
deny the essential truth of the Christian message.
Nothing reveals that so clearly as the tortuous and
dishonest methods which men have to adopt in their
attempts to try to undermine it. Can anyone deny
that the principles taught by the gospel are essentially
right and true? Here they are, 'love, joy, peace,
longsuffering, gentleness, goodness, faith, meekness,

[154]

temperance' (Gal. 5 : 22). Is there anything at all to be said against them? Is not the Christian type of life incomparably the best, the noblest and the highest? What have you really to say against a gospel which offers you pardon and forgiveness, which gives you a new nature and a new life, which calls you to lead a life which is worthy of sonship of God, and which is indeed to be a copy of that which appeared in the life of the only begotten Son of God, and which, at the end, promises you an eternity in the presence of God Himself? Can you really compare anything else with it? Can you honestly pretend to defend any other way or type of life? As Herod sat and listened to John, he *knew* that John was right. Do you not always feel that the gospel carries its own witness within itself, that it is so perfect in every respect that it must of necessity be the very truth of God? The man who fails to see that is utterly blind and dead. It is at least a sign that a man is alive and on the way that recognizes the essential truth of the gospel and admits that it is right, though that means that he condemns himself.

But there is clear indication in this account that there was still another factor working upon Herod, and that was a definite spirit of conviction. It was not only the personality of John, not only the truth that was spoken in and of itself, that affected Herod, there was something beyond that. These are the words which strike us, 'And when he heard him', and also, 'he heard him gladly.' Do you see the picture? Ever and again Herod would go down to the prison to visit John. He knew that in doing so he was displeasing Herodias and most of the members of the court. Yet he went and continued to go. There seemed to be a strange fascination for him in the prison with its remarkable prisoner and his extraordinary preaching. He felt himself drawn there. He knew what he would hear before he went, he knew it would condemn him and his life, nevertheless he went. He felt something drawing him there, something almost irresistible. Does he not remind you of a moth and a candle? He just could not keep away. And when he went and heard what John had to say, we are told that 'he heard him gladly'. He enjoyed the meeting, he was carried away in the service, he was always moved and affected. How are we to explain or to understand that? For me there is but one explanation – it was the work of the Spirit of God. And there are many who feel precisely the same thing under gospel preaching. They are convicted of their sin, they feel the truth of the gospel, they always hear it gladly and thoroughly enjoy being in religious services. Every time, they are deeply moved and affected, and though it may mean that they are condemned and left without any plea or excuse, like Herod of old, they are to be found listening to the gospel and feeling its effects upon their souls. Those then are some of the reasons which brought Herod almost to the right point, the reasons which explain why so many people today are 'almost' Christians – the Christian testimony and witness, the truth and the convicting work of the Holy Spirit. And yet, what is truly astonishing is that all this leads to nothing. So near and yet so far! Is it not almost incredible that a man who could have experienced as much as Herod did should nevertheless be capable of what happened afterwards? Yet such was the case. Why was it? How are we to explain him and understand him and all who are like him?

The following seem to me to be the explanations:
The first is that he never thought things right through, but was content merely with the registration of certain feelings. Or, to put it in another way, we can say of him that he was always a slave to his environment and too much under the influence of the particular circumstances and surroundings at any given moment. While listening to John he agreed with John and forgot Herodias. But while listening to Herodias he forgot John and all that he had said. It is not sufficient just to say that he was a

superficial person, for that does not get right to the root
of the problem. There was something more than that – a
certain spiritual laziness, a natural revolting from taking
decisions, a shrinking from any course of action which
could lead to difficulties. However, they can all be
summed up in this charge, that he had not faced the
position right through to the end, he had not followed the
argument all the way to its inevitable logical conclusion.
Had he done so it would have led to definite action on his
part. But he didn't. Almost as soon as he was out of the
prison he forgot all about John and the preaching, and so
it continued until he entered the prison again, and then
repeated the whole experience. He felt it deeply at the
time but he never worked it out. Had he worked it out he
would have said something like this, 'John is obviously
the right kind of man and he leads the right kind of life.
My life is different. Therefore I am wrong. What John says
is absolutely right; what I have said and done is therefore
wrong. There, under his preaching, I feel a power of God
which I never feel anywhere else. Obviously that is the
right way and I must put myself right with it. It will mean
separation from Herodias and many other things which
will pain me, but after all, right is right whatever it may
cost, and the only way to be true to myself and my
conscience is to act accordingly.'

Is not that incontrovertible? Yet that is the very thing
that men and women will not do! Have you ever faced it
right through like that? Have you ever followed the
gospel to its logical conclusion? If not, do so now. Here is
the argument. How simple and how logical it is. There is
God, the Judge eternal. Here am I, the sinner. God
demands certain things of me and has made them quite
plain and clear in His law, which is also attested by my
own conscience. I *have* to appear before Him. Do what I
will, it cannot be avoided. And I am guilty, and I am told
that for the guilty there is nothing but damnation and
hell. But here comes the gospel offer which tells me that

Christ having died for me, God is willing and ready to pardon and forgive me, and give me a new life, and that he calls upon me to leave my sin and give myself definitely to Him. It is the only way out, the only way of safety. Not only that, I believe it and believe it to be right. But it does ask me to give myself entirely to God and to do all I can to please Him whatever that may involve. Refusal means eternal damnation, acceptance means eternal life. I do not know how long I shall live; I have no control over the length of my life. The offer is there now, is open at the present moment. Surely, there is only one thing to do and that is to act at once. My going home and forgetting all about it will not change the facts. There they are and there they will remain. Oh! be logical! Do the only sensible thing. Act on your convictions. If you feel that it is right now, it will always be right. Right is right and wrong is wrong. If you feel the gospel is true, if you recognize the Christian life as being the best, if you want to get right with God, do so and do so now, at once. See how inconsistent, how illogical, how unreasonable, how ridiculous it is to recognize the right and then remain and persist in the wrong.

Another key to the understanding of Herod is his love of sin and, in particular, of his besetting or favourite sin. I cannot but feel that the real stumbling block was his illegal alliance with Herodias. I need not elaborate. The word here makes it quite plain and clear. We are told that 'when he heard him, he did many things'. Ah, yes, I can well believe it and I can easily understand it. 'He did many things'. Yes! everything but the *one* thing that was most important and that he should have done above all others. Yes! he probably remedied many evils and mitigated many wrongs in his kingdom and administration. He no doubt became kinder to everybody and gave more of his goods to feed the poor. He probably increased his subscription to the various charitable institutions and went out of his way to do all the good he could. No doubt also he gave up certain evil practices. Perhaps he drank less and gambled less and swore and cursed less. Yes! Yes! 'he did many things', but he never did the one thing that John asked him to do, he never gave up that immoral life and that illegal attachment to Herodias. Need I apply what I am trying to say? Is not this the trouble with all that are simply almost Christians? It is not always the same thing, not always precisely the same sin. But the method is always the same. We do this and that, we give up this and that, we are prepared to do anything and everything except give ourselves up *entirely* in a willing obedience and allow God to put His finger on anything He likes in our lives. And yet that is the condition. What is it that is holding you back? Examine yourself. Be wise and let it go! Are you going to jeopardize your eternal future for one thing, and that something which you know and confess to be wrong. 'Many things' are not sufficient. God just wants your entire submission, not your alms and good works, not the giving up of certain sins, but your entire will.

The only other thing to which I wish to refer is found in verse 26, where we are told that 'for his oath's sake, and for their sakes which sat with him', he failed to reject Herodias' daughter's request for John the Baptist's head. Ah! there it is – concern about his own reputation and the good opinion of others. In his heart of hearts he despised these people and knew that they were wrong. And on the other hand, he admired and feared John and knew him to be right, yet, such was his love for worldly pomp and popularity and for acclamation and applause, that he deliberately sacrificed the right for the sake of the wrong. Refusing God and His offer of eternal salvation in His Son, refusing all the treasures of heaven and eternal bliss simply because of the fear of men, simply because of being afraid of what certain people who will soon be dead will think and say! Oh, the madness of it all! Though the whole world may laugh and jeer at you, though all may agree that you have become insane and have made a fool of yourself, what does it matter as long as you are right with God? For He is the Judge!

Let me now draw the various obvious conclusions from this story.

The first is that all the good feelings and good actions in the world are useless and valueless unless we definitely decide for Christ. Not to decide for Him is to be against Him. Because he had not definitely done what John had repeatedly told him to do, Herod eventually gave the command to behead John. If you have not stood definitely and entirely on God's side, there is only one reason and explanation – you prefer the other. Beware of resting on good feelings, and good intentions and good actions. Do what God tells you. Believe in His Son and show the whole world that you have done so, by renouncing sin and evil and by leading the Christian life.

The only other conclusion is a terrible one and, in a sense, I had rather not mention it. But here it is in the record and it is true. Once a man has felt that the gospel is right and true he will never know rest or peace until he has given himself to it entirely. Poor Herod! How terrible his life was after he had beheaded John. He saw more of John after beheading him than he had ever done before. He haunted and tormented his life. Awake and sleeping he could ever see that charger coming towards him with the head of John the Baptist lying upon it. Wherever he went, there it was. And when he heard of the mighty works of Jesus Christ, he was quite sure that it was John risen again from the dead. Though you reject the truth you do not finish with it. It remains, and it will haunt you and condemn you for ever. It will give you no rest or peace. Jesus Christ, the Son of God, came from heaven and lived and died and rose again in order to save you, but if you do not believe in Him and accept Him, He will become your damnation. His love surpasses knowledge, but there is nothing so terrible and so awful as 'the wrath of the Lamb'. Try to picture Herod's life after he beheaded John. Such will be yours, but infinitely worse and more terrible, if you do not decide for Jesus Christ. I am not afraid of being charged, as I frequently am, of trying to frighten you, for I am definitely trying to do so. If the wondrous love of God in Christ Jesus and the hope of glory is not sufficient to attract you, then, such is the value I attach to the worth of your soul, I will do my utmost to alarm you with a sight of the terrors of hell. Eternal remorse, eternal misery, eternal wretchedness, unchangeable torment, such is the lot of all who content themselves with just agreeing with and enjoying the gospel, but who for some reason or other never forsake all else and embrace it with a whole heart. God save us all from it, as He is indeed waiting to do. For His Name's sake. Amen.

13: *False Assumptions*

٭

But they, supposing him to have been in the company, went a day's journey; and they sought him among their kinsfolk and acquaintance. Luke 2:44[1]

It is not at all surprising to find that the people who have pondered and thought about life most deeply have generally been sad. It is not at all strange that in the Book of Job and Ecclesiastes, and indeed in all the so-called wisdom literature of the Bible, the main note should be one of sadness. That the same is found to be true also of all other great and deep thinking about life, even outside the Bible, is, in the same way, not at all unexpected. For the very mystery of life itself is quite enough to cause all to pause and to become sober. The majesty and grandeur and greatness of life is stupendous, and almost overwhelming, even when we consider it only from the standpoint of nature as we see it round and about us.

But when we consider it in terms of human beings, all this is greatly intensified. I would venture to say that no one can face honestly and truly the fact and the spectacle of human life, and all that it involves and leads to, without being filled with a sense of alarm and tragedy, and without feeling also that he or she should do something about it. Look at the situation! Look round and about you in this world! Behold all these people, all these men and women. Who are they? What are they? What are they here for? Whither are they going? What is to be their ultimate destiny? Can you remain unmoved when you realize that they are

[1]Aberavon, March 19, 1933.

all beings who possess immortal and everlasting souls and spirits, that when they die and are buried they do not cease to be but pass on to a great eternal world of spirits which is divided into good and bad, and in which they will experience either infinite bliss and happiness or else unspeakable torment and agony. When you realize and remember that, can you remain unaffected? And when you realize further that they are all determining which of these two possible futures shall be theirs in eternity, now, in this present world and life, must not your concern of necessity be turned into alarm? For there is nothing that is quite so obvious about the majority of these people as their sheer unconcern and indifference about all this. Nothing so strikes us as their thoughtlessness and heedlessness and their apparent utter failure to understand their own nature and all the possibilities that are ahead of them. Observe them in their way of living, listen to their talk, and you will discover that they are interested in everything and concerned about everything except the one thing that is of most vital importance, namely, their souls. See how they give their time, their money and their very selves to pleasure, sport and sin; observe the laughter and the joviality and the apparent lightness and freedom from worry. Listen to them as they discuss men and affairs and as they become enthused and excited about the latest craze of the moment or of the hour. See how they quarrel and become bitter and try to destroy one another. Watch them as they strive for the so-called glittering prizes of this world, and scheme and plot and spend themselves day and night. Look at the world as it is today round and about us. Look at men and women. Would anyone imagine that life is really what it is? Do they live as realizing that the end must soon come, that soon they will have to go, and that in the meantime they are deciding and determining their *eternal* future? Is it not utterly terrible and alarming thus to see men and women going on the journey of life? What will happen to them? Is it not too terrible for thought?

Such are the thoughts that strike me and enter my mind as I read this well-known account of Joseph and Mary and of how the child Jesus was left behind at Jerusalem. Is it not a perfect picture of the life of the majority today? Watch these people as they go down from Jerusalem to their home in Nazareth. There they were going with the other people in the caravan, and as they journeyed they talked. Nothing seemed to worry them. Maybe they were discussing together the services they had just been attending at Jerusalem, commenting perhaps on the addresses they had heard. No doubt also the political situation was mentioned and the whole question of the Roman domination was raised and freely discussed. Quite likely also the relative strength of the various groups and parties of priests – the Pharisees, Sadducees, etc. – was considered and debated. Probably also the women in particular had their discussions as to the various things they had seen in the shops and bazaars of the city, the various purchases they had made and the whole difficulty and problem of life and living. On they went, so concerned about this, that and the other, and not thinking at all about the one thing that was really of greatest importance; not thinking at all as to whether the boy Jesus was with them or not. There, I say again, is a perfect picture of life and of the masses. On and on they go in life's journey, concerned about anything and everything and everybody, except the one thing that matters most of all and the one Person who alone really counts.

But in the vast mass of humanity there is one group that demands our especial attention, and that is the group that is so aptly and perfectly described in my text tonight as consisting of those who, 'supposing Jesus to be in the company', continue on the journey. And they demand this special consideration not only because they form a separate group on their own but, rather, because, of all the people in the procession or in the journey, they are beyond the slightest doubt the most wretched and the most to be pitied. There can be no doubt about that. The New Testament gives me authority to say that the hell of all persons is not identical; that to some it is much worse than to others (as, for instance, in the parable of the unworthy servants in Luke 12:47–48.) And obviously, therefore, of all the damned they must be most wretched who had fondly imagined themselves to be Christian and to be all right. For these people had gone forward on the assumption that they were in a good and right condition, and they therefore had various expectations. There are many in life who assume nothing and expect nothing. They live for this world alone and are concerned about nothing but the gratification of anything that is wrong within themselves. That they go to perdition is, of course, plain and obvious, and yet Holy Writ seems to indicate that the hell for such people will not be as terrible as the hell of those who had always assumed and imagined that they were Christians, and that therefore they were going to heaven. And this, of necessity, for the latter had had hopes. There is that extra sense of disappointment and painful surprise. Indeed there is no more terrible and horrible picture anywhere than the New Testament picture of the state of those who, having supposed and assumed, indeed having felt certain all their lives that they were Christians, on the Great Day turn to Jesus Christ saying, 'Lord, Lord', and are suddenly told, 'I never knew you; depart from me, ye that work iniquity' (Matt. 7:23). What an awful possibility! Irrevocable doom. Eternal disappointment. There is nothing so terrible as for a soul to assume that it is Christian and that all is well with it, and then to be suddenly disillusioned when it is too late.

Let us do all we can tonight to make such a position an utter impossibility in the case of all who hear these words. And let us do so by considering first *the grounds on which people tend to make this assumption.* I have often been struck, when talking to people about these matters, by the way in which, in the very terms they use, they confess that they had always assumed that they were Christians. This is their favourite term, '*Of course* I am a Christian', they say. Now, the very use of that term suggests that there is something wrong. There is no 'of course' about being a Christian. It is something entirely new. It is by no means inevitable or something which is bound to happen. Indeed, becoming a Christian is a crisis, a critical event, a great upheaval which in the New Testament is described in such terms as a new birth, or a new creation, or a new beginning. More than that, it is there described as being a supernatural act wrought by God Himself, something which is comparable to a dead soul being made alive. It means the direct intervention of God in a human life by His infinite grace in and through Jesus Christ His Son. It is something therefore which must stand out in one's life and to which one must always look with amazement and gratitude. In view of all this, therefore, the true Christian does not say, 'Of course I am a Christian', but rather, 'By the infinite grace and mercy of God I am what I am, I am a Christian'. But why is it that people should thus assume that they are Christians, or, in the more picturesque language of my text, why is it that people should thus suppose that Jesus Christ is with them in their journey through life and that He will be with them to the end? There are many things that account for this, many reasons why people tend to make this assumption. I desire merely to consider some of the more common reasons. Some of them, to some of you, will appear to be puerile and ridiculous, yet they obtain today in the case of many people, and maybe at one time you held such a view yourself. What are they?

There are some who actually assume that all is well with them for the simple and only reason that they belong to a so-called Christian country. This is so ridiculous that it need not be considered any further. To begin with, there is really and in actuality no such thing as a Christian country. Christendom, in the true sense, is made up of a number of individual Christians and no one can be a member of the kingdom of God who is not definitely Christian.

There are others who base their assumption of their Christianity on their upbringing. Sometimes they definitely relate it to that which was enacted when they were infants and when they were christened or baptized. They regard every baptized or christened person as of necessity Christian, and believe that we are thus made Christians by the actions of our parents when we are still in a condition which renders us incapable of thinking for ourselves. Having been baptized when they were infants, they assume that they are Christians and that all is well with them. This view is seen most perfectly, of course, among the Roman Catholics, but is to be found to an astonishing extent also among supposed Protestants. Or, it may be that such persons do not relate it quite so definitely to their baptism, but tend to say, rather, that they have always believed these things, that they were brought up to do so, and that they have never so much as thought of denying the truth of the gospel. They have heard of God and of His Son Jesus Christ ever since they can remember, and they have always taken it all for granted. 'Of course' they are Christians, therefore. Why, they have never been anything else! I wonder how many people there are on earth tonight who assume that they are thus Christians, but who in reality have never stopped seriously to consider what exactly it means to be a Christian according to the New Testament. Is it not amazing to note the number of people who never attend a place of worship and whose lives are patently and obviously unrighteous and sinful, who, nevertheless, feel insulted when it is suggested that they are not Christians. They have always supposed themselves to be true Christians.

[167]

Another group of persons base this assumption on the fact of church-membership or church-attendance. They have their names in the book, they attend with a fair regularity, they contribute towards the funds, they believe it is right and good and respectable to pay one's vows to God at least once on the Sabbath day, and on they go feeling quite happy and never doubting for a moment that God is well-pleased with them, and that Jesus Christ is proud of them and will honour them at the end. I wonder to what extent those of us who attend a place of worship regularly have really considered exactly what it means to be a Christian. How many assume that to be a member of a church is identical with being a member of the true church, which is the body of Christ. For that idea also is by no means confined to the Roman Catholics.

Then, there are those who suppose that a good life and good works mean of necessity that we are Christians and that Christ is with us. You are familiar with their talk – how they point out that they have never done anyone any harm, that they have always done their best to help others, and so on. They have not gone near a church or chapel, perhaps; they have not read their Bibles for years; their prayers have been fitful and intermittent; but that has not concerned them at all. On they have gone, assuming that all is well and that being a Christian just means leading a quiet, respectable, good sort of life.

The last group to which I would refer consists of those who make a still greater and wider assumption, namely, those who base their hope on the so-called love of God. These do not stop to find verses or explanations! Whatever may be said to them, they just wave their hands and say, 'God is love'. According to them, nothing else really matters, a man's life makes no difference at all. God's love will deal with everything and all will be well. And on they go, thoughtless and heedless, saying 'God is love'.

But the parallel provided by the story of Joseph and Mary is still closer. For we read here that they 'went a day's journey' before they realized that there was anything amiss. That is always the most fatal thing about this false assumption of being a Christian. *It always, for the time being, gives a false sense of peace, satisfaction and happiness.* Joseph and Mary went on without any worry or anxiety, assuming that the boy Jesus was with them, and, as I have suggested, they probably talked with the other people, who had also been up to Jerusalem, as they went on their way. The Bible does not tell us that this false assumption about our souls immediately reveals itself to be wrong. Indeed it tells us the exact opposite. It shows us how mankind at the beginning ridiculed Noah and everything he said, how they went on 'eating and drinking, marrying and giving in marriage', and refused to pay any heed or attention to the warnings of that righteous man. Then later we find the people of Sodom and Gomorrah absolutely refusing to listen to the warning of Lot and the angels, and so on through the Old Testament, past Samson and down to the time of the prophets and even in the ministry of our Lord Himself. How the children of Israel always laughed at and ignored God's true prophets and their greatest friends! A mere superficial reading of the Bible might well lead one to the conclusion that the godly life leads but to pain and trial, whereas the godless seem to be wonderfully happy and contented with their lot. Oh, yes! they went a day's journey quite happily. It is possible for men and women to go right through life's journey without feeling a hitch anywhere, or without being conscious that anything is wrong. For this false assumption is like a drug, it deadens pain and lessens fear and gives a false sense of health and well-being. That all seems well with you so far, proves nothing of necessity.

But *the real test arrives and arises when, for some reason or other, you look for Christ or look to Him.* Picture the

consternation as Joseph and Mary suddenly realized that
He was not with them – the flurry and the excitement, the
searching and the weeping! And realize that, or soon or
late, such a moment arrives in the life history of every
soul. And, after all, that is the only decisive test, that is
the only thing that really counts and matters. What is the
value of a religion if it does not help you at the critical
moment; what is the value of a Saviour unless He can save
and rescue you when you need Him most of all? That is
the test. Allow me to ask you a simple question therefore.
Do you know Him? Can you find Him when you need
Him most of all? Is He ever with you and near you? That
is what is meant by being a true Christian – that you can
trust yourself to Him always, everywhere, knowing that
He will always be there. Obviously, if there is any doubt
about it, you must be unhappy.

These are the questions. Is Christ always at hand when
you need Him in the hour of trial and temptation? Can
you always find Him then? Does He deliver, and has He
delivered you? Do you find Him near when you are ill and
laid aside and cut off from your friends and pleasures?
You have always assumed that you were a Christian, you
were christened, etc. but that is not the question. Does
He give you peace when you need it most of all? And face
to face with bereavement and sorrow can you always find
Him? When in your anguish, and with your heart nearly
breaking, you turn to Him and look to Him, do you find
Him? And, above all, on your death-bed and face to face
with the grave, are you certain that you will be able to find
Him easily? There will be no opportunity of going back
then. And face to face with judgment? Oh! let me plead
with you to face this question now. Have you ever known
Him? Have you ever found Him? Do you know what it
means to find Him? Cannot you see the fatal mistake of
assuming that you will be able to find Him at the end,
when you cannot find Him now? On what grounds do
you base this assumption? Let me remind you again of the

innumerable warnings in Scripture of people who had made that assumption and who were plunged into awful doom with those dread words, 'Depart from me, I never knew you'.

But let me now ask why it is that such people make such a terrible false assumption. Wherein lies their error? Well, this incident about Joseph and Mary supplies us with the true answer. They assumed that the boy would follow them, that His one business was to do so, and that therefore the matter need not be considered any further. But He corrects them with this word, 'Wist ye not that I must be about my Father's business?' Later on, indeed, when He was actually thirty years old, His mother makes precisely the same mistake again, in connection with the marriage feast at Cana of Galilee when she reports to Him the shortage of wine, obviously expecting Him to do something about it. The reply was, 'Woman, what have I to do with thee? mine hour is not yet come.' And there are other instances. The whole fallacy is to think that our Lord must accommodate Himself to us and not we to Him. We expect Him to come, we assume He will come. We think that we can come and go as we please and do anything that we like, but that He will always be there when we need Him. So we talk glibly and blasphemously about 'taking Christ with us' to various places – we leading, and Jesus Christ, the Son of God, the King of kings and the Lord of lords, following. Oh, the blasphemy of it all!

No! the first thing you have to realize is that there are conditions in these matters, and that the conditions are always to be laid down by Him. 'Wist ye not that *I* must be about my Father's business?' '*Mine* hour is not yet come'.

It is possible for us to be in such a position that we can always find Him and shall always be able to do so. On what authority do I make that statement? On the authority of His own word. Listen to it from John 14 : 23:

[171]

'If a man love me, he will keep my words: and my Father will love him, and we will come unto him, and make our abode with him'. There it is. He promises to dwell with, and abide with those who keep the condition. And the condition is, loving Him and keeping His word. Without that condition there is no promise. And keeping His word means believing what He said and doing what He has told us to do. It means believing that He is the only Son of God who came on earth to save us. It means believing that He died for me and that He is my only hope of heaven. It means giving myself to Him, turning from my sins and from the world and doing my all and utmost to please Him in everything. 'Do that,' says our Lord, 'and the Father and I will come to you and make our abode with you.' Not simply being baptized when you were a child, not simply being brought up in a religious home, not simply being a church member or doing a certain amount of good, but believing in and confessing Him everywhere as your only Saviour and Redeemer, and keeping His commandments. It is not your idea and mine of what a Christian is that matters, but His. If you want to be able to find Him always, keep His conditions. It is the only way. Oh! the folly and the madness of proceeding on any other supposition or idea.

That is His way and it works. Look at it in the case of Stephen. Do you remember the scene when he was on trial and how, when the authorities gnashed on him with their teeth, he 'looked up stedfastly into heaven, and saw the glory of God, and Jesus standing on the right hand of God', and how later, having been dragged out of the city and being stoned, he cried, 'Lord Jesus, receive my spirit' and 'Lord, lay not this sin to their charge' (Acts 7:59–60)? When Stephen needed Christ and looked for Him he found Him. Why? Because, as we are told in the 6th chapter of Acts, 'He was full of faith and of the Holy Ghost'. He had believed and kept the condition. But read the entire book of Acts for yourself and see it there.

Observe how in any difficulty they turned to Christ and found Him, whether it be Peter in prison or Paul in Corinth or in the shipwreck. At all moments of dire need and crisis He was always there: they had the witness within themselves. The Spirit testified with their spirit that they were the children of God. They trusted entirely to Him. They forsook the world and their sins for His sake. They looked to Him for strength and power, indeed for all. And He made it plain and clear to them that He was with them. 'I *know* whom I have believed', says Paul, 'and am persuaded that He is able to keep that which I have committed unto Him against that day'. That certainty is possible for all. The conditions are still the same. Read the history of the church ever since and find the same thing.

Are you content to go on just 'supposing' that He is with you and that all is well? If you do not know Him now, how do you know you will be able to find Him later on in the last crisis?

Be wise, give up all your vain and foolish ideas and accept His conditions!

For all who rely solely on Christ for salvation and whose main object in life is to show their love to Him by keeping His commandments and doing His will, the promise still is, 'I will never leave you nor forsake you'. Come, keep your side of the conditions tonight and the promise is definitely yours. For His Name's sake. Amen.

14: *True and False Religion*

*

*When the unclean spirit is gone out of a man, he walketh
through dry places, seeking rest; and finding none, he saith, I
will return unto my house whence I came out. And when he
cometh, he findeth it swept and garnished. Then goeth he,
and taketh to him seven other spirits more wicked than
himself; and they enter in, and dwell there: and the last state
of that man is worse than the first.'*
Luke 11 : 24–26[1]

There is nothing which is quite so interesting, and, at
the same time, quite so dangerous in connection with
religious life and thought as the way in which opinion
tends to swing always from one extreme to another. It is
interesting from the purely intellectual standpoint, for it
enables one to trace quite clearly how various movements
have arisen and how they in turn have led to something
else. Indeed, one can almost draw a graph depicting the
rise and fall, the actions and reactions, and by an
extension of that graph one can more or less accurately
predict what is going to happen. Those who think that
the history of religious thought is one of continuous
development, not only show a complete ignorance of the
Bible and the entire history of the Christian church, but
must also inevitably find themselves in hopeless difficulties when they try to explain certain modern
developments. For the fact is, as I have said, that the
history of thought in the church is not so much one of
development as of actions and reactions. One type of
thought hardly ever leads to and produces the logical
development of itself, but, almost invariably, its exact and
extreme opposite. Remembering this, the various move-

[1]December 12, 1933.

[174]

ments which at first seem to be very surprising and conflicting, at once fall into their natural places.

This phenomenon then is truly interesting from the merely intellectual standpoint. But, as I have already said, it is also exceedingly dangerous from the deeper and more spiritual standpoint, for it always tends to mean that the true position is hardly ever occupied. For the true position is never at one extreme or the other, but always in the middle. And thus it comes to pass that it is the one which is always missed and forgotten in the violent swinging of the pendulum from one side to the other. The very fact of this swinging proves in and of itself that there is something wrong with both extremes, but the tragedy is that people who tend to occupy extreme positions, when they begin to detect error and fallacy in their positions, always tend to go right over to the other extreme. They cannot see that the truth is simply that they have gone too far in a certain direction. They condemn the whole direction and, turning right round, fall into the same error in the opposite direction.

Now there cannot be the slightest doubt but that there is a marked tendency at the present time for religious thought to occupy an extreme position. This is seen very clearly in the most popular phrases of the day, and not merely in the phrases, but still more in the general attitude and what is called 'spirit.' The present insistence is upon 'power' and 'results' and the most oft-repeated phrase is to the effect that 'what matters most in connection with religion is not so much whether it is true as whether it works.' That is the great emphasis at the present time, and, like all extreme tendencies, it is loud and vociferous in its claims and tends to be contemptuous of every other position. Remembering what we have already said about the key to the understanding of the movements and changes in religious thought, there is nothing which is at all surprising in all this, and its exact history can be traced with the greatest ease. It is an almost inevitable reaction

[175]

to what has gone before.

Let me show you what I mean. Let us briefly trace the history of the present position. All we need to do is to go back some fifty years or so and remind ourselves of the movement in Christian thought which characterized that time, and which continued to be supreme until comparatively recently. It was a movement which claimed to be essentially and unusually intellectual in its outlook and in its methods. It said that religion formerly had been too much a matter of the heart rather than of the head, that feelings and sentiments had been much too prominent, that there was far too much insistence upon the personal element and the desire for what was called conversion, or experience of the grace of God in the heart. In other words, the whole point was that, according to this movement, religion had been too subjective and internal, and Jesus Christ had been pictured overmuch in supernatural and miraculous terms. What was needed, they said, was a realization that our Lord was more a teacher than anything else, that He was not so much Saviour as Master, that His concern was not so much with the individual as with society, that the thing to emphasize was not so much personal salvation and personal experience, as social salvation and the introduction of a new world order; and that religion primarily was not something to be enjoyed and experienced, but a programme which was to be worked out.

In other words the whole emphasis was placed upon the intellect, and the whole concern of religion was said to be with society in general. People who talked about personal salvation and a personal experience of the grace of God were ridiculed and regarded as being almost imbeciles, or, perhaps more generally, they were regarded as being simple, emotional, unintelligent creatures from whom nothing greater could be expected. That was the favourite view, that was the prevailing tendency. The social gospel was the order of the day. But as the years passed, it became increasingly obvious and evident that the social gospel not only did not improve the social conditions, and not only did not prevent the World War which was one of the greatest social catastrophies of all time, it also led to nothing but empty churches and chapels, and empty lives. Nothing became so clear as the utter barrenness of the movement. It led to no results whatsoever except the ones I have indicated, and year after year, under its influence, the statistics of church membership and church attendance told of a steadily increasing loss of interest in religion in general, while the public life of the country showed a still more obvious decline in morals and decent behaviour. Such were the results of the much-vaunted social gospel – empty chapels and churches, a spineless Christianity, a World War, a phenomenal rise in the number of cases of infidelity and divorce, gambling and sport of all descriptions more popular than ever before, indeed, all the present muddled state of society which we are witnessing.

At long last, all this became increasingly obvious even to the stoutest advocates of the social gospel. They had the sense and the wisdom to see that they were failing and that they were barren of all results. That was the commencement of the reaction, the desire for something to happen, the desire to see something tangible, to witness some results at any rate, to see some fruit following all their labour and their effort. And as the reaction grew and increased, the pendulum began to move and its speed accelerated until it became a violent swing, and by today we are at the extreme opposite end. By today, it is results alone that matter; nothing counts but experience and that a personal experience; truth and definitions are not merely regarded as being of secondary and subsidiary importance, but as actually being a hindrance and a stumbling block. The whole emphasis is upon the heart, not upon the head, and the personal note is being stressed with great force and vigour. Hence we get those phrases to which I have already referred, 'What matters is not whether a religion is true but whether it works', 'religion is caught, not taught'; and the endless talk about 'power', 'release' and 'experience', and also 'surrender' which is pressed so as to include not only mental relaxation, but also actual relaxation of the physical body. Such is the story and history of this violent reaction from a so-called intellectual and social gospel to the modern, personal, experimental type of religion which hates above all else intellect, theology, and precise definitions. As a piece of history alone it is really interesting and instructive. But, as I have already said, it is also exceedingly dangerous, and it is to this that I desire to refer most particularly. And I desire to do so in the light of these verses which I have taken as my text and in which this very matter is discussed by our Lord and Saviour Jesus Christ Himself.

You remember the facts. Our Lord had just cast out a devil from some poor sufferer, and the moment He did so, some of the Jews standing by said that He had done this and all similar works by the power of Beelzebub. Our Lord's reply to this takes two main lines, one of which is just to show that if He does this by the power of Beelzebub, it means that Satan is fighting against Satan, which is ridiculous. The other line of reply goes further and carries the attack right into the enemy's camp by asking the question, 'If I by Beelzebub cast out devils, by whom do your sons cast them out? therefore shall they be your judges.' In other words, He reminds these people that there are also other ways of casting out devils, of which they had never said a word. And then to complete His argument, He goes on to compare His method with all these other methods. The argument primarily was concerning the exorcising of devils, but it is equally true and equally applicable with respect to the whole field of religion and salvation.

Here we have a comparison between true religion and

false religion worked out for us by our Lord Himself. The most obvious thing that must strike us, face to face with this, is that there is a need for care, watchfulness, and above all for discrimination and thought. The mere fact of the comparison and the contrast suggests this at once and warns us therefore against the serious danger of the modern position which denounces definitions and thought and asks only for results. Now let us consider this in the light of the principles which our Lord lays down here in such a clear and definite manner.

The first principle is, that we must always remember that there are other powers, beside that of Christ, which can give 'results'. It is truly astonishing to note how that obvious truth is being forgotten or ignored at the present time, and that in spite of the fact that the world is almost literally teeming with cults which demonstrate it upon all hands. As it was possible in our Lord's own days on earth, and as He admits in this paragraph, it is possible for men and women to get relief from many of their ills and troubles apart altogether from the gospel. It would be ridiculous and foolish for us, or for anyone else, to say that all sorts of improvements are not possible without the gospel. For round and about us we see men and women in whose lives there have been great changes, who are able to testify to great release and relief and help obtained from many a different quarter. How many thousands of people there are who are ready at all times and in all places to extol the virtues of Christian Science and to speak of what it has done for them. Others speak in a like manner for theosophy, others again for Couéism[1], others for the psycho-analyst and his method, and others for just plain common-sense.

Ah! how many people there are in the world today whose one big argument for refusing to believe the

---

[1]Dr Coué was, among other things, a great advocate of auto-suggestion, e.g. 'Look at yourself in the mirror every morning, and say, "Every day and in every way, I am getting better and better".'

gospel and to become Christian is that they are 'all right' without it, that by one or other of these means they have already found the solution to their problems. I have known people who have been delivered from the craving for drink and drugs, from fears and terrors, from worries and anxieties and all sorts and kinds of problems and difficulties by one or other of these means and methods, and when confronted by the gospel, the question they ask is, 'What more can it do for me?' To say, therefore, as so many are saying today, that the only thing that matters about religion is not its truth but whether it works or not, is obviously to sell the pass and to miss the really distinctive thing about the gospel. For if results are the only criterion, if effects and changes are the only standard, wherein lies the uniqueness of the New Testament gospel? Wherein does it differ from all the cults and fads and even the pagan religions, many of which can produce the most remarkable phenomena? Results and effects, therefore, in and of themselves are clearly not enough. Certain of the Jews themselves could cast out devils.

But that is not all. Every relief is not true relief. Every result is not always what it appears to be. False and quack treatments can often relieve pain as well as the correct and the orthodox treatment. What we need to do above all else therefore is to do the very thing that our Lord does in this paragraph. We need to think, and to sift and examine the evidence. 'All that glitters is not gold'. The counterfeit is amazingly like the genuine. The devil is so subtle and has such power as 'to deceive', if it were possible, 'the very elect' themselves. That a thing works and produces certain results is therefore no guarantee of its rightness. That a man finds himself in a better state than he once was, free from certain sins and feeling happy and carefree, does not prove of necessity that he is a Christian. Oh! the blindness which ignores our Lord's own warning, and contents itself merely with results and improved conditions. To put it at its very lowest, it is just not Christian, for the very term *Christian* suggests a limit and a definition, and brings us face to face with a very precise standard. What matters most of all is not *what* has happened to me but rather *how* it has happened. Who has delivered me? What has given me the release? Why am I what I am? Is it but will-power, or Couéism, or common-sense or one of the innumerable modern cults, or is it because of the grace of God through the Lord Jesus Christ? Is it the result of the working of a human power or is it produced by 'the finger of God'? For, as I have said, there are other powers in this world and they can produce strange results. Are we aware of them and are we alive to the dangers?

All this becomes much more urgent when we consider the second principle which our Lord enunciates, which is, *that if our lot or our lives are improved by any power save His own, our state is actually worse than it was before.* This is an astonishing doctrine at first sight, yet there it is in verse 26 where we are told that the evil spirit which had gone out of the man, after he had wandered vainly looking for another lodging place, at last returns again, and finding the place ready and waiting for him, then 'taketh to him seven other spirits more wicked than himself; and they enter in, and dwell there: and the last state of that man is worse than the first.' The exact nature of the power that works the improvement is as important as that. What apparently makes us better may actually be making our condition very much worse. But how is this so? I have often heard it interpreted in this way. The case is taken of a man ceasing to be a drunkard by means of the exercise of his will-power and because he sees the wrongness of it all. That is how the casting out of the devil is explained. Then the return of the devil with the others is interpreted by saying that the man, after becoming sober, now becomes, for instance, a miser, and so his last state is worse than his first. First state, drunkenness only! Last state, miser, unpleasant, and so on! How false is such an interpretation which is based on the difference between one sin and another, as if one sin differed from another in the sight of God, or that some sins were worse than others. No! that is not the explanation. All sin is sin to God and miserliness is no worse than drunkenness. Both are equally repugnant to Him, and equally to be punished. It is we who classify sin, not God – to Him all sin is sin, whatever particular form it may take. How then are we to say that the man whose life is improved by one of the various means we have described is actually in a worse state than he was before? I suggest the following answers.

(1) The first is, that as all these other methods are false, those who have been treated by them are always subject and liable to relapses and frequently experience them. And then, they become the subject of what we might call the relapse complex or mentality. Let me illustrate what I mean by using a medical example. Imagine a man who has been suffering for a long time from a certain trouble. He has tried many medicaments, all of which have proved to be quite useless. He meets a man who tells him that he has got a certain cure. He admits it is expensive and that it will probably mean the patient spending most of his money, yet it is a certain cure and therefore well worth while. Many others have tried it successfully and are ready to praise it. After much hesitation, the man decides to try it, come what may. He spends the money and obtains the treatment. At once it seems to put him right and he begins to tell everybody that he is cured. It is simply marvellous and he is eternally grateful to the man who introduced him to it. But after a while he begins to feel the old trouble returning and soon he is back exactly where he was before. But is he exactly where he was before? No! He is in a much worse condition. He is disillusioned and disappointed. He feels he has a grievance. He becomes distrustful of everyone and everything. He loses faith all round and though a real cure should be found one day,

and his friends try to persuade him to go in for it, and spend some money on it, he will turn to them and say: 'Oh! I suppose it's only like the last one. Cure for a while and then relapse. No! I prefer to waste no more money. Nothing can be done for me. All you say is very wonderful, but all that was said for that other thing which let me down'.

And precisely the same thing occurs in the realms of thought and religion. There are no more hopeless people on earth than those cynics who were once great idealists and optimists. They set out with a certain view. Education, political and social reform were going to put the world right. They trusted to certain people who seemed to be in agreement. Everything was going to be right. But after a while they found themselves being betrayed and let down upon all hands. The world, they discovered, was not what they had thought it to be, and gradually they sank into cynicism, and by today they believe in nobody and nothing. This is one of the terrible dangers of adopting a false philosophy, or believing a false doctrine. It seems to do so much at first and to give such great satisfaction. But after a while it begins to pass off and leaves you, not merely where you were before but actually in a worse condition, for now you tend to distrust everything, even that which is true. Had you not tried the false teaching you would have been more ready to try the true one. There is no type of mentality which is so difficult to treat as that of a person who has been disappointed by someone or something in which he once believed. Having been let down once how difficult it is to bring yourself to try the second time! Yes, how much more difficult than it was the first time! At least eight times as difficult, according to our Lord! Beware therefore of believing in and pinning your faith to something that is not true. The tragedies left in the train of all cults are terrible.

(2) But I can imagine someone criticizing my argument

by saying that if the whole of my case rests upon the possibility of relapse, then it is incomplete, for some do not relapse. To which I reply that even if they do not actually relapse, their case is nevertheless still worse than it was before they were improved at all. And that I demonstrate in this way. Before they were improved they were at least conscious of their trouble and aware of their disease. The real danger of the false cure is, that by relieving symptoms it tends to persuade us that our disease is cured. In how many ways could this be illustrated. It is toothache that takes most people to the dentist; it is pain that draws attention to the disease and makes people seek medical advice. Nay more, it is one of the royal rules in medicine that pain should not be relieved by an injection of morphia until the cause of the pain has been discovered, and one of the greatest medical crimes is to break that rule. The trouble with drugs and quack-remedies is that, by lessening the pain and palliating the symptoms, they tend not only to hide the real cause of the disease, but also tend to keep the people away from the true physician. As our Lord Himself said, 'They that are whole have no need of a physician, but they that are sick', by which He meant that those who imagine themselves to be whole and to be all right are always the last to accept salvation. As long as the man committed a certain sin, or was in a certain position, he felt himself to be wrong and was prepared to listen to the gospel. But having got rid of his sin and having improved his lot by one or other of the various methods to which we have referred, he now feels that he is all right and that he no longer needs to attend a place of worship. He is satisfied with himself. The pain has gone, so he fondly imagines that the disease has been cured, and he stays away from the heavenly Physician. Yes! the very last people to be converted are always those who feel and imagine they are all right, and the very first to get saved are those who are most conscious of their need. Have you met Jesus Christ?

Do you owe all to Him? Are you what you are by the grace of God? Believe me if you have not known Him, you are but fooling yourself as to your true condition and state.

(3) But the last state is worse than the first also in this respect, that the people in that condition actually believe a lie, and are held firmly in the grip of a delusion. As I have said, they believe they are all right and that they have been put right by means of their will, by their creed, or whatever. But according to the Bible that is a lie, for there is but one way in which a man can be put right, and that is by believing on the Lord Jesus Christ, which means believing that He *alone* can put us right and that without Him we are entirely and utterly helpless. To believe that you are all right without seeing the necessity of His death and resurrection is, according to the New Testament, the height of falsehood and delusion and error. No worse state is possible. How much worse it is than the state of the man who just believes nothing at all! He at any rate does not believe a lie, does not delude himself. He feels and knows that he is wrong and is prepared to admit it. All he needs is to accept the positive truth. But as for these other people who follow the various cults, or who trust to themselves and their own works of moral reformation – the humanist and idealist – before they can be put right, before you can get them to believe the true doctrine, you have to break down and tear away their false doctrine. It is better to believe nothing than to believe a lie. That is why one of the most terrible pictures ever drawn by our Lord was the picture of those people who thought they were all right, and who cried out, 'Lord, Lord' but to whom the door was closed. The Pharisee, in the parable of the Pharisee and publican, who went up into the temple to pray, thought that all was right with him but it is the publican, who knew he was all wrong, who was blessed! There is infinitely greater hope tonight for that

[185]

man who is grovelling in the gutters of sin than for the man who believes himself to be all right outside Jesus Christ and His salvation. All that is needed by the former is to be picked up. The latter has to be knocked down first, in addition!

So much for the work of the false cures and the terrible dangers accompanying them. Let me, in conclusion, point you to the other side, to the true cure. How gloriously does the superiority of the true stand out in this paragraph! How divinely supreme is our Lord above all others! No, I am not going to compare Him with the others! It is not a question of comparison but of contrast. Why do the foolish people turn to, and try, any other? Consider His superiority along the following lines.

Note, for one thing, that He has conquered the very chief of the devils. These other powers can cast out an occasional devil here and there. They can produce their little results in this respect and that, and deal with certain of our troubles. But there is only One who is stronger than 'the strong man armed', and who, coming upon him, can overcome him, take from him his armour in which he trusted, and divide his spoils! The other powers can deal at times with particular sins; Jesus Christ the Son of God has conquered sin itself and has overcome Satan himself. And He offers to deliver you, not in this respect or in that respect, He offers and gives *complete* deliverance. 'For this is the will of God, even your sanctification' – a complete renewal and a new nature which is the nature of God Himself. He does not merely promise to deliver us from this sin or that sin, from this devil or that devil, but to free us from all sin, to emancipate us entirely from the dominion of Satan, and at the end to present us '*faultless* before the presence of His glory with exceeding joy'. He faces all the possibilities and defies and conquers them all. He *has* bound the strong man armed.

[186]

Sinful earth can ne'er oppose Him;
Hell itself quails at His word.

He is so strong and His salvation so complete and certain and entire that Paul could safely say, 'I am persuaded that neither death, nor life, nor angels, nor principalities, nor powers, nor things present, nor things to come, nor height, nor depth, nor any other creature, shall be able to separate us from the love of God, which is in Christ Jesus our Lord' (Romans 8 : 38, 39). Results! What else can give such results? What else can enable you to sing in the storm and to be exultant even in the moment of death? You say your life is better and that you have conquered this sin and that. But are *you* free? Really free? Free from the power of sins and trials and tribulations and sorrows? Are you ready to die and to meet God in eternity? 'If the Son therefore shall make you free, ye *shall* be free indeed'. Believe in Him and trust yourself to Him, and be made 'free indeed' and not merely in the appearance.

But His superiority and that of His way of salvation is seen also in that, unlike the other ways, He does not leave the house untenanted when He casts out the devil. He occupies it Himself and fills it with His own presence. All these other ways and powers can certainly help in this respect and that, but they leave the house exactly as it was. You are precisely and exactly as you were before. That old trouble has gone, but you yourself have got to keep it out, you yourself have the fight and the struggle. You have to go on repeating your formula, you have to continue with the process of self-hypnotism and auto-suggestion. And when you get tired and weary it obviously fails and you just relapse and break down. It gives you nothing new. How gloriously different is the gospel of Jesus Christ! Listen to it, ye who are struggling and fighting: 'Come unto me, all ye that labour and are heavy laden, and I will give you rest'. No wonder that Paul

[187]

said, 'I can do all things through Christ which strengtheneth me'! To all who allow Him to do so, He enters in and keeps them safe and free. He promises never to leave us nor forsake us but to be with us always even unto the end. If ever we fail or fall or falter, it is never His fault but always our own, for being foolish enough to trust to ourselves for a second, instead of trusting only, ever, to Him. And as time goes on, in contradistinction from the effects of the other powers, the salvation and the release become greater and greater and ever more and more wonderful. As time advances we grow in grace and in the knowledge of the Lord – the house becomes increasingly filled by His presence. The gospel of Christ not only delivers from sin, it fills you with a new life which grows and ever increases.

Then, last of all, in addition to, and over and above all I have said about the advantages and superiorities, consider by whom, and how the gospel is provided. Here is the contrast: 'But if *I* with the finger of God cast out devils, no doubt the kingdom of God is come upon you'. 'I'! 'The finger of God'! Who is it that speaks? The Son of God Himself come on earth to live and die and rise again in order to set us free! And note His power and His easy mastery. 'By the finger of God'! No wonder He said, 'And the truth shall make you free' to those who believed in Him, for He Himself is 'The way, the truth and the life'. Believing on Him we are not only freed from the devil and sin, we are also put right with God. The salvation offered in the gospel is God's salvation. It is His power unto salvation. It is the truth and the only truth. There is no other way. All others are 'thieves and robbers' and false. God Himself guarantees this. 'This is my beloved Son', He says, 'in whom I am well pleased; hear ye him'. Have you done so?

Consider your life and your eternal soul now. Are you free? Truly free? 'Free indeed'? What is it that enslaves you? What is it that holds you back and fetters you? What is it that you are struggling against vainly and hopelessly? It does not matter! Look unto Him. He has bound the strong man armed. All things are possible with Christ. He will not only set you free, He will keep you free, and above all that, He will put you right to all eternity with God. He not merely gives this relief and that for a short time while we are here on earth. He does that! Oh! yes! He saves in life. But beyond that – He saves in death and to all eternity.

> *He is able,*
> *He is willing; doubt no more!*

15: *The Wonder of the Gospel*

*

For with God nothing shall be impossible.

Luke 1 : 37[1]

The New Testament, in describing the effects and results produced by the gospel and its preaching upon true believers, will be found to do so invariably in terms of what it calls 'the heart' of man. In other words, it constantly states that the one and only true response to the gospel is one which involves the whole personality and the entire being. For in the Bible 'the heart', the very depth and centre of one's soul, expresses what man truly is. This truth is brought out in a number of different ways, both in our Lord's own teaching and in the subsequent teaching of His inspired apostles. They are always warning us against a partial response and against the danger of persuading ourselves on insufficient evidence that we are Christians. And the test we are to apply is this test of a complete and entire response. We are warned that to believe certain things is not sufficient in and of itself, and to believe in God and in the deity of Jesus Christ does not, of itself, prove a man to be a Christian, for the very devils believe all these things and are in a sense perfectly orthodox if the statement is merely intellectual. The gospel of Jesus Christ is not preached merely to produce response in the brain and in the intellect.

Yet, on the other hand, the gospel is not something which merely produces a response and a reaction in the realm of the feelings. How often are we given pictures of people

[1] Aberavon, December 12, 1933.

[190]

who seemed to feel things profoundly but whose feelings led to nothing! Who can forget the picture of the seed that fell into stony ground, or the account we have of those people who followed our Lord up to a point and then 'went back' when the doctrine became what they regarded as hard? Who can forget the son pictured in our Lord's parable who, when asked by his father to go to the vineyard to work, at once responded and said 'I go, Sir', but actually did not go? No! the gospel of Jesus Christ is not meant to appeal merely to the feelings and to produce certain emotional results and nothing more. It is meant to go deeper, to include the will also, and to affect the life and the conduct. But again it is made equally plain and clear that the gospel is not merely meant to produce a response in the will and to lead to a certain type of life and living, for we are constantly warned against mere external rectitude, the leaven of the Pharisees and the awful danger of asceticism, or what Paul calls 'will worship'. And on we could go showing how the New Testament in its teaching warns us against trying to shut up or confine the effects of the gospel to but one part of our make-up and personality. Its case always is that the gospel is to affect and to include the entire man – mind, feelings and sensibilities, will, indeed everything we are and that we possess. And we are told that, unless we can thus say that we have 'obeyed from *the heart* that form of doctrine delivered' unto us, we have no right to regard ourselves as Christians (Rom 6 : 17). A Christian is not one who only believes certain things, or only feels and experiences certain things, or only does certain things. The Christian believes, feels *and* does. His response is entire and complete; every part of him has been moved and affected; nothing remains as it was before; his whole being is changed and with the writer of the hymn he says,

> *Let my whole soul an offering be*
> *To my Redeemer's praise,*

[191]

or with the psalmist he sings, 'Bless the Lord, O my soul, and all that is within me, bless his holy name. (Psa 103 : 1).

Such is the New Testament account of the effect of the gospel. Such is its description of the true Christian. And what we find thus enunciated in the teaching, we find abundantly proved and demonstrated in the illustrations that are to be found everywhere in it and subsequently in the history of the Christian church. Look at these New Testament saints. Start right away at the very beginning, in the very first chapter of Luke's Gospel. What has been the effect of the coming of the Lord Jesus Christ upon all who had recognized Him? For the answer turn to the first two chapters of this Gospel. Could anything be further removed from the speculative arguments and disputations of the man who is only a philosopher, and who regards feeling and emotion as vulgar because they are the opposite of philosophic calmness and poise of mind, and of that impartiality and control of which he likes to boast? Could anything be so essentially different from the vapid, enervating and sickly emotionalism and sentimentalism, with its fleshly riot of the senses, than the noble, elevated, soul-stirring and stimulating songs which we find here and which cause us to desire to rise to our feet and to be up and doing? Or could anything provide such a contrast to the mechanical correctitude and legal righteousness of those who regard the gospel merely as an ethical code or new social outlook? Look at them! Read them again and again. Why! even before our Lord was actually born, His mother Mary, filled with the Holy Ghost, poured out from the depths of her soul those blessed words which we call the *Magnificat*, commencing with the words, 'My soul doth magnify the Lord, and my spirit hath rejoiced in God my Saviour' (Luke 1 : 46, 47). Likewise, Zacharias, the father of John the Baptist broke forth into the famous *Benedictus*, beginning with the words, 'Blessed be the Lord God of Israel; for he hath visited and redeemed his people' (Luke 1:68). No-one surely can forget the *Gloria in Excelcis* of the angels heard by the shepherds, nor in turn the way in which we are told that the shepherds themselves, having seen the Babe in the manger, returned 'glorifying and praising God' (Luke 2 : 20). And lastly consider also the *Nunc Dimitis* sung by the aged Simeon as he stood and looked at the face of the Son of God who was lying helplessly as a little babe in his arms (Luke 2 : 29). What are the characteristics of all these songs and hymns? As we have already indicated, they clearly come from the very depth of the soul, and what they express is gratitude, wonder and adoration. That is the response produced by Jesus Christ even when He was a Babe.

As we follow His story right through we find it to be continually the same, both during the days of His earthly ministry and afterwards. Look at the different people who fall at His feet and worship Him. Listen to them as they praise God for what they have seen and heard. Read the writings of the various apostles and observe how constantly they break forth into praise, wonder and adoration. Indeed there is nothing which is quite so typical and characteristic of the writings of Paul as the way in which he constantly interrupts his theme and his argument with a hymn of praise to God as he contemplates the great salvation wrought in Jesus Christ. And the same is true of all the others and of all the saints that have lived ever since.

In other words, it is abundantly plain and clear from a mere superficial study of the history of the Christian church that a Christian is one whose whole being has been moved and affected by the gospel. Of course he has believed certain things; of course he has felt certain things; of course he has given up his sins and has been doing his utmost to live a new and a better life; but above all else he is one who, like these people at the very beginning, desires to praise God and to magnify His holy Name with his whole soul and being. That surely, therefore, is the test we must apply to ourselves here tonight. Does the thought of Christmas urge you to praise God? Has the coming of Jesus Christ into this world moved you to your very depths? Do you feel that He has made all the difference and that without Him you would be lost? Have you ever thanked God for Him with your whole being?

But let us ask and consider the question as to why the gospel produces that effect upon all true Christians. What is it about this great salvation which is offered to all that leads always invariably to 'wonder, love and praise'? The answer is suggested by the text which I have taken, and which is really the key to the understanding, not only of these first two chapters of Luke's Gospel, but also the key to the understanding of all the amazing and stupendous things which have happened as the result of the coming of the Son of God into this sinful world of time. And in considering this, we shall see clearly why it is that many today, who call themselves Christians and whose lives are often above reproach, fail at that crucial test which we have already been considering.

The first truth is, that salvation is entirely of God. There is nothing which is quite so extraordinary, in connection with the whole question of religion, as the way in which men and women, who persuade themselves that they believe and accept the gospel, at the same time entirely deny this obvious truth. Throughout the centuries man has tried to attribute to man what is so clearly of God. And the tendency is still the same today. Salvation is conceived of in terms of what *men* think and of what *men* do. It is perfectly astonishing to note how people are able to talk and write about salvation without even mentioning any sort of activity on the part of God. All the emphasis is upon what we have to do and what we have to think. Never has human effort and human power and human organisation been so highly praised. God is pictured merely as a goal or as One who passively waits and watches and who is ready to reward us for all our wonderful efforts and achievements. The whole conception of salvation is that it is something which man has to win and work out for himself by study and research, by quest and investigation and by living up to certain definite standards. Man is active. God is passive. Not only is this believed, but what is even more astonishing, it is gloried in and regarded as being greatly superior to that old and true view which ascribes salvation entirely to God. And yet the moment one begins to study the matter in the Bible itself, nothing is so plain and clear as the fact that salvation is entirely of God, and that what has led all the saints to praise Him and to laud and magnify His Name is just that very thing. For, after all, if salvation is just something that we earn, there is not any incentive to praise; if we merely get our wages and our deserts, it is rather irrational to sing the *Magnificat* and the *Nunc Dimitis*. No! you can only explain these inspired songs and all the great anthems of all the ages on one hypothesis, and this is the one reached here, namely that salvation is entirely the result of something done by God.

'How shall this be?' asks Mary, when she is informed by the angel of the promise. 'The thing is impossible', she says. Here is the answer, 'With God nothing shall be impossible'; as if the angel turned to her and said, 'Ah! Mary, you are still thinking in the old terms and in the old human way. What I am announcing to you is quite different. God is going to act now. Humanly speaking you are right, but this is not to be human, it is to be divine. God is going to break into the world, 'The Holy Ghost shall come upon thee and the power of the Highest shall overshadow thee'. No, no! the story of salvation is not the story of God waiting for us to do something, waiting for us to repent and to turn to Him and to do good works; neither is it just the story of God responding to what we have done and rewarding us by pardoning us

[195]

and forgiving us. All that would be wonderful, but it is as nothing in comparison with the story which the Bible reveals. For here we find not a passive God but an active God, not a God who is merely ready to receive us, but a God who actually goes out after us and seeks for us; not a God who can be persuaded by our lives and actions into forgiving us but a God whose love is actually so great that He not only forgives but also persuades us to be forgiven; whose mercy is so boundless that He is not only ready to be reconciled to us but actually Himself so deals with us as to reconcile us to Himself! 'With God nothing shall be impossible.' It is God who does everything.

That is the story of the whole Bible. Look at it right from the very beginning to the end. It is not so much the history of people as the history of God's dealings with them. It was He who chose Abraham even when he was a pagan. It was He who made those promises to him and opened his eyes to the glorious future. All Abraham did and had to do was to believe Him and obey Him. God made the first move and God continued to move. Watch Him as He manipulates Isaac and Jacob and founds the nation of Israel. Is anyone so foolish as to try to say that the children of Israel became what they were as the result of their own efforts? Did they arrive at their knowledge as the result of their own efforts, their own research and investigation and their own holy lives? Look at the record! Their habits and practices were previously those of the people who lived round and about them, unless indeed they were actually worse. All they ever did was to sin and to wander away from God. How were they preserved? How do you account for their history? There can be but one answer. It is God. He went after them. He fed them and clothed them. He protected them and led them. He conquered their enemies and rescued and restored them. All the knowledge they had of Him was not the result of their efforts to find Him but His revelation of Himself to them. It was God who gave the law, it was God who raised and inspired the prophets. The whole Old Testament is but the history of the attempts of the Israelites to foil the purposes of God and to resist His holy will.

And if this is clear in the Old Testament, how much more clearly does it shine out in the New! Look at the first chapter of Luke's Gospel. Who spoke to Zacharias and prepared John the Baptist as a forerunner? How did Jesus Christ come into the world? How was He able to speak as He did and to perform those miracles? Look at the history! Consider the facts and above all consider our Lord's own answers to the questions. It is all of God. Why! John the Baptist cannot be explained in mere human terms, quite apart from Jesus Christ Himself. Just when this old world had reached its lowest point of sin and decadence, when all seemed most hopeless, an angel appeared to Zacharias in the temple and spoke to him. And that marks a turning point in the entire history of the world and the human race. That was the beginning and it was God who began it all. Listen to the words of Jesus Christ as He says repeatedly that the Father has sent Him and that all He does and all He says are but the result of the Father's will and the Father's desire. Nothing is so astonishing as the way in which He persistently attributes everything to God. It was God who sent His Son to work out the great salvation. It was God who sustained Him, it was God who raised Him from the dead, it was God who gave to Him the whole world and its care, and the gift of the Holy Spirit.

Even the church is 'the church of God' and those who are truly members in it have been drawn by the power of God. All is of God. That is why the saints have always praised and magnified His holy Name. Many of them had been trying to climb to heaven. They had constructed their ladders with rung after rung of good thoughts and noble actions, pious hopes and good deeds, but the highest rung was still infinitely short of the heavenly goal.

[197]

They had done all and could do no more. They had exhausted all their efforts and expended all their reserves. They looked down in despair, and crashed to the ground. Then suddenly they, like Jacob of old, became conscious of the fact that there was a ladder hanging in front of them, not erected from the earth but suspended from heaven, there waiting for them, constructed without their knowing it – the cross of Jesus Christ – and they began to sing:

> *As to the holy patriarch*
> *That wondrous dream was given,*
> *So seems my Saviour's cross to me,*
> *A ladder up to heaven.*

Yes! God so loved the world that he gave his only begotten Son (John 3 : 16).' Yes! 'God commendeth his love toward us, in that, while we were yet sinners, Christ died for us' (Rom. 5 : 8). To realize what that means, as far as we can realize it, is to be a Christian. It is also to praise God with your whole being. For think of it! the God you have defied, the God you have ignored and disobeyed, not only has not damned and destroyed you, but actually has sent His only begotten Son to die for you and to redeem you. The way of salvation, the way to heaven, is open tonight and, wonder of wonders, it was made by God Himself. Yes, let us join Zacharias in saying, 'Blessed be the Lord God of Israel, for he hath visited and redeemed his people.'

The second truth about this great salvation, of which we are reminded here, is that *it is essentially supernatural and miraculous*. Those who are unaware of, or who refuse to believe, what we have said already, obviously fail to appreciate this point also and generally oppose it even with violence. And yet there is nothing which is so glorious about the entire scheme, nothing which has so moved the saints to sing God's praises. Whichever way you look at it or from whatsoever angle, the marvel and the wonder of it all shine out more and more gloriously. The salvation which we are offered in the gospel, far from being the result of man's efforts and endeavours, far from being a human and an earthly product is essentially divine and supernatural. Let us look at this in two different ways:

Let us regard it, first of all, from the standpoint of the way in which it was worked out. Nothing is so clear as the supernatural, the miraculous, element. The very birth of the forerunner, John the Baptist, was in itself a miracle. On human grounds the thing was an utter and an entire impossibility. The course of nature was superseded even in the case of the herald of the gospel. But in the case of our Lord Himself, this was still more obvious. His birth was a miracle. The only alternative really is unthinkable. He simply cannot be explained in human terms. He is unique. He stands alone. Then look at His life. These are the only possible comments: 'Never man spake like this man.' 'We never saw it on this wise before.' And as for His miracles and marvels and mighty deeds, they just proclaim Him to be the Son of God, as He repeatedly said. He had power over the wind and the sea, over all manner of devils and diseases and could even command the grave to yield up the dead. All His works have the stamp of God and are supernatural. Never was anything like it seen before. But most astonishing of all was His own resurrection on the morning of the third day after the crucifixion and that cruel death. Then the appearings to the disciples and the people and the final ascension into heaven. It is all the extreme opposite of human effort and endeavour and achievement. It is unusual. It is new. It is miraculous. It is divine. It introduces an entirely new order. It cuts right across everything that had gone before.

But this miraculous and supernatural aspect is seen quite as clearly when we consider the way in which this salvation which had been so wrought in Christ is linked up to man. Look at that which happened in Jerusalem on the day of Pentecost. Can the apostles really be explained in human terms? They constantly deny that themselves, and attribute all to Jesus Christ. And they astonish and amaze the authorities in Jerusalem, for what puzzled them was that 'unlearned and ignorant' men such as Peter and John should be so bold and should be capable of such mighty deeds. We are told that they 'marvelled'. And indeed it is not surprising, for we have but to compare and contrast these men, as we find them in Acts and in their own epistles, with what we read of them in the Gospels, to see at once that they are utterly and entirely different. It is no process of development and gradual growth. Suddenly they are transformed and filled with power. There is no physical miracle in the New Testament that is in any way more remarkable than the change in these men. It is not the result of what they had done, but of what God had done to them. And as they look at themselves they feel that there is nothing to do but to praise Him and to go on praising Him.

Had you realized that the gospel was like that? Had you realized that it offers a superlative salvation, which means that you will be not only forgiven and pardoned and shown a new way of life which is to be lived, but that above and beyond all that, it offers you a new birth and a new nature, a new life within you with all its power, and that the life of God Himself. Ah! the misery and the poverty of those who fail to see that salvation is supernatural and who continue wearily and uselessly to trust to their own efforts and endeavours. It is not surprising that they never produce great hymns and anthems of praise. For how can one sing in a state of bondage? How can one shout one's hallelujahs when face to face with an impossible task in an impossible world? No! before we can sing we must have life and power, vigour and abandon, victory and conquest. And that is precisely what is offered you in the gospel. In the words of John Calvin, 'The Son of God became the son of man in order that the sons of men might become the sons of God.' It is possible for you tonight, as a result, not merely to become a better man but to become an entirely new man. Ah! you may admire the life of Jesus Christ and feel that His words and works were wonderful; you may shed tears as you think of Him as the babe born in that manger, or as you watch Him at the end forsaken of all and crucified; you may feel a great desire to follow Him and to imitate Him and His life, but you will never feel your whole soul and entire being going out to God in gratitude, wonder and adoration, until you are conscious of the fact that He died for you and until you have experienced His life and power flooding your own, changing it and transforming it, infusing power into it, turning your defeats into victories and liberating you from the power of sin. And that is offered to you tonight in the gospel of Jesus Christ.

But there are probably many who, face to face with all this, are saying to themselves as Mary said of old, 'How can these things be?' which reminds us of the third principle, namely, that salvation being of God is therefore supernatural, it is something which *not only cannot be achieved by man but also cannot be understood and comprehended fully by us*. Indeed, I could have gone further and I could have said quite definitely that this great salvation which is offered to us by God is to the natural man something which is inherently incredible. Our standards of judgment are earthly and human. We are accustomed to the things of flesh and of sense. Our categories are limited and finite. We are born into a certain order of events and into a world which believes wholeheartedly in itself and in its own powers. Salvation, as far as we can see it in every department of life, depends upon will-power, grit, determination and hard work. It is the realist who succeeds, the man who, as we say, 'faces the facts' and who suffers from no illusions. Is it surprising, therefore, that when confronted by the whole gospel scheme of salvation we, like Mary at the beginning, should ask, 'How can these things be?' Ah! it has been said all along, not only by Mary, but also by that learned man Nicodemus who, when our Lord spoke to Him about the re-birth, said precisely the same thing; also by the Greeks who put it into stronger terms by saying that the preaching of the cross was folly. It is still being said by thousands tonight who say that they will not believe a thing unless they can understand it, and who inevitably cannot understand the gospel. For who can understand it? Who can understand the virgin birth and the incarnation? Who can understand the miracles and the mighty deeds? Who can understand the cross and the death and the whole question of the atonement? Who can fathom the power and the mystery of the resurrection and the person of the Holy Spirit? Who can understand the mechanism of the re-birth and the new life with all the promise of a new beginning and all things being made new? It is baffling. It is staggering. It is so unlike all we have known and have thought and have felt. 'How can these things be?' 'Are they really possible? Can it really happen?' Such are our reactions. Such are our feelings. We are confronted by something that our minds cannot grasp, that even intellectuals cannot span. We are face to face with the infinite and the eternal. And there, we have only two alternatives. We can either refuse to believe because we do not understand and reject because we cannot explain, or we can imitate the example of Mary who, though she did not understand and although she could not see, when told that it was of God and that with Him nothing shall be impossible, submitted and accepted and yielded a ready acceptance and obedience saying, 'Behold the handmaid of the Lord; be it unto me according to thy word' (Luke 1:38). That then is the question for you tonight. I do not ask you to try to understand these things. No-one can. I just ask you to accept them and to yield yourself to them. The gospel in the first place does not ask you to do anything. It does not even demand an understanding or a great intellect.

Let me say a word more on that last point, for it is indeed the most glorious of all. In our logical sequence we would put it thus, *that in view of the fact that salvation is of God and therefore supernatural, although we cannot understand it, it holds out a hope for all.* 'For with God nothing shall be impossible.' It is our only hope. It is the only way. It is the only gospel, the only really good news. It is the one thing that enables me to stand in the pulpit and preach with confidence and assurance. The gospel is 'the power of God unto salvation' and not merely an indication of how men can save themselves! It is God's work, and because it is His work, it is possible for all and can be offered to all. Were salvation something human and natural it would be impossible for all, yes, even for those who talk most about it in that way. For it is one thing to talk, it is a very different thing to live and act! It is all very well to use idealistic phrases and to talk beautifully about love, and, to consider exalted ethical standards and to talk glibly about applying the principles of the gospel to the problems of life. But the question is, Can they be applied? Do those who talk thus apply them in their own lives? Can they do so? And can all this teaching be 'applied' to the world? Look at the world today in spite of all this teaching. And what has such teaching to offer to the failures, the broken and the maimed in life, to those who have lost their will-power as well as their character? Oh! how I thank God that salvation is something which He gives to us, for we can all receive a gift, the weakest as well as the strongest. There is literally hope for all. 'How shall this be?' asked Mary. 'Nothing shall be impossible with God', came the answer. And in due time Jesus Christ was born in Bethlehem. The impossible happened. And

[203]

oh! the hundreds and thousands of cases in which that was repeated during His earthly ministry! Which are the cases that the people and the disciples take to Him? Oh! always the most hopeless, always the ones which had baffled and defeated everyone else and all their powers – the born blind, the deaf, the paralysed, yes, even the dead. The hopeless of the hopeless, the most helpless of the helpless. Can Jesus do anything for them? 'How can these things be?' Can it really happen? 'Go and shew John again those things which ye do hear and see: the blind receive their sight, and the lame walk, the lepers are cleansed, and the deaf hear, the dead are raised up, and the poor have the gospel preached to them' (Matt 11 : 4–5). Yes, it happened. There was no limit to His power. The most desperate case was no more difficult than any other, for 'with God nothing shall be impossible.' Is that so? Is that really true? Surely there is a mistake! For one afternoon He is to be seen hanging upon a cross utterly helpless, and the people standing near by say, 'Others He saved, Himself He cannot save.' So mighty in life, apparently conquered by death! 'Nothing impossible'? And He there, dying, yes, dead and buried in a grave! But wait! He bursts asunder the bands of death and rises from the grave. Even death could not hold Him. He has conquered all; yes, again I say, 'With God nothing shall be impossible.'

'But how does that affect us?' asks someone. Well, I am here to tell you that whatever your problem, however great your need, it is still the same for all who ask. The gospel just asks you to allow God to forgive you, to pardon you, to cleanse you, to fill you with a new life by believing that he sent His only begotten Son into the world, to live and die and rise again in order to make all that possible. 'How can these things be?' 'With God nothing shall be impossible.'

16: *Devotion to Christ and Its Source*

✽

*And Jesus answering said unto him, Simon, I have
somewhat to say unto thee . . .
And he said to the woman, Thy faith hath saved thee; go in
peace.* Luke 7 : 40, 50.[1]

I choose these two particular verses as my text as they
seem to me to be the key to the true understanding of the
well-known incident which happened in the house of
Simon the Pharisee, and our Lord's well-known comment
upon it in the parable of the two debtors. In a dramatic
incident like this there is a grave danger of our 'missing
the wood for the trees', and that danger becomes greatly
exaggerated when we come to consider the parable with
its many comparisons and contrasts. The parable is one
which is notoriously difficult and which, as I hope to
show you, can be seriously misunderstood if we are not
very careful. The way to avoid all these dangers and
pitfalls is to keep our eye fixed upon these two persons,
Simon the Pharisee and the woman 'which was a sinner.'
For they are the *dramatis personae* in the parable as well as
in the incident that took place in Simon's house. The two
verses I have taken as my particular text indicate to us
very clearly the most striking of all the points of
difference between these two persons, namely the result
in the two cases of their meeting with Jesus Christ. The
one is surprised, reprimanded, condemned, and probably
felt annoyed and disgruntled – the other finds exactly
what she expected, is praised, blessed and goes away with

[1]Aberavon, September 9, 1934.

[205]

the peace of God in her heart. Is it not a perfect contrast? Look at it, look at the two persons! Is it not truly amazing and almost unbelievable? Here are two people in the presence of the same Person. They both desire to see Him. There they are, both of them in His presence. As far as He is concerned the power to give is obviously the same in both cases and yet how utterly different is the result. The one is condemned, the other is pardoned and receives the gift of salvation.

Have we not here a perfect picture of what happened constantly and everywhere during our Lord's earthly ministry, though the exact form was not always quite so dramatic? The best way to classify all the people who appear in the Gospels, is according to what they received from Him. But is it not also a perfect picture of the way in which He has divided mankind ever since, the way in which He divides them even tonight? There was Jesus of Nazareth, the very Son of God, to whom all power and judgment had been given, who was able to work miracles, heal diseases, forgive sins and give rest to troubled and tormented souls – there He was in the house of Simon, full of power, yea more, full of a love to mankind which made Him long to exercise and use that power for their welfare. There He is in the house, and two people come into contact with Him. But how utterly different are the results of that contact. He is not here in the flesh now, but the great fact remains the same. As the result of His life on earth, above all as the result of His atoning death and resurrection and ascension, He is present among us in this world by the Holy Spirit, and is waiting and ready and longing to impart unto us the greatest gifts and blessings that man can ever receive, the gift of pardon and the knowledge of it, power over sin and temptation, a new life of joy and happiness, a removal of the fear of death and the grave and a certain hope of heaven and eternal bliss. But how different and varied has mankind been in its reactions to this across the centuries, and how evident still is the division this evening. Is it not present even here and now? Have *you* had the blessing? Do you love Him as this poor woman did, has He given rest to your troubled soul and put peace into your heart? Why are there people who are still miserable and unhappy, the slaves of sins and passions, weak and troubled and perplexed in mind and soul and spirit? With all the fulness of the Godhead in the One who is offering and waiting to bless, why is the world as it is? why are men and women as they are? indeed, above all, why are you as you are and what you are?

Now I would like to emphasize the fact that this is not merely a difference between those who are interested in our Lord and His religion and those who are not so interested. Indeed, in a sense, the whole point of the parable is just to show that that is a very light and superficial distinction, which may very well only conceal the all-important truth. For Simon himself was interested in our Lord and His teaching, otherwise he would never have invited Him to his house at all. He had heard of Him, had probably heard Him himself several times. His interest and his curiosity were definitely aroused. We must say that to his credit. His attitude is definitely a great improvement on that of the majority of the Pharisees who certainly did not invite our Lord into their houses, but clearly showed their dislike and their hatred. No! this man is interested and goes out of his way to show that interest. He makes a move on the basis of that interest quite as definitely as the woman takes action on the basis of her interest. The difference here then is not between two people, one of whom is interested in Christ and the other is not.

I make this point for the simple reason that there is a tendency today to say that nothing matters but that we should be interested in our Lord and His teaching. People do not like to be questioned today about the exact nature of that interest; they object to insistence upon certain fundamental conditions and definitions in connection with it. It seems to be taken for granted that each one can go to Christ in his or her own way and find anything they like, and that as long as each one is satisfied personally and obtains some particular experience, it ill befits anyone else to inquire into it. All this is being expressed in terms of tolerance and in talk about uniting, and we are to regard all as truly Christian who in some way or another invite Christ into their house to dine with them because they are interested in Him. But how wrong and misguided is all that in the light of this incident with its searching questions as to the nature of that interest and above all the result of that interest. Again, that is why, we chose verses 40 and 50 as our text, for they emphasize the really important distinction and shew that it applies as a test, not only to those outside the church, but also to many who have been members for years, perhaps for life, and all their life-time have been 'interested' in Christ and His religion as they see it. Simon could say that he was acquainted with Christ and with His teaching and that he was very interested in both; but what he could never say was that he had been blessed by Him, that Christ had made a fundamental difference to him and to his life and that he felt that he owed all to Him. But that is what the woman *could* say, and that, after all, is what makes a true Christian. All the interest in the world cannot replace that, all the knowledge possible about His life and His teaching cannot compensate for that. In which of the two positions are you? That of Simon or that of the woman? Let us, first of all, proceed to consider these two positions as they are represented by the conduct of Simon and the woman, and then let us consider the underlying principles which go to determine these respective attitudes as they are enunciated by our Lord in the parable of the two debtors.

The nature of our relationship to Jesus Christ can be easily discovered by the application of two simple tests which are suggested by this account of the incident in

Simon's house. Both Simon and the woman are interested
in Christ and both treat Him in a certain manner. Our
interest in Him and treatment of Him either correspond
to those of Simon or else to those of the woman.

Now it is perfectly clear that Simon's interest in our
Lord is mainly and primarily intellectual, if not entirely so.
As we have already indicated, he had probably heard Him
several times, had perhaps been intrigued by His
personality and interested by the teaching. For, after all,
there was much that was novel and strange about that
teaching. And Simon had sufficient intelligence to
appreciate that, and to realize that it merited further
investigation and was not merely to be dismissed on the
basis of his old prejudices and training. Simon was a
student of life and of religion. Here he met with
something that he had never met before. He was
therefore curious and prepared to investigate. Further-
more he had heard some astonishing claims put forward
by this strange new teacher. He claimed to be the
Messiah, He put Himself above the law and called for and
demanded utter obedience. 'Is this right or is it not?' Such
was the question that Simon asked himself. And he
decided to investigate. He would invite this teacher to
dine with him and there observe Him at close quarters
and test both Him and His teaching. Such was the nature
of Simon's interest. It was purely intellectual. Christ and
His teaching were an intellectual problem worthy of his
consideration and worthy of his examination. How
different is the case of the woman! Her interest is by no
means purely intellectual. She comes rather on the basis
of her need, on the basis of the failure of her life, on the
basis of her shame. She does not come merely because her
intellectual faculties are intrigued and because that here is
a moral view and philosophy of life worthy of the exercise
of all her critical faculties. She does not come to examine
and to test; she comes rather to listen and to receive.

Another, and perhaps a better way of putting all this is

to say that Simon himself as such was not involved in the
meeting at all. It was only a part of him. Do you not feel as
you read the account that there is a strange detachment
about him? How calm and cool and collected he appears
to be. He is entirely master of himself. No doubt he was
appropriately polite and charming and appeared to be
engrossed in the conversation at the table, and yet the
whole time he was thinking his own thoughts and drawing
his own conclusions and proceeding with his own
intellectual analysis of his guest. The whole thing was
outside him, outside his true self. It was merely his head
that was engaged. Not for one moment does he give the
impression that this meeting is the most vital and
momentous occasion in his life, that here and now he may
obtain something which will make an eternal difference to
him. No! there is no thrill, no excitement, no tension. He
is calm and detached. How different is the woman! Her
whole personality is involved, she is anxious and
quivering with excitement and thrilled with the thought
of approaching Jesus Christ. It is not merely a part of her
personality that is involved. Far from being detached and
controlled, she cannot restrain herself. The tears flow
down her cheeks – she is moved to the very depth of her
being. How have you approached Jesus Christ? How do
you approach Him and His religion? Are these things
merely problems to you? Are you interested in them
merely from the intellectual standpoint? Is Jesus Christ
merely an historical person to you, merely a man, better
than all others perhaps and greater, but still only a man
who did certain things and who propounded a certain
view and philosophy of life? And are you interested in all
this merely as a problem for your mind? Have you realized
that Jesus Christ and His religion are not merely to
concern your mind or a certain part of you, but *you*
yourself, your life and all you are and hope to be? When
you consider Him and His gospel to what extent are you
yourself involved?

But this question can really be answered at once by observing how these two different approaches to our Lord inevitably affect the way in which we treat Him. I do not apologize for using that phrase, for it is literally accurate, as I shall show you. Observe how Simon treats Him. He does not hesitate to sit at His side and to look into His eyes without a blush. He does not even treat him with the civility and politeness which is due from a host and which he invariably showed to the majority of his guests. He does not provide Him with water to wash His feet, he does not welcome Him with a kiss and he does not anoint His head with oil. Oh yes! he invites Him into his house. He is interested. But there is no real warmth in the invitation. The Lord is not honoured as many a guest has been honoured in that house and at that table. How different is the action of the woman! She falls at His feet, is ashamed to show her face and to glance into His all-pure eyes. She kisses His feet, washes them with her tears, dries them with the hair of her head, and actually anoints them with ointment. Oh! yes, the approach, and the reasons for it, at once show themselves in the conduct and the behaviour!

How do you treat Him? Do you give Him *the* place of honour in your life? He is not the first or the only guest to enter your house. Who receives the finest entertainment, He or one of the others? To whom do you pay the greatest attention, to whom do you show the greatest amount of respect? On whom do you lavish the greatest tokens of respect and admiration? This woman had kept the box of ointment for years. It was one of her greatest possessions and treasures. That is what she brings forth and breaks for the anointing, not of His head, but actually of His feet. Her very best is unworthy of Him. On whom do you use that box of ointment which you have? To whom and to what do you give yourself utterly and entirely? Who attracts your interest, who calls forth your praise and your thanksgiving? What is your attitude

[211]

towards Jesus Christ this evening? Is He merely a man, a teacher with a certain view of life that interests you and which you are prepared to consider and perhaps to try as far as it suits you? Or do you recognize in Him the Son of God come down to earth, the Saviour of your soul? Do you look upon Him as more or less of an equal with whom you can sit at the table and whom you can examine and criticize, or do you realize that He is the Lord of glory? Have you fallen at His feet in utter shame and humiliation, casting yourself upon His mercy and looking only to Him for deliverance and pardon? And have you realized that He is prepared to receive you? And has that led to an outburst of love and affection within you towards One who is so amazing? For that is the truly Christian interest in Christ which leads to surrender, love and adoration. He is no longer here in the flesh as He was in the days of Simon and the woman. You can no longer fall at His physical feet and wash them and kiss them and anoint them. But the question of the way in which we treat Him is as vital and as relevant as ever. Do you remember what He said to Saul of Tarsus on the road to Damascus? The question was, 'Why persecutest thou me?' making it clear to Saul that it was *He* who was being persecuted, though Saul's intention was to harry Christians. And how often are we warned against grieving Him and crucifying Him afresh? You show your love to Him today by forsaking sin, obeying His commandments and praising Him with your lips and by your life before your fellow men and women, and by telling all that He has the central place in your life.

There then we see the two attitudes towards our Lord analyzed and portrayed. We see that the true Christian attitude is one of loving interest which leads to worship and adoration and surrender to Him. Now we must ask a second question. What is it that leads to this attitude? Or, if you prefer it, why is it that some people are only distantly and coldly interested in our Lord, and keep themselves detached from His religion like Simon of old, while others worship Him and love and adore Him like the woman, and feel the desire to give their all to Him? According to our Lord Himself, in the parable there are two main answers to that question.

(1) In the first place, Christ says, our view of Him and our attitude towards Him depend upon our view of ourselves, or our view of our need, or, if you like, our view of sin and sinners. This is the great point of the parable which Jesus addresses to Simon (vv 40-43), the point therefore which we must elucidate and work out carefully. You remember the facts. There was a man who had two debtors, the one owing five hundred pence and the other fifty. Neither had anything wherewith to pay or to meet the debt, whereupon the creditor frankly forgave both and told them that they could regard their debts as having been settled. On the basis of this our Lord asks Simon, 'Which of them will love him most?' To which Simon answers, 'I suppose that he, to whom he forgave most'. To which our Lord answers, 'Thou hast rightly judged'.

Now what does all that really mean? There are some who do not hesitate to say quite frankly that our Lord's teaching is that those who have committed the greater number of sins and to whom therefore a larger number of sins have to be forgiven, of necessity love God more than those who have committed but a few sins. They expect open obvious sinners who have touched the dregs and the depths to be more grateful for their salvation than those who have always lived good, moral and respectable lives. They regard the first group not only as needing more forgiveness but also as receiving more forgiveness, the one five hundred and the other but fifty. They expect a more demonstrative and loving, passionate type of religion from those who were once violent sinners than they do from those who have been brought up in a religious atmosphere and manner. In other words, they expect

[213]

people like this woman to love God and our Lord more than people like Simon, for the reason that she had been a notorious sinner and evil liver, whereas Simon had always been a good, upright, moral man.

The more subtle way in which this is often put is that all people do not need to be converted. The drunkards, gamblers, wife-beaters etc. – certainly! But not your good moral man. And obviously therefore the change-over in the first one will be greater than in the second. 'Preach salvation', they say, 'in the slums and amongst the profligates and insist upon conversion. But all that is needed amongst chapel-going people is instruction and knowledge'. Now all this is the exact opposite of what our Lord was out to teach, for the point of the parable is not to justify Simon for his lack of love, and to explain why his love was less than that of the woman, but rather to condemn him and to show him how utterly false his view of sin was. And that is true of necessity, otherwise we shall be saying that our Lord taught that good could come out of evil, and that the best way to learn to love God was to sin violently against Him; which is ridiculous, of course, for in that case our Lord Himself would have loved God less than those who much needed to be forgiven because of their sins! No! such an error must not be thought of for a moment. This was the very error into which Simon and all the Pharisees had fallen. They judged people solely by the number of sins which they committed, or by their apparent degree of sinfulness. He and all the people in the town condemned this woman simply because she committed sins of a certain type. She was the sinner! They were not! Why? Simply because of the nature of her sins. But everywhere in His teaching our Lord condemns that type of thought and actually tells the Pharisees and 'good' people that the publicans and the harlots are crowding into the kingdom before them. His case always everywhere is that the one group is as much in need of forgiveness and salvation as the other.

'What then,' asks someone, 'is the meaning of the five hundred and the fifty in the parable? Why the contrast?' The question is easily answered. It is a figure which is meant to show, not the need itself, but the realization of the need in the two cases. But let us make this plain by looking at these two people figured in the parable. The teaching is, I say, that what matters is not the number of sins we may or may not have committed, but our sinful *state* or *condition*. And in that respect we are all identical. 'But surely,' argues someone, 'you are not going to say that all people are exactly the same and all commit the same sins?' No! I am not saying that at all. What I am saying is that ultimately all that makes no difference at all, and that what makes a sinner is not the number of sins but the sinful state, the desire to sin, the nature that is biased towards evil. How perfectly is that shown here. Here are these two men. Both are debtors. Both have nothing to pay. Both are probably cast into prison. And both are forgiven in precisely the same way. They are identical! 'But what of the five hundred and the fifty pence?' you say. It makes no difference at all. Though the one only owed fifty as against the other's five hundred he was a debtor and quite as much a debtor. Though his bill was but fifty and not five hundred that did not create money wherewith he could pay. He was equally penniless. Though it was only fifty and not five hundred he was quite as definitely condemned by the law, and in prison. And though it was only fifty and not five hundred he was forgiven in exactly the same manner as the other. The position of the two men is identical! Debtors, penniless, helpless! Try to make use of the fifty and the five hundred as you will, except in the way I have already indicated, and you will find it is quite useless. The state of these two men was identical. Simon thought that his state before God and that of the woman were very different. Our Lord's reply is that they are identical. It is only in the realization of their state that they differ.

[215]

Is this clear to you? It is in a sense the most vital truth of the Christian religion. It is only those who realize their need of the Saviour who will ever find Him and thank Him for His glorious salvation. Do you feel grateful to Him? Do you love Him? If not, why not? Have you felt your need of Him? Do you realize your sinful state before God? Are you still thinking in terms of particular sins or the number of sins you have committed as compared with someone else? Cannot you see that that is the very error our Lord here condemns? Do you see that child's copy book with the perfectly white page for which the master will commend him? But an accident occurs, one blot drops on to the page. Oh! that is nothing, you say. It is just one drop. But the child knows better. It spoils the record. It is as bad as if there were several blots. Or take a walk round the horticultural show. What a perfect apple that is! Surely it must have had the first prize. Its shape and colour are so perfect. And yet it has clearly had no prize at all. Why? There is just one blemish, just one spot of degeneration. You have to turn the apple upside down before you see it. But the judge has done so and there it is! Do you see that magnificent specimen of a horse – perfect as regards breed, holding himself perfectly and moving very much more perfectly than any machine has ever done. And yet he does not receive the prize. Indeed he is placed at the very bottom of the class. Why? Oh! it is only a very small blemish in one of his feet. The uninitiated could never have seen it or noticed it. But there it is and it means that the horse is unsound and will probably transmit that unsoundness to its progeny. Very small! True. But the vet saw it and it is enough to condemn the horse.

Do I need to go on multiplying my illustrations? If man is so careful about slight blemishes and so sensitive to such minute faults; if man's judgment is so keen, how much more so God's? He has told us the terms of the competition in the law. He has there indicated His expectations and desires and demands. Have you fulfilled these? Can you satisfy them? 'Ah!' you say, 'I have not sinned much, very little indeed as compared with so and so. I have not broken many laws, indeed, as far as I can see, I am almost perfect.' To which the reply of James is 'Whosoever shall keep the whole law, and yet offend in *one* point, he is guilty of all'. Are apples and horses and animals expected to be perfect and yet man, the lord of creation, on whom God has showered His greatest gifts and from whom He expects most of all, to be allowed to be imperfect? The Lord God Almighty created man perfect and expected him to remain so. His demand is an absolutely white page. One blot is as bad as hundreds, one blemish, one defect, is enough to condemn. 'Yes', says the apostle Paul, who had done his utmost to live the perfect life and to justify himself, 'there is *none* righteous, no, not one'. Whether there are many sins in your record or few, you are a sinner, you are a debtor. More than that, you have no plea to offer. If you have only committed one sin in your life, you cannot erase it, you cannot atone for it, you cannot remove it. 'Surely', you argue, 'it will be easy to rub out that one blot in the copy. If there were many it would be impossible, but it is just that one. Fetch me a rubber.' But can you? You may succeed in removing most of the ink, but the mark, and the roughness, and the irregularity will remain. You can never reconvert that page into the perfectly white page it once was. You cannot cut the one blemish out of that apple without leaving traces of its existence. You cannot remove the fault from the bone in the foot of that horse. If only that could be done, what a difference it would make! Man, of course, has not been slow to try it. All sorts of schemes and devices have been tried. Wax has been used to fill gaps, varnish has been employed. Man has exercised all his ingenuity and inventive power in an attempt to remove and cover up these slight faults and blemishes. The ordinary man is sometimes fooled by these things but never the expert.

[217]

Can you deal with your sins? You say that they are but few and these comparatively slight and unimportant. Very well! Can you get rid of them? Can you remove them? Do they leave you alone? Do you really feel that the record is clear? Are you quite happy? Have you blotted them out? You have left off that sin, you have done a lot of good, but has the sense of shame gone, has the feeling of condemnation left you, do you honestly feel as if you had never sinned at all? Come, be wise and admit it. Not only are you a debtor like all others, but it is as true of you as of them to say that you have nothing wherewith to pay. You cannot clear your record. You cannot satisfy God. All your actions and all your best works can never atone for the injury that you have done Him by even one sin. You are in debt to Him and His law. You are estranged from Him and can never reconcile yourself to Him. You stand condemned by the Judge whatever you may say for yourself and about yourself – the rules of the competition are clear. One blemish debars. Do you realize that as you approach Jesus Christ and His gospel? Realizing that truth about yourself, do you really think that the right place for you is to be seated by Him at the table, and that your attitude should be one of a critical examination of Him to see what He is like and what He has to say? As you look at Him and consider His perfect record and remember that, when challenged to do so, no one could convict Him of sin, do you still feel that you can approach Him in a cool and detached manner? Fall at His feet in tears of contrition and failure! Listen to Him! Drink in His words! Realize that it is madness for the condemned criminal to judge. Cast yourself entirely upon His mercy and accept His every word! Those who have been blessed by Him are always those who, like this woman, approach Him with a deep consciousness of their failure and their sense of need.

(2) The other condition of blessing is that we should be perfectly clear that we are right in our view and idea of

[218]

salvation. And this follows of necessity, of course, from what we have been saying already. Here again there is that amazing contrast between Simon and the woman. Simon's view of salvation corresponded to his view of sin and his view of himself. The woman had no real view of salvation at all until she came to Christ and heard what He had to say. She had heard the Pharisees' view many and many a time and it had utterly condemned her. She knew that there was no hope for her. For the Pharisees' view was that a man earned salvation for himself by keeping the law, by fasting, by doing good, and so on. It utterly condemned her. There was no hope. She was an utter failure. Simon felt no need of Christ and His help because he felt that he had done so well. His life had been good. We have it all already. 'Good' people see no need of a Saviour and therefore do not love Jesus Christ, nor feel that they owe all to Him. But how different it is when one sees oneself as a condemned sinner, when one realizes that that one spot is enough to damn us to all eternity and makes us quite as bad as the violent sinner. How different it is when one realises that one is a debtor, yea, a penniless debtor, who has *nothing* whatsoever to pay. Ah! one then begins to cry out for help, for a Saviour. One is then exactly like the woman, conscious of the utter, the desperate need. And, oh! how sweet are the words of Christ to such a soul and in such a condition! Listen to them, 'And when they had nothing to pay, he frankly forgave them both' (v.42). Still, there is no difference between them. But look at what He says. They were helpless. They were penniless. They could do nothing. Their case is hopeless then, and the law must take its course? No! blessed be His Name, He frankly forgave them both. Salvation is not something that we have to achieve, it is something that has been done once and forever by the Son of God Himself. *He* does it! 'While we were yet without strength ... Christ died for the ungodly' (Rom. 5 : 6). When we could not pay, He paid.

[219]

Salvation is entirely His work. Without Him we remain damned. Do you not long to fall at His feet and kiss them and wash them with your tears of joy and anoint them with ointment?

But look at the way in which He does it. 'He frankly forgave them both'. What a glorious word that word *frankly* is! It not only means freely but also the way in which it is done. It is full of grace and of charm. There is no law anywhere near it. He does not go to the two debtors and say, 'I want to treat you both exactly alike, and forgive you exactly the same number of sins, which means that you who owe fifty are free and that you who owed five hundred now only owe four hundred and fifty and therefore still have to remain in prison.' No! No! that is man's legalistic way of computing forgiveness according to the number or type of sins forgiven. That is not the Lord's way, glory be to grace! He does not consider the number of sins but the state. Both were debtors, both were failures, both were in the same condition, so He frankly forgave them both. Both were cleared, both were free, the five hundred as well as the fifty. Yes! and in one moment. No conditions laid down for the five hundred because he had owed more than the other. Forgiveness free and full, without any conditions at all, and no mortgaging of the future because of the past. Both are at liberty, both have the same possibilities for the future. As they were identical in the prison, so they are identical outside. The woman that was a sinner is as forgiven, and as free, and as much a child of God as the one who had always lived an outwardly respectable life. She is given the new beginning and the new life as much as the other.

And on I could go, but I must close. You are not surprised at her action now, and its marked contrast to that of Simon. She knew she was a sinner. She was miserable and unhappy. She felt hopeless and lost. She was afraid of life but especially afraid of death and that meeting with God beyond the grave. She knew she could do nothing. But then she heard this new teacher who assured her that God forgave freely and utterly in Him, that all the past could be blotted out, that God would smile upon her and she could start on a new life. She did not realize the whole truth about the way in which this was made possible. She did not know that that forgiveness depended upon His dying in her stead and taking her sins upon Himself. All she knew was that she trusted Him and that He had entirely changed her life. He had done what she could never do, He had solved her problem and removed her burden.

Face Him tonight then in the depth of your being, in your weakness, in your fear and in your secret shame. Listen to Him as He tells you that He has died for you, that He has reconciled you to God, that your past can be blotted out, and that your eternal future is safe. Listen to Him as He opens out to you a *new* life, with new possibilities and new powers. Whatever you may have been, the offer is open to you. The gate lies open. You have but to walk out to liberty. Do so by acknowledging Him before all, by confessing your sinfulness, accepting His salvation, and by trusting only to His power to enable you to live a life which will be pleasing in His sight. For His Name's sake. Amen.

17: *The Parable of the Prodigal Son*

*

And he said, A certain man had two sons: and the younger of them said to his father, Father, give me the portion of goods that falleth to me. And he divided unto them his living. And not many days after the younger son gathered all together, and took his journey into a far country, and there wasted his substance with riotous living. And when he had spent all, there arose a mighty famine in that land; and he began to be in want. And he went and joined himself to a citizen of that country; and he sent him into his fields to feed swine. And he would fain have filled his belly with the husks that the swine did eat: and no man gave unto him. And when he came to himself, he said, How many hired servants of my father's have bread enough and to spare, and I perish with hunger! I will arise and go to my father and will say unto him, Father, I have sinned against heaven, and before thee, and am no more worthy to be called thy son: make me as one of thy hired servants. And he arose, and came to his father. But when he was yet a great way off, his father saw him, and had compassion, and ran, and fell on his neck, and kissed him. And the son said unto him, Father, I have sinned against heaven, and in thy sight, and am no more worthy to be called thy son. But the father said to his servants, Bring forth the best robe, and put it on him; and put a ring on his hand, and shoes on his feet: and bring hither the fatted calf, and kill it; and let us eat, and be merry: for this my son was dead, and is alive again; he was lost, and is found. And they began to be merry.

Now his elder son was in the field: and as he came and drew nigh to the house, he heard music and dancing. And he called one of the servants, and asked what these things meant. And he said unto him, Thy brother is come; and thy father hath killed the fatted calf, because he hath received him safe and sound. And he was angry, and would not go in: therefore came his father out, and intreated him. And he answering said to his father, Lo, these many years do I serve thee, neither transgressed I at any time thy commandment: and yet thou never gavest me a kid, that I might make merry with my friends: but as soon as this thy son was come, which hath devoured thy living with harlots, thou hast killed for him the fatted calf.

The Parable of the Prodigal Son

And he said unto him, Son, thou art ever with me, and all that I have is thine. It was meet that we should make merry, and be glad: for this thy brother was dead, and is alive again; and was lost, and is found.   Luke 15:11–32[1]

There is no parable or saying of our Lord which is quite as well-known and as familiar as the parable of the prodigal son. No parable is quite so frequently quoted in religious discussions, or made use of in order to support various theories and contentions with respect to these matters. And it is truly astonishing and amazing to note the almost endless number of ways in which it is so used and the almost infinite variety of conclusions to which it is held to lead. All schools of thought seem to claim a right to it; it is held to prove all sorts of theories and ideas which are mutually destructive and which exclude one another. It is quite clear, therefore, that the parable can be very easily and readily mishandled and misinterpreted. How can we avoid that danger? What are the principles that should guide us as we come to interpret it? It seems to me that there are two fundamental principles which must be observed and which, if observed, will guarantee a correct interpretation.

The first is that we must always beware of interpreting any portion of Scripture in such a manner as to come into conflict with the general teaching of Scripture elsewhere. The New Testament must be approached as a whole. It is a complete and entire revelation given by God through His servants, a revelation which has been revealed in parts and sections, all of which go together to make a complete whole. There are obviously, therefore, no contradictions between these various parts, no clashes, no irreconcilable passages and statements. This is not to say that we can understand every single statement. What I do say is that

[1] January 6, 1935.

there are no contradictions in Scripture and that to suggest that the teachings of Jesus Christ and Paul, or the teachings of Paul and the other apostles, do not agree is subversive of the entire claim of the New Testament itself and of the claim of the church for it throughout the centuries, until the rise of the so-called higher-critical school some hundred years ago. I need not go into this matter this evening. Let it suffice to say that it is only the more superficial critics, who are by now many years behind the times, who still try to make and force an antithesis between what they call 'the religion of Jesus' and the 'faith of St Paul'. Scripture is to be compared with Scripture. Every theory we evolve must be tested by the solid body of doctrine and dogma which is to be found in the entire Bible and which has been defined by the church. Were this simple rule remembered, the vast majority of the heresies would never have arisen.

The second rule is a little more particular. It is that we should always avoid the danger of drawing any negative conclusions from the teaching of a parable. This applies not only to this particular parable, but to all parables. A parable is never meant to be a full outline of truth. Its business is to convey one great lesson, to present one big aspect of positive truth. That being its object and purpose, nothing is so foolish as to draw negative conclusions from it. That certain things are not said in the parable means nothing. A parable is important, and matters only, not from the point of view of what it does not say, but from the point of view of what it does say. Its value is entirely and exclusively positive and in no respect negative. Now I suggest to you that the failure to remember that simple rule has been responsible for most of the strange and fantastic theories and ideas which have been propounded supposedly on the basis of the parable of the prodigal son. That this should have been possible at all is surely astonishing, for if those who have done this had only looked at the two other parables which are in the same chapter, they would have seen at once how unjustifiable was their procedure. Why not draw negative conclusions from those also? And so with all parables?

But apart from that, how utterly ridiculous and illogical it is to base and found your system of doctrine upon what is not said. How dishonest it is! For it does away with all authority and leaves you with no standard save your own prejudice and your own desire and your own imagination. Now that, I say, is what has been done so frequently with this parable. Let me illustrate that by reminding you of some of the false conclusions that have been drawn from it. Is this not the parable to which they constantly refer who try to prove that ideas of justice and judgment and wrath are utterly and entirely foreign to God's nature and to Jesus' teaching concerning Him? 'There is nothing here,' they say, 'of the father's wrath, nor the father's demands for certain actions on the part of the son – just love, pure love, nothing but love.' This is a typical example of a negative conclusion drawn from the parable. Because it does not positively teach the justice and the wrath of God, we are told that such qualities do not belong to God at all. That Jesus Christ elsewhere emphasizes these qualities is of course also completely and entirely ignored. Another example is, the way in which we are told that this parable does away with the absolute necessity for repentance. I have heard of a preacher who tried to prove that the prodigal was a humbug even when he returned home, that he had decided to say something which sounded right, though he did not believe it at all, in order to impress his father, that his exact repetition of the words proves the case. The ultimate point is that in spite of this, in spite of a sham repetition, in spite of all, the father forgave. The final clinching argument of this preacher, was that the father said nothing about repentance. Therefore, because he said nothing, it does not matter; because repentance is not taught and impressed upon the son by the father, repentance towards God does not matter!

But perhaps the most serious of all the false conclusions is that which tells us that no mediator between God and man is necessary, and that the idea of atonement is foreign to the gospel and is to be attributed rather to the legalistic mind of Paul. 'There is no mention in the parable,' they say, 'of anyone coming between the father and the son. There is no talk at all about another paying a ransom, or making an atonement; just the direct dealing between father and son conditioned solely upon the latter's return from the far country.' Because those things are not specifically mentioned and stressed in the parable, it is agreed that they do not count at all and really do not matter. As if our Lord's object in the parable was to give a complete outline of the whole of the Christian truth, and not just to teach one aspect of the truth. Surely it must be obvious to you that if a like procedure were adopted in the case of all parables, the position would be utterly chaotic and we should be faced with a mass of contradictions.

The business of a parable then is to present to us and to teach us one great positive truth. And if ever that should be clear and self-evident, it is in this particular case. It is no mere accident that this parable is one of three parables. Our Lord seems to have gone out of His way to protect us against the very danger to which I have been referring. But apart even from that, the key to the whole situation is provided in the first two verses of the chapter which provide us with the essential background and context. 'Then drew near unto him all the publicans and sinners for to hear him. And the Pharisees and scribes murmured, saying, This man receiveth sinners, and eateth with them.' Then follow these three parables, obviously dealing with that precise situation and obviously meant to reply to the murmurings of the Pharisees and scribes. And, as if to enforce it still further, our Lord draws a certain moral or conclusion at the end of each parable. The great point, surely, is that there is hope for all, that God's love extends even to the publicans and sinners. The glorious truth that shines out in these parables, and which is meant to be impressed upon us, is that amazing love of God, its scope and its reach, and especially by way of contrast to the ideas of the Pharisees and scribes on that subject.

The first two parables are designed to impress upon us the love of God as an activity which seeks out the sinner, which takes infinite trouble in order to find him and rescue him, and to show the joy of God and all the host of heaven when even one soul is saved. And then comes this parable of the prodigal son. Why this addition? Why the greater elaboration? Why a man, rather than a sheep or a lost coin? Surely there can be but one answer. As the first two parables have stressed God's activity alone without telling us anything about the actions or reactions or condition of the sinner, so this parable is spoken to impress that aspect and that side of the matter, lest anyone should be so foolish as to think that we should all be automatically saved by God's love even as the sheep and the lost coin were found. The great outstanding point is still the same, but its application is made more direct and more personal. What, then, is the teaching of this parable, what is its message to us this evening? Let us look at it along the following lines.

The first truth it proclaims is *the possibility of a new beginning*, the possibility of a new start, a new opportunity, another chance. The very context and setting of the parable, as I have reminded you already, shows this perfectly. It was because they had sensed and seen this in His teaching that the publicans and sinners drew 'nigh unto Him for to hear Him.' They felt that there was a chance even for them, that in this man's teaching there was a new and a fresh hope. And even the

Pharisees and scribes saw precisely the same thing. What annoyed them was that our Lord should have had anything at all to do with publicans and sinners. They had regarded such people as being utterly and entirely beyond hope and beyond redemption. That was the orthodox view to take of such people. They were so hopeless that they were to be entirely ignored. Religion was for good people and had nothing at all to do with bad people, and certainly had nothing to give them, and most certainly did not command good people to mix with bad people and treat them kindly and tell them of new possibilities. So the Pharisees and scribes were annoyed by our Lord's teaching. Anyone who saw any hope for a publican or sinner must, to them, be entirely wrong and a blasphemer. The same point exactly emerges in the parable in the different attitudes of the father and the elder brother towards the prodigal, the point being not as to how he should be received back, but rather as to whether he should be received back at all, whether he deserved anything at all.

That then is the thing which stands out on the very surface. There is a possibility of a new start, a new beginning, and for all, even for the most desperate. No case can be worse than that of the prodigal son. Yet even he can start again. He has touched bottom, he has sunk to the very dregs, he has gone down so low that he could not possibly descend any further. Never has a more hopeless picture been drawn than that of this boy in the far country amidst the husks and the swine, penniless and friendless, utterly hopeless and forlorn, utterly desolate and dejected. But even he gets a fresh start, even he is called to make a new beginning. There is a turning-point which leads on to fortune and to happiness even for him. What a blessed gospel, and especially in a world like this! What a difference the coming of Jesus Christ has made! What new hope for mankind appeared in Him! There is nothing that so demonstrates and proves that the gospel of Jesus

Christ is the only really optimistic philosophy and view of life offered to man, so much as the fact that publicans and sinners drew nigh unto Him for to hear Him. And the message which they heard, as in this parable of the prodigal son, was something entirely new.

But I would have you note that it was not only new to the Jews and their leaders, but also new to the whole world. The hope held out to the vile and hopeless by the gospel not only cut across the miserable system of the Jews, but also the philosophy of the Greeks. Those mighty men had been evolving their theories and their philosophies. Yet not one of them had anything to offer to the down and out. They all demanded a certain amount of intelligence and moral integrity and purity. They all had to postulate much in the human nature for which they catered. Nor were they realists. They wrote and spoke in a learned and fascinating manner about their utopias and their ideal states, but they left mankind exactly where it was, and were entirely divorced from ordinary life and living. The only people who have ever been in a position even to try the idealistic and humanistic methods of solving the problems of life have been the wealthy and the leisured, and even they have invariably found that they do not work. There was not, and there never had been, any hope for the hopeless in the world before Jesus Christ came. He alone taught the possibility of a new start and a new beginning.

But that teaching was not only new then, during His days on earth, it is still new. And it is still surprising and astonishing and amazes the modern world quite as much as it amazed the ancient world of nearly two thousand years ago. For the world is still without hope and its controlling philosophy is still profoundly pessimistic. This is to be seen most clearly, perhaps, when it tries to be optimistic, for we see always that when it tries to comfort us it always has to point us to the future with its unknown possibilities. It tells us that in the new year things surely

[229]

must be better, that they cannot at any rate be any worse. It argues that the depression must have lasted so long that surely the turn of the tide must of necessity be at hand. It is glad that one year has ended and that a new one is beginning. What is the real secret of a new year? Its real secret lies in that we know nothing at all about it. All we know is bad, therefore we try to comfort ourselves by looking to what is unknown and by fondly imagining that it must be brighter and better. Then listen to it as it talks about its schemes and plans for the uplift of mankind. All it can tell you is that it is trying to make a better world for its children, trying to build for the future and for posterity. Always in the future! It can do nothing for itself, it can only hope to make things better for those who are yet unborn. And the longer it goes on talking about that and trying to do it, the more hesitant does it become. To prove this, just compare the language of 1875 with that of 1935, or even that of 1905 with 1935.

But if the situation is like that with regard to society in general and at large, how infinitely more hopeless and filled with despair is it when we face it in a more individual and in a more personal sense! What has the world to offer by way of solution to the problems that tend to distress us most of all? The answer to that question is to be seen in the frantic efforts that men and women are making in their attempts to solve their problems. And yet nothing is more clearly seen than the fact that all their attempts are failures. Year after year men and women make their new resolutions. They realize that above all else what is needed is a fresh start and a new beginning. They decide to turn their backs on the past, to turn over a new leaf, or even to start a new book of life. That is their desire, that is their firm conviction and intention. They want to break with the past and for a time they do their utmost to do so, but it doesn't last. Gradually but inevitably they slide back to the old position and to the old state of affairs. And after a few such experiences they no longer try, and come to the

[230]

conclusion that all is hopeless. Up to a point, the fight is kept up and maintained, but sheer weariness and fatigue eventually overcome them, the pressure and the might of the world and its way seem to be entirely on the other side and they give in. The position seems to be utterly hopeless. I wonder how many there are, even in this service now, who feel like that in some respect or other! Do you feel that your life has gone wrong, has gone astray? Are you for ever mocked by 'the haunting spectre of the might-have-been'? Do you feel that you have got yourself into such a position, and into such a situation, that you can never get out of it and put yourself right again? Do you feel that you are so far away from what you ought to be, and from what you would like to be, that you can never get there again? Do you feel hopeless about yourself because of some situation with which you are confronted, or because of some entanglement in which you have got involved, or because of some sin which has mastered you and which you cannot conquer? Have you turned to yourself and said, 'What is the use of making any further effort, what is the use of trying again?' I have tried and tried many and many a time before, but all to no purpose, and my trying now can lead to but the same result. I have made a mess of my life, I have forfeited my chance and my opportunity, and henceforth I have nothing to do but to make the best of a bad job.' Are such your thoughts and your feelings? Is it your position that you have missed your opportunity in life, that what has been has been, that if only you had another chance things might be different, but that cannot be, and there it is? Is it that? Alas! How many there are in such a position. How unhappy are the lives of the average man and woman. How hopeless! How sad! Now the very first word of the gospel to all such is that they should lift up their heads, that all is not lost, that there is still hope, still the possibility of a new start and a new beginning, here and now without any delay at all, and without looking to the slightest extent on

[231]

something imaginary which may belong to the unknown future, but rather by leaning upon something which happened in the past nearly two thousand years ago, but which is as strong and as powerful today as it was then. Even the prodigal can get right. There is a possible turning-point even along the blackest and the most hopeless road. There is a new beginning offered even to publicans and sinners.

But I must hasten to point out in detail what I have already indicated in passing, that this message of the gospel is not something vague and general like the world's message, *but something to which definite conditions are attached.* And it is here we see most clearly why it was that our Lord spoke this particular parable in addition to the other two. To avail ourselves of this new beginning and new start which is offered by the gospel we must observe the following points. And oh! let me impress upon you the importance of doing this. If you merely sit there and listen and allow yourselves to be moved in general by the glowing picture of the gospel you will go home exactly as you were when you came. But if, on the other hand, you attend carefully and note each point and act upon it, you will find yourself going home an entirely different person. If you are anxious to avail yourself of the gospel's new hope and new start, you must follow its methods and its instructions. What are they?

The first is that we must face our position squarely, honestly and truly. It is one thing to be in a bad and difficult position, it is quite a different thing to face it honestly. This prodigal son had been in a thoroughly bad situation for a very long time before he truly realized it. A man does not suddenly get into that state in which he is described here. It happened gradually, almost unbeknown to himself. And even after it happened, he did not properly realize it for some time. The process is so quiet and so insidious that the man himself scarcely sees it at all. He looks at his face in the mirror every day and does not see the changes that are taking place. It is someone who only sees him at intervals who sees the effects most clearly. And often when we begin to sense our terrible plight, we deliberately avoid thinking about it. We brush such thoughts aside and busy ourselves with other matters, more or less saying to ourselves as we do so, 'What's the use of thinking, here I am anyhow.' Now the very first step back is to face the issue, to face the situation honestly and clearly. We are told that this young man 'came to himself.' That is actually what the man did! He faced things out with himself and did so quite frankly. He saw that his troubles were entirely due to his own actions, that he had been a fool, and that he should never have left his father, and should certainly never have treated him as he had done. He looked at himself and could scarcely believe that it really was himself. He looked at the husks and at the swine. He faced it right out.

Have you done that? Have you really looked at yourself? What if you put all your actions of the past year down on paper? What if you had kept a record of all your thoughts and desires, your ambitions and imaginings? Would you consent to their publication with your name beneath them? What are you now in comparison with what you once were? Look at your hands – are they clean? Look at your lips – are they pure? Look at your feet – where have they trodden, where have they been? Look at yourself! Is it really you? Then look around you at your position and surroundings! Do not shirk it! Be honest! What are you living on? Is it food or swine's husks? On what have you spent your money? For what purpose have you used money that should perhaps have gone to feed wife and children or to clothe them? On what have you been living? Look! Is it food fit for men? Look at what you enjoy. Face it calmly. Is it worthy of a creature created by God with intelligence and understanding? Does it honour man, leave alone God? Is it swine's food or is it really fit for human consumption? It is not enough that you should just bemoan your fate or feel miserable. How did you ever get into such a state and condition? Look at the swine and the husks and realize that it is all due to the fact that you have left your Father's house, that you have deliberately gone against your conscience, deliberately flouted religion and all its commands and dictates, that it has been entirely and utterly of your own doing. You are where you are today entirely as the result of your own choice and your own actions. Face that and admit it. That is the first essential step on the way back.

The next is to realize that there is only One to whom you can turn and only one thing to do. I need not work out that point in detail in connection with the prodigal. It is perfectly clear. 'No man gave unto him.' He had tried and had exhausted his own efforts and the efforts of all other people. He was finished and no one could help him. There was but one left. Father! The last, the only hope. The gospel always insists upon our coming to that point. As long as you have a halfpenny of your own left, the gospel will not help you. As long as you have friends or agencies to which you can apply for help and which you believe can help you, the gospel will give you nothing. Actually, of course, as long as a man thinks he can keep himself going by some of these other methods, he will continue to try to do so. And the world is far from being bankrupt in our estimation still. It still believes in its own methods and ideas. And how pathetically we cling to them! We bank on our own will-power and our own efforts. We draw upon the new years of our calendar – as if they made the slightest difference to the actual state of affairs! We invoke the aid of friends and companions and of relations and dear ones. Ah! you know all about the process, not only in your attempts to put yourself right, but also in your attempts to put others right about whom you are concerned and worried. And on we will go until we have exhausted all. Like the prodigal we go on until we become frantic and until 'no man gives unto us'. Then and then only do we turn to God. Oh! how foolish. Let me try to explode the fallacy here and now. Face it frankly. Realize that all your efforts must fail as they have always failed. Realize that the improvement will only be transient and temporary. Cease to fool yourself. Realize how desperate the position is. Realize further that there is only one power that can put you right – the power of Almighty God. You can go on trusting to yourself and others and trying with all your might. But a year tonight the position will not only be the same, but actually worse. God alone can save you.

But as you turn to Him, you must realize further that you can plead nothing before Him save His mercy and His compassion. As the prodigal left home his great word was 'give'. He demanded his rights. He was full of self-confidence and even had a feeling that he was not being given his due and his rights. 'Give'! But when he returns home, his vocabulary has changed and his word now is 'make'. Before, he felt he was someone and somebody and something which could demand rights worthy of itself and of himself. Now he feels he is nobody and nothing and realizes that his first need is to be made into something. 'Make me'! If you feel that you have any right to demand pardon and forgiveness from God, I can assure you that you are damned and lost. If you feel that it is God's business and God's duty to forgive you, you will most certainly not be forgiven. If you feel God is hard and against you, you are guilty of the greatest sin of all. If you feel still that you are somebody and that you have a right to say 'give', you will receive nothing but misery and continued wretchedness. But if you realize that you have sinned against God and angered Him, if you feel you are a worm and less, and unworthy even of the name of man, quite apart from being unworthy of God, if you feel you are just nothing in view of the way you have left Him and turned your back upon Him, and ignored Him and

flouted Him, if you just cast yourself upon Him and His
mercy, asking Him if in His infinite goodness and
kindness He can possibly make something of you, all will
be different. God never desired to see you as you now are.
It was against His wish and His will that you have
wandered away. It is all of your own doing. Tell Him so
and tell Him further that what worries and distresses you
most of all is not merely the misery you have brought
upon yourself, but the fact that you have disobeyed Him
and insulted Him and wronged Him.

Then having realized all this, act upon it. Leave the far
country. You have stood up in the field of the swine and
the husks by your mere action in visiting this chapel. But
walk right out of that far country. Leave the swine and the
husks. Turn your back upon sin and give yourself to God.
Feelings and desires and inclinations will avail you
nothing. Do it! Make a break. Get to God and get right
with God! Take your stand. Commit yourself! Venture
on Him! Trust Him! How ridiculous it would have been
for the prodigal to have thought of all he did and yet not
do it! He would still have remained in the far country. But
he did it. He acted upon his decision. He carried out his
resolution. He went to his father and cast himself upon
his mercy and compassion. You must do the same in the
way I have already indicated.

And if you but do so, you will find that in your case, as in
the case of the prodigal, *there will be a real, solid new
beginning and new start*. The impossible will happen and
you will be amazed and astounded at what you will
discover. I pass over the joy and the happiness and the
thrill of it all tonight, in order that I may impress upon
you the reality of the new start which the gospel gives. It
is not something light and airy. It is no mere matter of
sentiment or feelings. It is no mere drug or anæsthetic
which dulls our senses and therefore makes us dream of
some bright realm. It is real and actual. In Jesus Christ a

real genuine new start and new beginning are possible. And they are possible alone in Him! The greatness of the father's love in the parable is seen not so much in his attitude as in what he did. Love is no mere vague sentiment or general disposition. Love is active. It is the mightiest activity in the world and it transforms everything. That is why here also, the love of God alone really can give us a new start and a new chance. The love of God does not merely talk about a new beginning, it makes a new beginning. 'God so loved the world that He *gave*.' The father did things to the prodigal; God alone can do that to us and for us which can set us on our feet again. Let us observe how He does it. Oh! the wondrous love of God that really makes all things new and that alone can do so.

Observe how the father blots out the past. He goes to meet the son as if nothing had ever happened, he embraces him and kisses him as if he had always been most dutiful and exemplary in all his conduct! And how quickly he commands the servants to strip off the rags and the tatters of the far country and remove from his son every trace and vestige of his evil past. He wipes out the past by all those actions, in a way that no one else could do. He alone could forgive really, he alone could wipe out what the boy had done against the family and against himself, and he did so. He strips off every trace of the past. That is always the first thing that happens when a sinner turns to God in the way we have been describing. We go to Him and expect just as little as the prodigal who had expected to be made a servant. How infinitely does God transcend our highest expectations when He begins to deal with us. All we ask for is a kind of new beginning. God amazes and surprises us, in His very first action, by blotting out our past. And that, after all, is what we desire most of all. How can we be happy and be free in view of our past? Even if we no longer do a certain action, or commit a particular sin, there is the past, there is what we have done already. That is the problem. Who can deliver us from our past? Who can erase from the book of our life what we have done already? There is but One! And He can! The world tries to persuade me that it does not matter, that I can turn my back upon it and forget it. But I cannot forget it, it keeps on returning. And it makes me miserable and wretched. I try everything but still my past remains, a solid, awful, terrible fact. Can I never get free from it? Can I ever be rid of it? There is only One who can strip it off my back. I only know that my rags and tatters have really gone when I see them on the Person of Jesus Christ the Son of God who wore them in my stead and became a curse in my place. The Father commanded Him to take my filthy rags off me and He has done so. He bore my iniquity, He clothed and covered Himself with my sin. He has taken it away and has drowned it in the sea of God's forgetfulness. And when I see and believe that God in Christ has not only forgiven but also forgotten my past, who am I to try to look for it and to find it? My only consolation when I consider the past is that God has blotted it out. No other could do so. But He has done so. It is the first essential step in a new beginning. The past must be erased, and in Christ and His atoning death, it is!

But in order to have a really new start, I require something further. It is not enough that every trace of my past be removed. I require something in the present. I desire to be clothed, I must be robed. I need confidence to start afresh and to face life and its people and its problems. Though the father met the boy and kissed him, that alone would not have given him confidence. He would have known that everyone was looking at the rags and at the mud. But the father does not stop at that. He clothes the boy with a dress that is worthy of a son, and places a ring on his finger. He gives him the status of a son and the external proofs of that station. He announces to all that his son has returned, and so clothes him as to make him feel unashamed when he meets people. No one else

[238]

could do that but the father. Others could have taken the boy in and have helped him, etc. But no one could make him a son but the father, and give him his position and provide him with the wherewithal.

It is precisely the same with us when we turn to God. He not only forgives and blots out the past, He makes us sons. He gives us new life and new power. He will so assure you of His love that you will be able to face men unashamed. He will clothe you with the robe of Christ's righteousness, He will not only tell you that He regards you as a child, but make you feel that you are one. As you look at yourself you will not know yourself. You will look at your body and see this priceless robe, you will look at your feet and see them newly shod, you will look at your hand and see the ring and signet of God's love. And as you do so you will feel that you can face the whole world without apology, yes, and face the devil also, and all the powers that fooled you in the past and ruined your life. Without this standing and confidence a new start is a mere figment of the imagination. The world only tries to clean the old suit and make it look respectable. God in Christ alone can clothe us with the new robe and really make us strong. Let the world try to point its finger and remind us of our past, let it do its worst, we have but to look at the robe and the shoes and the ring, and all is well.

And if you require a clear proof of the actuality of all this, it is to be found in the fact that even the world has to acknowledge that it is true. Listen to the servant speaking to the elder brother. What does he say? Is it, 'A strange-looking man in rags and tatters has come from somewhere'? No! 'Thy brother is come'. How did he know he was the brother? Ah! he had seen the father's actions and had heard the father's words. He would never have recognized the son, but the father did, even while he was yet a long way off. The father knew! And God knows you, and when you go to Him and allow Him to clothe you, everyone will get to know it. Even the elder brother knew it. It was the very last thing he wanted to know, but the conclusion to be drawn from the singing, and the noise of jubilation and happiness was unavoidable. He is too mean to say 'my brother,' but he, even he, has to say 'this thy son'. I do not promise that all will like you and speak well of you if you give your self to God in Christ. Many will certainly hate you and persecute you and try to laugh at you and do many things to you, but, in doing so, they will actually be testifying that they also have seen that you are a new man and that you have been made anew and have been given a new start.

What more do you require?

Here is an opportunity for a real new beginning. It is the only way. God Himself has made it possible by sending His only begotten Son into this world, to live and die and rise again. It matters not at all what you have been, nor what you are like at the moment. You have but to come to God confessing your sin against Him, casting yourself upon His mercy in Jesus Christ, acknowledging that He alone can save and keep, and you will find that

> *The past shall be forgotten,*
> *A present joy be given,*
> *A future grace be promised,*
> *A glorious crown in heaven.*

Come! Amen.

18: *Jairus – Complete Salvation*

*

And, behold, there cometh one of the rulers of the synagogue,
Jairus by name; and when he saw him he fell at his feet...
Mark 5:22 ff [1]

There are times when one feels strongly the need of a
complete revision of the little synopses which are to be
found in the majority[2] of Bibles at the head or
commencement of each chapter. This feeling arises
because it seems to us sometimes, that the authorities
responsible for the synopsis have not picked out and
selected the most important or the most vital thing or
that they have given undue emphasis to something which,
to us, does not seem to merit it. This does not mean that
we are not grateful for the synopsis or that we would in
any way detract from its great value, but that we feel that
we would have made a different selection. A synopsis is of
very great value, in spite of the opinion of those pedants
and purists who are more concerned with the Bible as
literature than as truth, and to whom the appearance of a
page is more important than its contents. For the
synopsis reminds us that we are dealing with facts and
that we must not lose sight of the great outstanding facts
or principles, as we wend our way through the details. Our
case tonight is certainly not that we do not need a
synopsis; we are concerned rather with the content of the
synopsis, the particular choice. And the more one
ponders this subject and reflects upon it, the more
interesting and illuminating does it become. Indeed we

[1]Aberavon, June 2, 1935.
[2]This was true of the King James Version which was in general use at the
time and which Dr Lloyd-Jones used to the end.

[241]

have not proceeded very far in our consideration of it before we find ourselves becoming conscious of the fact that to decide what to place in the synopsis and what to leave out is one of the most difficult problems with which we can ever be confronted. And this in turn leads us to modify our criticism of the work of those who have furnished these synopses for us, and to marvel and to wonder that they have done their work so well.

The essence of the difficulty is to be found in the fact that the Bible is not a mere text-book of history or indeed a mere text-book of philosophy or anything else, even including theology. It is all that, but very much more. And it is this other element, this divine element, this supernatural inspiration, that makes the task of making a synopsis almost impossible. In an ordinary book, it is a comparatively easy matter to classify material into important, less important and comparatively unimportant. But when dealing with the Bible such categories lose their meaning and should scarcely be mentioned at all. Everything becomes important and one's feeling is that everything should be included in the synopsis. A further difficulty is to be found in the fact that our appreciation of the contents of the Bible is not something static and fixed, but rather something which tends constantly to fluctuate and to change according to our degree of spirituality and the amount of spiritual insight and discrimination that we possess. We have all had the experience of constantly making new discoveries as we read the Bible. Something which we had always passed over in the past, almost without noticing it at all, suddenly strikes us as one of the greatest and most important things we have ever read, and were we to draw up our synopsis at that moment, that, and almost that alone, would receive our attention. Our synopsis, therefore, would change from time to time and we would never be satisfied with any one particular attempt or effort. Perhaps therefore the wisest rule for us is to be content with the one provided for us, which certainly can claim to be a good average of the various feelings that thus suggest themselves to us from time to time. Let us use it and, in our minds, criticize it and quarrel with it! That will be excellent for us, for if we do so honestly and in a logical manner, it will but serve to remind us once more, and impress more firmly than ever upon our minds, the fact that the Bible is God's Word, that it is a divine book which transcends all our categories and increasingly supplies our finite minds from its inexhaustible store of treasures. Here are gems and pearls of all types and kinds, of all colours, shades and sizes. Who can really assess their respective values?

I have been drawn into saying all this by noting the synopsis at the head of this particular chapter of Mark's Gospel. According to the synopsis, the big thing is the dealing of our Lord with the daughter of Jairus and His act in raising her again to life. But, to me for the moment, a matter of still greater significance is the dealing of our Lord with Jairus himself! What I mean is that it would be a real pity, if, in our preoccupation with the striking and amazing miracle that our Lord performed upon Jairus' daughter (which is recorded at the end of this remarkable narrative) we should fail to see and to appreciate the equally vital and important things that happened before that dramatic end was reached. It is not that we desire to compare and to contrast the events as such, or 'per se', with each other, for, as we have already seen, that is ridiculous. But we can claim that there is that about our Lord's dealing with Jairus which is even more unique, and therefore more profitable for us, than His dealing with Jairus' daughter. The great and glorious lesson to be learned from the latter is one which we can learn equally well from the story of the widow of Nain's son, and also from the case of Lazarus, the brother of Martha and Mary. But there is a lesson to be learned from our observation of our Lord's dealing with Jairus himself which, in a sense, cannot be found anywhere else in quite the same form. And it is a lesson which is of vital and central importance, as we shall see, and which deals with that precise form of the difficulty which many people feel today with regard to the whole question of religion and salvation. By this I mean that what makes the incident unique, when we regard it from the standpoint of Jairus himself rather than from that of his daughter, is that we are given a view of a vitally important aspect of our Lord's work which is not so clearly demonstrated in any other incident and which also does cause considerable perplexity to many who are concerned about religion and salvation. The uniqueness lies in this, that we find Jairus, not only coming to our Lord, but also continuing with our Lord and travelling in His presence.

If we compare and contrast the case of Jairus and his daughter, we shall see the difference very clearly. In the case of the daughter, our Lord restores her to life in a wonderful and miraculous manner. And then we find her eating. But at that point the narrative ends. From that we can draw a glorious lesson as to the restoring power of our Lord and as to the whole possibility of resurrection from the death of sin to newness of life. But we are taken no further. And it is just because of that, that many experience difficulty. 'I believe all you say about forgiveness etc,' says a man. 'I am quite ready to accept all you say about God's love, but what of tomorrow? How am I to face the future with all its difficulties? I might stay behind here tonight and join the church. I feel the truth of the message and I long to be a Christian and to lead a new life. But the difficulties are so great and I am so weak. I am afraid of the future.' Such is the talk of many and it is a real and genuine difficulty. Now it is that very aspect of the matter that is brought out and stressed in such a wonderful manner when we consider our Lord's dealing with Jairus rather than with Jairus' daughter. Indeed we can venture to claim that there is no incident in the entire New

Testament in which this aspect of the matter is brought out quite so clearly.

The same thing of course is taught in our Lord's dealings with the disciples, but here we have it all compressed into a short space and presented in a dramatic form. Our Lord not only receives Jairus, but they continue together, 'And Jesus went with him'. And it is this journey which is so important and so full of interest. For here we see the difficulties met and the problems of the journey solved. How grateful we should all feel to the woman who came and touched the hem of our Lord's garment and thereby caused a delay. For that very delay created problems and difficulties for Jairus which he himself could not solve, precisely like the difficulties and trials and temptations which come to meet us all in this life and in this world. Here in this narrative there are delays, disappointments, evil forebodings, fears, anxieties – they all appear and are all solved. Nowhere does our blessed Lord shine forth so gloriously in all the fulness of His Person as Saviour. Are we clear about the principle, about the teaching? It is this, that salvation is entirely and altogether in and of Jesus Christ Himself. He is the alpha and the omega of salvation, He is the author and finisher, the beginning and the end. He does not merely start a process and then allow us to continue it in and of ourselves – He continues to work in us, He carries the work to a triumphant conclusion.

Ah! how they sin and spite themselves, and rob themselves of the most glorious aspect of salvation, who depict our Lord as merely a man, or even a God-man, who just came to announce to the world the fact that God was prepared to forgive our sins and pardon our transgressions and iniquities, and then to indicate to us that we should live a better life and conform to a certain standard. He does that, it is true, but the glory of the gospel is that He does very much more. For, according to the gospel, He is alive and though unseen yet 'for ever at hand'. He

accompanies us on the journey, enters into our life and
being, does not leave us to ourselves, but is with us to the
very end. Salvation does not just mean forgiveness of sin
already committed, nor sin which will yet be committed.
It also means conquest of sin, and deliverance from its
tyranny; triumph, freedom, victory and an ultimate
arrival at perfection. To believe in the Lord Jesus Christ
does not just mean that you are forgiven, and that then
you go back, and out into the dark and difficult world to
face its trials and temptations and problems all on your
own and in your utter weakness and helplessness. It
means that, being forgiven, you go out to meet them all,
accompanied by Christ and all that that means. Have you
ever had this experience? Would you like to have it? Let us
study together this case of Jairus in order that we may see
exactly how it is to be obtained and how exactly Christ
works it. Every single section is worthy of a separate
discourse in and of itself, but I am anxious tonight that we
should see and grasp the great, broad, general principles.
The details of the Christian life are to be worked out
afterwards at leisure. Our object tonight will be to take
just one glimpse at the great panorama as it stretches out
before us in this story.

The first question that arises, obviously, is this, *How is
Jesus Christ to be approached?* We have said that salvation
is entirely in Him and of Him from the beginning right on
to the end. How, then, is He to be approached? What a
vital question this is! One has only to read the New
Testament in a very superficial manner to see this most
clearly. Observe the different people that approach our
Lord. How different is the treatment which they receive!
Some are received with the greatest kindness and
gentleness, their requests are granted and they go away
rejoicing. Others are repelled from the first moment,
their questions are returned to them in the form of other
questions, and they go away murmuring, disgruntled and

angry, determined to persecute Him and to kill Him. Our Lord did not smile on all. He did not bless all. The people who came to Him fell into these two definite groups. Why the difference? It is not in Him. He was ready and waiting to bless all. He is patient and kind and pleads even with a Judas to the very end. 'Whosoever cometh unto me, I will in no wise cast out.' Those are His words and such was His attitude. Why the difference then? There is but one answer. It is in the people themselves and in the way in which they approach Him. Jairus is received, his request is granted and he is blessed. He clearly approached our Lord in the right way, in the only way which leads to blessing. What is that way?

In the first place, there is clearly in it a deep consciousness and realization of need. It was because of that, that Jairus set out on his journey to our Lord. His little daughter was desperately ill, at the very point of death. He hurries on his journey; it is a race against time. It needs little imagination to read between the lines the further fact that Jairus had already tried many other means and methods and expedients to heal the child and save her life. But all had proved to be vain and futile. The disease progressed, the fever continued, the situation had become desperate. He had heard of our Lord and His powers, so as a last resort he comes to Him. And observe how the sacred record impresses upon us Jairus' consciousness of his need. These are the words he 'besought him greatly ... I pray thee come and lay thy hands on her that she may be healed.' The man was desperately conscious of his need. There was no ambiguity, no uncertainty whatsoever in his mind on that score.

Read the New Testament for yourself and you will find that that is always present in the case of all who were blessed by our Lord. They have all been deeply, terribly conscious of their need. Have you known His blessing? Face the other question first! Have you realized your need? When you have thought of Him and approached Him, why have you done so? Have you realized your desperate need? Are you aware that it is very much more desperate than that of Jairus? How easily we see physical and external needs, and how blind we are to the infinitely more important needs of the soul and of the spirit simply because they are unseen and immaterial! In the case of Jairus' daughter it was only a matter of the death of the body. But what of the death of the soul and that to all eternity? Jairus was well aware of the crisis and the urgency of the situation. Are you? He felt death was drawing nearer and nearer to his daughter and might occur at any moment. Do you realize that the same is true of you? Are you ready for it? For after death comes the judgment when we shall all be tried and have to answer for what we have done. The standard of judgment is clearly revealed in the laws of God. Nothing unclean and impure shall be allowed to enter into the holy city. No one is admitted unless clad in the spotless white robe of righteousness and holiness. 'God is light,' and all who hope to spend eternity with Him must be like Him. Are you ready? Have you the robe? It is no use talking about the wonderful garb you have made for yourself as the result of all the sins you have not committed and all the good works you have done. Have you the robe of God's righteousness? Have you kept His laws, have you honoured Him?

But come, look at yourself in a more personal and direct sense and manner. Are you a success? Are you quite pleased and satisfied with yourself? Is all well in your soul? Do you never fall, never sin? Does not your own heart condemn you? How much more, then, a holy God! And we must face Him, and the time 'draweth nigh'. We can no more postpone it than Jairus could hold death at bay in the case of his daughter. And the disease is as desperate as in her case. Can you cleanse your soul and purify your spirit? Can you erase your own past? Can you, with all your striving and efforts, merit for yourself that spotless robe of righteousness? Without it you are doomed to eternal death and misery. It is no use trying not to think about it and to forget it. 'The day' is drawing ever nearer, 'the night is already far spent.' Are you ready? Oh! realize the desperate position in which you are placed and fly to Jesus Christ.

But in addition to the realization of his need, we note in Jairus a very marked and striking humility. Though he is one of the rulers of the synagogue, a man of importance, a man in authority, he falls at the feet of Jesus Christ who is apparently only the son of a carpenter of Nazareth, a peasant, a mere nobody. Jairus prostrates himself at the feet of Jesus Christ. Again we say that this is something which is found to be present, invariably and without exception, in the case of all those who have been blessed by Jesus Christ. The people who came to examine and to test Him invariably went away disappointed and confused, feeling that they themselves had been tested and examined to the very depth of their being. Those who came to trap Him and to entice Him in His words, and to get Him into difficulties, invariably went away confounded and condemned and hating Him with bitter hatred. But those who fell at His feet, who acknowledged Him and His greatness, never failed to obtain a blessing. Let there be no mistake about this. If you approach Him in the mere spirit of curiosity He will not reveal Himself to you; if you come with your own ideas and conceptions in order to judge and to estimate and to try Him, He will confound you by holding forth before you a standard of life to which you can never attain and an example and a pattern which make your highest and noblest efforts trivial and childish. Approach Him as if He were merely a man among men, albeit the greatest and best and noblest, to whom you *are* prepared to shew great respect and deference and whose example and pattern you propose to follow – approach Him in any one of these ways on your feet, and relying even to the slightest extent on yourself and your own powers, and you will not know His blessing. You may persuade yourself of many things, and even persuade yourself that you are happy and that you are living a wonderful life, but you will never know what He really does to and for His own, and what He is waiting and ready to do for you. He only blesses those who come on their knees those who, looking at Him and conscious of their own sinfulness and helplessness, realize that this is the very Son of God come on earth to deliver us. He is hidden from the wise and prudent but revealed unto babes. He will not submit Himself to our conceited and self-satisfied inspection, but He will reveal Himself to our broken, humble, contrite hearts,

> *Not the righteous –*
> *Sinners Jesus came to save.*

And this is certain. Once you realize that you are a desperate and hopeless sinner, you will cease to criticize and merely consider Him, but urgently and desperately begin to cling to Him. You will never understand Him. All the efforts of the critics for the past hundred years have utterly failed. He defies all categories and transcends all definitions. He has staggered and astonished all the critics since His birth. The greatest saints have fallen prostrate at His feet. It is the one way to be blessed by Him.

But there is one other thing we must note, and that is Jairus' faith and obedience. He believes that Christ can heal and save his daughter's life. He begs and implores Him to go down at once to lay His hands upon her. He has faith in our Lord's power and places himself entirely and unreservedly in His hands and submits to be led by Him along the way. Had you noticed that? After his first request, Jairus does nothing but simply follow our Lord and cling to Him. He does not remonstrate at the delay

caused by the woman, he does not grumble and complain.
It is clear that he does not understand and he must have
felt bewildered and perhaps heart-broken within. But he
says nothing. He just listens to our Lord's words and
submits to His leadership. He believes in Him, submits
himself entirely to Him and is content to be led by Him,
come what may. Our Lord does not insist upon our
understanding, but He does insist upon our trusting Him
and yielding ourselves to Him. He does not demand a
thorough philosophical apprehension of the way in which
He has achieved our salvation, and, His ability to save, but
He does ask us to believe it, and especially to believe in
Him, to believe in Him utterly, and to be prepared to
follow Him whithersoever He may lead and direct us, and
in spite of what may happen on the way. Have you done
that? Are you prepared to do so? Have you seen the
wisdom of doing so, and the sheer folly of still clinging to
your own understanding? We have already seen our
situation and its desperate nature. All our own efforts can
never save us. Men cannot help us. There is only One
who can help, but He insists upon our confession of
failure, our acknowledgement of our own utter helplessness, and He demands our entire surrender of ourselves –
and all we have and are – unto Him. Those are His terms.
That is the way to approach Him!

Let us now consider *What happens to those who so
approach Him*. We can divide it most easily and most
conveniently by indicating *what they discover about Him*.

What remarkable discoveries Jairus made that day and
especially about the person of Jesus Christ! He had
certain ideas about Him before He left his own home.
And on the basis of such ideas he had approached Him.
But his experience that day taught him that Jesus Christ
has to be known personally before He can be properly
known. How small and unworthy were Jairus' ideas of
Him before He had met Him. And how they grew as the

intimacy continued! You will never really know Jesus Christ until you submit to Him. The moment you do so you will begin to discover some of the most astonishing and glorious things that can ever be known.

You will find, for instance, that He is ready to receive you and prepared to respond to your humble cry. What glorious words are those simple words, 'And Jesus went with him.' He had heard his cry, He had recognized his faith, He had yielded to his entreaties. He had accepted Jairus and his plea. Could anything be more gratifying or more wonderful? Jesus Christ does not turn him away and refuse to receive him, but actually goes with him. Let us say it again, and never tire of saying it, and never cease to go on saying it, Jesus Christ receives all who, in their desperation, turn to Him in humility and cast themselves upon His love. He will never say you 'nay' if you come in that way. Though He is 'very God of very God', though He is holy and perfect and spotless and pure and without sin, He yet 'receiveth sinful men.' He sat with publicans and sinners, He said He had not come to call the righteous, but sinners to repentance. He received those who had been regarded by all as outcasts and hopeless sinners. Whatever you may have been, however you may have treated Him, He is still ready and waiting to receive you. He has actually borne your sin in His own body on the tree, died your death and suffered your punishment. He will receive you if you but approach Him in the right way and He will grant you the desires of your heart. Venture on Him!

Then afterwards you will begin to learn about His solicitude for you and His watchful care over you. Once He receives you He will take charge of you and guide you and protect you and watch over you. He will lead you on. Had you thought of the real meaning of verses 35 and 36? The people who came from the ruler's house spoke to Jairus, but they were answered by Jesus. Before Jairus has a chance to answer a word, our Lord speaks these blessed words, 'Be not afraid, only believe.' But I want you rather to concentrate on those other words, 'as soon as Jesus heard the word that was spoken'. And how 'soon' it was! Before Jairus even had time to think or to feel the shock! How tender is Christ's care! He watches over Jairus. In a sense there is no doctrine in the New Testament that is so vitally important as this. It is to be found in the Old Testament as well as the New. Once you yield yourself to Jesus Christ you are not left alone. He is with you. 'Unseen, yet for ever at hand.' He is with you, protecting and guarding you as well as guiding you. Think of all the promises that are made to God's children and by which they are surrounded. 'I will guide thee with mine eye.' 'I will never leave thee, nor forsake thee.' 'I will send you another Comforter.' 'The Lord knoweth them that are his'. And many more! Before we ask, He answers. In His love He will not allow us to be tempted above that we are able to bear 'but will with the temptation also make a way to escape' (1 Cor 10: 13). As he watched over Jairus so He will watch over you. He will take you under the shadow of His wing and care for you. Had you not thought that the Christian life just meant a hopeless struggle, on your own, against impossible odds? Realize the glorious truth tonight and yield yourself to His guiding and protecting care.

But, in addition to this, you will become conscious of His power. Before he went to Christ, Jairus had believed that He had a certain power, but his idea of it was hopelessly inadequate, as he soon discovered. He had believed that Jesus could prevent his daughter's death and heal her and cure her of her illness. He believed that by actually going down to the house and laying His hands upon her He could do that. In one sense his faith was great; in another it was very small. There came a certain man to Christ one day, you remember, who realized that there was no need for our Lord to be present and to lay on his hands in order to heal. That man realized that all He had to do was to speak the word, no matter how far away He might be. Jairus had not realized that, neither had he realized that our Lord could raise from the dead quite as easily as He could heal a sickness. But that day he was taught that great lesson. He had already believed that our Lord had certain powers. He was to learn, and did learn, that our Lord had *all power and that nothing was impossible to Him.* We tend to measure Jesus Christ and His salvation by our own ideas and by our own powers. How inadequate they are! We talk about the difficulties and the problems and our weaknesses, instead of thinking in terms of His might and His strength. He is not only willing to receive you and to take you under the shadow of His wing, He is able to sustain you and to hold you with His mighty hand. Crying to Him, then, and casting ourselves upon Him without reservation, we find that He is sympathetic and kind, watchful and tender, mighty and strong to save.

But we are also shown in this incident not only what Jesus is like, but also what He does. For His activity is as wonderful as His Person, His work for us in salvation as great as His nature. Truly salvation is entirely in Him and of Him and through Him. We can only note these things briefly.

For one thing He answers all our doubts and questionings and fears. After the delay caused by the woman, those messengers come to tell Jairus that it is too late, that the little girl is dead, that there is no point in troubling the Master any further. And at once, as we have seen, Jesus Himself replies with these words of comfort and consolation, 'Be not afraid, only believe.' What a perfect picture that is of the Christian life! Ah! It is not a life without problems and trials; doubts will come and will be suggested. The evil one will do his very utmost to make us give up in despair and hopelessness. He will come and suggest all sorts of things which we, in and of ourselves, will be quite unable to answer. He will come and say that the case is hopeless, that in spite of our having thought that all was going to be well, all is not well. He will suggest that we have sinned too deeply and sunk too low into the mire ever to be put right. He will say that had we only sinned a little, all would have been well, but that in view of our actual record, all is hopeless. Or he will come and say that it is too late, that if we had turned to Christ and to religion many years ago, while we were still very young and comparatively untarnished and unsoiled, all would have been well, but that it is no use turning now. The devil will remind us of the law and its demands and our failure. He will resurrect our past sins and fling them into our faces. He will do his utmost to shake our faith and cast us into the depths of despair, and we shall begin to shake and to feel that we have no defence to offer. Our feelings will agree with the enemy's suggestions. It is Christ alone that can overcome our doubts and fears and evil forebodings. The devil tells me that I have sinned too deeply ever to be forgiven, and I tend to agree. But Christ tells me the story of the prodigal son and I know that all is well. The devil assures me that it is too late and that only those who give themselves while they are young can be saved. But when I hear my blessed Lord saying to the dying thief on the cross 'Today shalt thou be with me in paradise', again I am happy. The terrors of the law and the holiness of God alarm and terrify me and fill me with a sense of hopelessness and despair, and I almost give up and give in, but when I hear the words, 'It is finished', and Paul's assurance that 'Christ is the end of the law for righteousness to every one that believeth' I again sing with Toplady –

> *The terrors of law and of God*
> *With me can have nothing to do;*
> *My Saviour's obedience and blood*
> *Hide all my transgressions from view.*

[255]

In Jesus Christ all my doubts are resolved and all my questions answered, and whatever messages and messengers may come to me from Satan, I answer them all in Him and through Him.

But, according to this incident, He does still more. For we read that when they come to the house, they hear the tumult and the weeping and wailing, and after our Lord speaks to them and assures them that all will be well, they laugh Him to scorn. And then follows the significant thing. He puts them all out! He expels them! He drives them forth. Jairus, you observe, seems to play no part whatsoever in that incident. Our Lord does it all. The opposition is no longer content merely with sending messages to Jairus, it now becomes more active and more arrogant and pits itself against our Lord Himself. But all its efforts are futile and it is routed by Him. He literally turns on the enemy. In the Christian life we are assailed not merely by doubts and fears and evil forebodings; there are subtle temptations of flesh and spirit, evil powers and forces with which to contend. Left to ourselves we are helpless, but, thank God, we are not left to ourselves. He works in us and upon us. He does not lead us forward just as we are, He purifies and sanctifies us. He fights a battle within us; He is purifying unto Himself a peculiar people, zealous of good works. Follow Him and keep close to Him and He will cast out lusts and passions, evil desires and evil thoughts, and deliver you from the dominion of Satan and all his hordes. Follow Him and trust yourself to Him and nothing shall be able to withstand you, or to thwart you, or hinder you – follow Him and He will make you more than conqueror over the world, the flesh and the devil. As he cast out those people from the room in Jairus' house, so He will cast out and cast down every enemy of your soul.

Yes! and He will continue to do so until He brings the work to a triumphant conclusion. He will continue and go on to the end. Our Lord does not stop at answering the objections and doubts and merely casting out the wailers and weepers who laughed Him to scorn. He goes in and takes hold of the damsel's hand and raises her again to life. That was the objective for which they had originally set out and in spite of all hindrances, delays and obstructions they arrive there and the work is completed. Oh! yes, we can always be confident with Paul that 'he which hath begun a good work in you will perform it until the day of Jesus Christ.' He is not only 'able to keep us from falling', but will also one day 'present us faultless before the presence of His glory with exceeding joy.' He will not only lead us to the river, He will be with us in the river, and beyond it to all eternity. He is not only faithful in life, but also in death. He will be with us to the end. To the end? Throughout the countless ages of eternity! For ever! What more can you need? What further could be offered? What greater salvation can possibly be conceived? It is all in Jesus Christ and it is complete and entire. It will meet you just where you are now, it will clear your past, give you immediate peace and joy, quicken you and lead you through the remainder of this your earthly life, and enable you to live victoriously, and at the end present you to God in heaven.

In your need, in your desperate position, face to face with God and His law, come to Jesus Christ confessing your sins and believing that He died for you. Yield yourself to Him and follow Him, singing with us as you do so:

> *All the way my Saviour leads me:*
> *What have I to ask beside?*
> *Can I doubt His tender mercy,*
> *Who through life has been my Guide?*
> *Heavenly peace, divinest comfort,*
> *Here by faith in Him to dwell!*
> *For I know whate'er befall me,*
> *Jesus doeth all things well.*

[257]

All the way my Saviour leads me,
Cheers each winding path I tread;
Gives me grace for every trial,
Feeds me with the living bread.
Though my weary steps may falter,
And my soul a-thirst may be,
Gushing from the rock before me,
Lo! a spring of joy I see.

All the way my Saviour leads me;
O the fulness of His love!
Perfect rest to me is promised
In my Father's house above.
When my spirit, clothed immortal,
Wings its flight to realms of day,
This, my song through endless ages—
Jesus led me all the way.

Come! Amen.

19: *True Christian Discipleship*

From that time many of his disciples went back, and walked no more with him. Then said Jesus unto the twelve, Will ye also go away? Then Simon Peter answered him, Lord, to whom shall we go? Thou hast the words of eternal life.   John 6 : 66–68[1]

I feel it is always an interesting and profitable subject to try to decide which is the more dangerous position for a man to be in - either to state openly and avowedly that he is not at all interested in Christ and religion, or to follow Christ for the wrong and for the false reason. I know every theologian in this congregation will be led to say at once that, ultimately, there is no difference between these two men; that the one who follows Christ for the wrong and false reason is as much outside the kingdom as the man who makes no pretence to follow Christ at all. That is perfectly true: but I do think there is an important distinction between the two when you regard things merely from the human standpoint: for the difficulty with the man who follows Christ for a wrong or false reason is that he not only deludes himself, but he deludes the church also. But when you are confronted with one who says he does not believe in Christ, then you know exactly what to say and what to do with him. When a man presents himself as a religious person, the church tends to take him for granted, to think that it would be an insult to question him. The church assumes that, because he acknowledges himself to be a religious man, therefore, he is a Christian. One of the most dangerous places for a man to be in is the church of the living God.

I am not at all sure but that one explanation for the

[1]Preached on the morning of Dr Lloyd-Jones' first visit to Westminster Chapel, December 29, 1935, and earlier at Sandfields.

[259]

present state of things in the church today is to be found just at that point. She has been far too ready to associate church membership with true discipleship, and to assume that all who join the church are really following Christ. I know the church may have a very good motive for doing so. She has felt that it is a very good thing for people to be within the home of the church, that she may protect them from the temptations of the world. But the tragedy is that so often she takes it for granted that these people are truly Christians. The church has addressed, to such, messages which are quite appropriate for the true Christian, but are not of much value to those who lack the essence of the faith. Thus, I say, it comes to pass that the church can be a very dangerous place. It may be that because these people are in the church they will never have addressed directly to them some of the primary, fundamental questions which all true Christians must be able to answer. There is a real danger of our assuming that we are Christians for wrong and false reasons, and I do not hesitate to say that it is a very real and great danger. Were you to ask me to substantiate those adjectives I could do so very easily from the pages of the New Testament itself.

There, is surely, nothing quite so striking as you read the story of the life of our Lord in the Gospels as to observe the way in which He seemed to be acutely anxious that men and women should not come after Him for the wrong reason. You will find Him constantly pausing, and asking men and women whether they are following Him for the right reason. He seemed to be concerned that He should not attract those who had not really laid hold of the right and true things. There is no greater travesty of the life of our Lord than to declare that our blessed Lord was disappointed at the end of His life when He found Himself deserted by His friends: that Christ's heart was broken at that point because He had never anticipated such desertion, and that He was taken by surprise. There is nothing so false to the New Testament picture that we have of Him. We are told that our Lord was aware of this possibility from the very beginning. He actually predicted it. He was constantly at great pains to question His followers, because He knew for certain what was ultimately going to take place. We all remember those wonderful words that our Lord uses at the end of the Sermon on the Mount: 'There will be many at the last day who will come to me, and say, Lord, have we not done this and that and the other in thy Name. Then will I say unto them, I never knew you: depart from me.' They thought that everything was all right, and in that day they will discover that everything was all wrong. We remember, too, the parable of the house built on the rock, and of the house built on the sand. 'Take heed how ye hear,' says our Lord. 'Examine yourselves: sift yourselves.' Then we all remember the parable of the Sower in which our Lord seems to lay it down as a fundamental principle that of the hundred per cent who go after Him only some twenty-five per cent really have grasped the truth. I would remind you also of the parable of the drag net, in which there were a number of fish, some good and some bad, pointing to the great division of the people. But perhaps the most perfect illustration of this principle is that which is to be found in one of the three pictures you find at the end of the 9th chapter of Luke's Gospel. You remember how the young man came running to our Lord, and said: 'Lord, I will follow thee whithersoever Thou goest. I do not know about these other people, but as for myself I am all out.' Surely, says someone, that is the kind of man that the church of God is looking for at the present time. Surely our Lord received him with open arms. But it was to that man that Jesus said, 'The foxes have holes, and birds of the air have nests: but the Son of man hath not where to lay His head.' Christ turns to this zealot, and says: 'You are full of zeal and enthusiasm and ecstacy, but wait a moment, do you realize exactly what it may mean to follow me? It means ostracism, perhaps giving up the things that you value most in life. Make certain you know exactly what Christian discipleship means.' As you read the Gospels you will find that our Lord is constantly at pains to warn people

[261]

and to show them that there is a possibility of their going after Him for the wrong and spurious reason.

The writers of the Epistles reiterate the same message, which they impress upon the early Christians.

Is it not a good thing that we should examine ourselves, and ask ourselves the same question, as to whether we are following Him for the right or the wrong reason? Why are we following Him? What is the precise meaning and significance that we attach to our own church member-ship? That is the question I would like to consider with you in the light of my text. It always seems to me that this chapter is a kind of *locus classicus* of the whole subject. The evangelist under the divine inspiration seems to have gathered together into this one chapter most of the false and spurious reasons for which men are content to follow Christ: they are all grouped together here. You notice the division in the text.

'From that time many of his disciples went back.' On the other hand, the twelve remained. Here is the division – the many who returned: and the few who remained. Many had gone after Him for the wrong reason. The few had gone after Him and had companied with Him for the right and true reason.

Let us glance, first of all, at some of these false reasons that men have for following Christ. There are some people who become attached to the church for the simple reason that many other people are doing the same thing. You see quite clearly in the New Testament, as you see subsequently in the history of the church, that there is a good deal of mob psychology. There are people who are always ready to join a crowd, who are always fascinated by the thing that everybody else tends to be doing. There are people who are in the church for the simple reason that they have been taken there, or they have seen others going there. They have never asked themselves the question, 'Why am I in the church?' It seems to be the right thing for them to do: their parents and their grandparents did it: it is a tradition in their town: others are doing it: and, therefore, they do it. There are people who are merely carried down the stream. They do things because others do them. God forbid that any of us should be in the church thoughtlessly, and because we have never actually faced the question of true membership of the church, and what it involves. There were many who went after our Lord simply because they saw the crowds surrounding Him. May the Lord deliver us from that category!

Another reason is the one indicated by our Lord in the 26th verse: 'Jesus answered them, and said, "Verily, verily, I say unto you, Ye seek me, not because ye saw the miracles, but because ye did eat of the loaves and were filled."' What does he mean? He suggests that these people have a purely mercenary and materialistic reason for going after Him. They come running after our Lord, and apparently seem to be worshipping Him: but they are not really interested in the spiritual, in the divine and in the supernatural. Why did they follow Him? Because they got from Him the thing that appealed to them – the loaves. They were anxious to be given food, and for that selfish reason went after Him because they got from Him what they desired. I do not know that this is a very common reason for people joining the church, because religion is not as popular at the present time as it was; but we must agree that, perhaps, the real tragedy was that men tended to attach themselves to the church because it gave them position and status and power and influence. Alas, men even joined the church because it helped their business, or profession; they made use of the church to further some personal interest and desire. These are the people who go after Christ because they are anxious to eat of the loaves, and be filled. Perhaps in this category we ought to place those who go after Christ simply because they are interested in the doctrine of the forgiveness of sins, because they want to make use of His cross; they do not want to suffer eternal punishment; they do not like the notion of hell. Christ announces pardon of sin, and they go after Him, not because they desire holiness, or because they really love Him, but because they fear hell, they are afraid of eternal punishment. These are the people who make merchandise even of the cross of Christ; they use it as a cloak to cover their sins. They use the cross to further their own personal, mercenary desires. They follow Christ solely to serve their own ends, and not because He is the Son of God, and the Saviour of the world.

Then in verse 2 of this chapter we find another interesting thing. 'And a great multitude followed him, because they saw his miracles which he did on them that were diseased.' Now this is a very interesting type of person; we meet them frequently in the pages of the New Testament. We get a description of the same type of people in the second chapter. 'Now when he was in Jerusalem at the passover, in the feast day, many believed in His name, when they saw the miracles which he did.' (John 2:23) This group of those who are concerned with the externals of religion tends to be a rather large one at the present time. These are the people who are interested in the phenomena of religion; they go after Jesus because they see the miracles which He does. Christ's miraculous power appeals to them. If there is a display of supernatural power, they are always there. They are attracted by the phenomena of religion rather than by the truth of religion. Our Lord Jesus Christ performed many miracles; and He did so deliberately. His object and purpose in performing miracles was to manifest His power. Yet the interesting thing is this. He does not commit Himself to those who are more interested in the miracles than in the man, to those who are more interested in the phenomena than in the power. Jesus Christ, by the grace of God, still performs miracles in this sinful world, and still changes the lives of men. There are still glorious phenomena in connection with the kingdom of God in Christ Jesus. But Christ, the Son of God, did not come to earth merely to work miracles, to do mighty deeds, and so to manifest His power. He did not come even to change our lives; He came primarily to purify to Himself a peculiar people zealous of good works. He came to reconcile men to God, and to bring us to a knowledge of the truth. We must beware of following Him simply because we are more interested in the phenomena than in the truth itself.

[264]

And that brings me to my last group, which is to be found in verses 14 and 15, where we read: 'Then those men, when they had seen the miracle that Jesus did, said, "This is of a truth that prophet that should come into the world." When Jesus therefore perceived that they would come and take him by force, to make him a king, He departed again into a mountain himself alone.' Here we have an interesting group of people who follow him because they completely and entirely misunderstand Him and His message. What was the miracle that they had seen? It was the feeding of the five thousand. These people, according to the context, had been following our Lord for a number of days, perhaps weeks. They had listened to Him; but it was only when they saw the miracle that they said 'This is the Messiah; this is the Prophet that was to come.' Then we are told that they conspired together and agreed that they must approach Him, and take Him by force to Jerusalem to make Him a king. But Jesus observed their intention, and withdrew Himself into a mountain, and remained there alone. These Jews had a political conception of the kingdom of heaven. They conceived of the Messiah as a political liberator, as one who would deliver them from the Roman bondage, and would establish himself as king in Jerusalem, where He would reign supreme over all their enemies, and over the whole world. And these men approached Him with that idea in their minds; but He repulsed them. Ultimately they become members of that company that went from Him. How many there are still who think of Jesus as a political agitator, or as a social reformer. How many there are still who think of the kingdom of heaven as being mainly secular and political. How many there are who think that one of the main functions of the church is to deal with the social condition of the world, to take its place in various departments and walks of human life, and to decide great questions in regard to industry and politics and international affairs. How many there are still who think of Christ as a social reformer, as a political agitator. And how many others there are who think of Him rather as the pale Galilean who

[265]

holds men aloof, as too sensitive even to touch the world. Some there are who think of Him as the great Artist, or the great Ascetic, or the incomparable Philosopher. There are those who approach this Book as if it were merely a collection of literary gems. If we took out of the church all these various groups, I wonder how many we would have left. I fear that the 'many' would assume an alarming proportion.

I make no apology in asking you, 'Do you follow Christ? Have you faced this question? Have you stood face to face with these possibilities?' These people I have mentioned were going after Christ. They had been with Him for days: they called themselves His disciples. Then, we read, many of His disciples, His followers, those who had listened to His words, walked no more with Him. Why have we gone after Him? Have we the right reason, or are we guilty of one of those false reasons? What is the true reason for following Christ? The answer, of course, is to be found in that great word of Simon Peter. 'Then said Jesus unto the twelve, "Will ye also go away?" Then Simon Peter answered Him, "Lord, to whom shall we go? Thou hast the words of eternal life. And we believe and are sure that Thou art that Christ, the Son of the living God"' Now we can be very happy about this answer, for, as the context shows us, the Lord tested the faith of the twelve. The many were going back. 'There they go; you see them,' says our Lord, turning to the twelve. 'They have heard the same sermons that you have; they have seen the same miracles; you and they are in exactly the same position. Do you want to go with them? Have you been following me for the same reason that they have? For, if you have, then I prefer not to have you. Will ye also go away?' And Simon Peter answers with confidence and with certainty. We have here in his words the irreducible minimum of true Christian discipleship. What do these words of Peter mean? We have to break them up and analyze them. 'Lord, to whom shall we go?' he says. Is that sentence to be interpreted merely in some emotional manner? Was it that Peter turned to our Lord, and said:

'We have been having such a wonderful time together that life would be impossible without you?' Was it just some emotional attachment? Yes, it was that, and also very much more. It was a profound, basic definition of faith. 'To whom shall we go if we leave you?' Why go to anyone? Why does Peter ask this question? Because there we discover the primary statement in the Christian profession. Peter asks, 'To whom shall we go?' because he realizes he cannot save himself. Peter had long since realized his own helpless condition. He had been looking for someone outside himself for salvation. And Peter, having faced the law, and having seen John the Baptist, and having looked into the face of Christ, had long since realized his own state before God. He, together with his countrymen, had been looking for the Messiah. But Peter does not merely admit that he cannot save himself. He also states here very definitely that he is absolutely certain that no one else can save him but Christ. What other one is there whom we can follow? There is none other. 'I cannot save myself, and no other man can save me,' says Peter. There is always this negative statement in the basic, primary Christian confession. I wonder to what, and to whom, we are pinning our faith? The man who has any conceivable alternative to Christ is not a Christian. What do we hold on to as we think of death and eternity? Are we still trusting in that delusion of a world that is supposed to be advancing and developing? Are we still fondly imagining that mere intellectual attainments can fit us for heaven?

'I cannot save myself,' says Peter. 'Man cannot save me. The world cannot save me. But I believe that Thou canst.' And he gives his reason. 'Thou art the Christ, the Son of the living God. Thou hast the words of eternal life.' In the face of Jesus Christ Peter saw God.

Have you ever taken your stand with Simon Peter? Have you ever realized your own bankruptcy and sinfulness? And have you said to Christ, 'Thou must save, and Thou alone'? Peter is not content merely with avowing that Christ is the Son of the living God. He says, 'We cannot leave thee, for Thou hast the words of eternal life.' It was these words of His that had caused the others to go back. These people had gone after Christ; they had listened to His sermons; they had appreciated His miracles. Then our Lord, in one of His sermons, compares Himself with the manna that came down from heaven, and He goes on to say that He is the living Bread, and that unless men eat of His flesh they can never have eternal life. 'And many of his disciples, when they heard this, said, "This is a hard saying."' And ultimately they went back because of these words. He spoke of men eating His flesh, and drinking His blood, and He made that the postulate of eternal life. 'How can that be?' they said. It was these very words that offended them. But Peter says: 'I do not understand it all, but I believe it.' My friends, it is not enough that we should ascribe to Jesus of Nazareth deity in a unique sense. It is not enough that we should believe in His miracles and in His supernatural works. We only really and truly follow Him when we believe that He ultimately achieves our salvation through His broken body and His shed blood. 'I do not understand the doctrine of the atonement; I cannot fathom it; it seems abstruse, almost immoral,' you say. I am not asking you to understand it all. Simon Peter did not understand it, but he accepted it, and he committed his life to Christ. Jesus Christ offers Himself to us crucified, risen again, One who was bruised by the stripes that we deserved, and who gave His life as a ransom for many, and who by His Holy Spirit offers to dwell within us: who not merely delivers us from the guilt of our past sin, but who delivers us from the power of sin, and from the very pollution of sin, and who stands before us, and says, 'Take of Me.'

'Will ye also go away?' Thousands are going away from Him. Alas, the country and the world are becoming increasingly irreligious. Man in his intellectual pride is rejecting the Word of God. 'Will ye also go away?' Shall we all together turn to Him, and with Simon Peter, say, 'Lord, to whom shall we go? Thou hast the words of eternal life. And we believe and are sure that Thou art that Christ, the Son of the living God.'

[268]

20: *The Narrowness of the Gospel*

*

> *Enter ye in at the strait gate: for wide is the gate, and broad is the way, that leadeth to destruction, and many there be which go in thereat: because strait is the gate, and narrow is the way, which leadeth unto life, and few there be that find it.*
> Matthew 7:13, 14.[1]

There is no charge which is quite so commonly and frequently brought against the Christian way of life as the charge of narrowness. It is a charge also that is constantly brought against the individual Christian believer by that type of man, who, in his desire to show his own breadth of mind describes himself as a man of the world. He is so broad that nothing but world dimensions can give you a true impression of the width and largeness of his views! He is a man of the world in contrast to this narrow and confined man who calls himself a Christian! I fear at times also it is true to say that there is no charge concerning which the average Christian believer is quite so frightened as this charge of narrowness. To some Christians at the present time, it is more or less immaterial what men may say about them as long as they do not describe them as narrow. Of course, there is a sense in which that is a very good and healthy reaction. God forbid that we should ever really become narrow in the sense that the Pharisees were narrow, or that Judaism was narrow. God forbid that we should ever really reduce this glorious gospel of liberty to a mere number of prohibitions and restraints. But that is not our danger at all. Our danger is that in our fear of being thought narrow, we should so swing over to the opposite

[1]Preached on the evening of Dr Lloyd-Jones' first visit to Westminster Chapel, December 29, 1935, and earlier at Sandfields.

[269]

extreme as eventually to become quite nondescript.

I sometimes feel that a simple, well-known story in Æsop's Fables has a good deal to say to many modern Christians. I am referring to the well-known story of the frog and the ox. One day, it says, a little frog in a field suddenly lifted up his head and observed an ox standing near by. He looked at the ox, and began to admire him, and wished that he was as broad and as big as the ox. 'I am so small and insignificant,' he said. 'How marvellous it must be to have the breadth and width of that ox.' And the story goes on that the frog began to imitate the ox, and he began to expand, and to grow larger and larger, and broader and broader, and eventually he reached a point at which he just exploded and ceased to be. Now that, unless I am mistaken, is the precise thing which has happened to the so-called faith of many a Christian during the last fifty years. In his desire to become broad and wide, the little Christian faith that man ever had has long since exploded and ceased to be. What the exact explanation of the phenomenon is I am not quite sure, but I think we must recognize that there has been a tendency, particularly during this century, for the church to pay great respect and regard to the man of scientific knowledge. He has become the last authority on all these questions. The church has gone to very great lengths in order to please him; she has been prepared not to stress certain doctrines in her creed and to delete certain portions of the Bible and she has in so doing wandered very far from the example set for her by her Lord and Master. I never find Jesus Christ changing His gospel in order to make it suit the people. Rather I find Him changing the people in order to make them fit into His gospel. We can be perfectly certain that there will be no true revival in this country, in spite of what may be happening round about us, until we return to the royal pattern.

My commission is this:

Ye servants of God, your Master proclaim,
And publish abroad His wonderful Name.

Whether men like it, or dislike it, our business is to preach the truth which was once and for all committed unto the saints. There is a very real danger that we should develop a kind of inferiority complex in the fear of being thought narrow, and ultimately make shipwreck of our faith. But all this is merely an aside.

For my text is not a negative text, but a very positive text. It tells us that we must not only not be afraid of being called narrow, but it actually goes on to say that if we really want to be Christians worthy of the Name, we must go out of our way to become narrow: we must enter in at the strait gate and walk on the narrow way! Now this, surely, is rather a startling and amazing thing. Is it not wonderful that when our Lord came to choose the designation to express His way of life, He should have selected the very word by which we are most frightened – that the very word of which we tend to be afraid is the very word in which He exults, the very word which He puts upon His flag? I would say also, for the purpose of encouraging and stimulating any frightened Christian who happens to be here, the next time one of these so-called men of the world tells you that you are narrow, instead of trying to run away, just stand your ground, look him straight in the face, and say, 'Of course I am narrow: and it would be a very much better thing for you, and for your wife and children, if you also became narrow, and ceased to boast of a largeness and a breadth which are in reality nothing but a cloak for laxity and looseness.' He would not worry you quite so frequently in the future!

But why does our Lord speak about entering in at the strait gate, and walking on the narrow way? Christ never said anything accidentally. He had all the letters of the alphabet at His command, yet He deliberately chose these words to describe His way of life. He spoke thus because there must be certain respects in which the gospel of Christ is really narrow. I want to try to consider with you some of the respects in which this is so.

The first respect in which we observe its narrowness is this,

[271]

that the gospel confines itself to one particular subject. The gospel of Christ narrows itself down to one question – the soul of man and its relationship to God. In the Bible there is a good deal of history – history of men and nations – and geography, and some people find in it geology and biology. All sorts of subjects are dealt with in this Book, and yet it is not an encyclopædia. It is not a Book which gives us a little knowledge about many things. It is a Book which gives us much knowledge about one thing. It is the textbook of life, the handbook of the soul. It is a manual dealing with one subject, the reconciliation of man with God. If ever there was a specialist's textbook in this world it is this Book. This is true also of the Master of the Book. If ever there was a specialist on the face of the earth it was our Lord Jesus Christ. There is a sense in which He preached only one sermon, and the theme of this sermon was this – the soul of man and its relationship to the Eternal Father. All the knowledge and information He possessed, He used in order to illustrate this important and vital subject. Let me give you some instances.

One day our Lord was in the country, with His disciples standing round about Him. And He observes a farmer sowing seed into the ground. Very clearly our Lord was not only interested in agriculture, but He knew a good deal about it. But the sight of that farmer does not prompt our Lord to deliver an address on agriculture: but as He watches that farmer He sees an illustration for His sermon. 'You see that man,' says our Lord. 'He is sowing seed into the ground. There are different types of ground into which it is sown: and the ground will be judged by its response to the seed that the farmer is sowing into it. I am like that farmer: I am sowing the seed of the Word of God which leads to eternal life. Ultimately men will be judged by their reaction to that seed sown in their lives.'

On another occasion when in the country our Lord beholds the various fruit-trees in an orchard. It is quite clear that our Lord knew a good deal about horticulture, but that does not lead Him to deliver an address on that subject. 'Look at those trees,' says our Lord. 'They may bear either good or bad fruit. Ultimately they will be judged by the kind of fruit that they bear.' And turning to His disciples, He says, 'You are exactly like those trees. By your lives and by your works you will bear either good or bad fruit. So take heed.' On another occasion our Lord was in the country and He observed the lilies of the field and the birds of the air. 'If God is so concerned about the lilies of the field that He clothes them, and about the birds of the air, that He feeds them, how much more is He concerned about you,' Christ says. So I could go on taking you through our Lord's discourses, and you will find how He is constantly making use of things around Him to illustrate His one great theme – the soul of man and its relationship to God.

We hear a good deal nowadays about the simple gospel. The secret of the simplicity of the gospel is this. Jesus of Nazareth, being the Son of God, and living in perfect correspondence and communion with His Father, had all knowledge. He knew what was important, and what was unimportant: and He ignored the unimportant, and gave Himself solely and entirely to the important things of life. He disregarded the irrelevant, and gave Himself utterly and only to the relevant, and to that which ultimately matters. The secret of the simplicity of the gospel lies in the fact that He brushed aside everything but the one supreme question of the soul's need. That is, clearly, an utter contradiction of all our modern ideas and conceptions. We, today, tend to judge the greatness of a man, not by his simplicity, but by his complexity. Yet here was the very Son of God, and even little children got something from Him: ordinary fisherfolk followed Him —'the common people heard Him gladly.' Why? Because He always talked about something which they understood. You, my friend, may be very well versed in many of the arts and sciences. You may be an expert on politics: you may be an authority on quite a number of subjects. But I would like to put a very simple question to you – do you know how to live? 'What shall it profit a man if he gain the whole world,' of knowledge, as well as wealth, 'and lose his own soul?' 'Enter ye in at the strait gate.' Come back to the beginning. The important and vital question is that of the soul.

But the narrowness of the gospel does not end at that point: it is merely a beginning. We discover that the gospel even narrows that. The ancient Greek pagan philosophers were very interested in the soul as a concept, as a thought, and they talked and argued much concerning the soul. But our Lord was not interested in the soul as the Greek philosophers were. It was the individual soul in which our Lord was interested. Someone says, 'I do not like such a gospel – it is so personal.' It is profoundly true that the gospel is personal, and on that account it annoys certain people. We find a perfect illustration of the personal nature of the gospel in the fourth chapter of the Gospel according to St John in the story of our Lord's meeting with the woman of Samaria at the well. Our Lord that afternoon was very tired, too tired to accompany His disciples into the city to buy food, and He rested by the side of the well. A woman came to draw water: and immediately they had a religious discussion. Did that well really belong to the Jews or to the Samaritans, and where exactly should worship take place? This woman seems to have been very astute: she was certainly an expert in the art of repartee. They were engaged in this religious discussion, when suddenly our Lord actually becomes personal! He turns to the woman, and says, 'Go, fetch thy husband,' revealing, thereby, that He knew all about the kind of life she was living. It was as if He said, 'My dear woman, you have really no right, being what you are, to talk about worship and about God. You cannot even manage your own life, you have no right to express an opinion on these great eternal themes. Start with yourself first. 'Go, fetch thy husband.' When you put your own life in order then you will be entitled to speak.'

Yes, the gospel is a personal thing. We cannot be saved in families: we cannot be saved as a congregation. We cannot be saved collectively because we are all doing a certain amount of philanthropic work. We are saved one by one. It is a question of you and God. Have you entered in at the

[274]

strait gate? Are you prepared to meet God face to face? Are you ready for the Judgment? Do you know in whom you have believed? Is all well with your soul? Have you a personal conviction of sin, and a personal knowledge of God?

But the narrowness of the gospel does not end even there. It tends to become still narrower by insisting upon having a say in our conduct and behaviour. It is not content merely with bringing the soul into a personal contact with God. But it insists upon dictating to us the kind of life we have to live. Someone says, 'That is precisely why I have long since finished with organized religion, and turned my back upon it. It is too narrow. I maintain that I am entitled to live my own life in my own way. I will not be fettered.' Yes, the gospel is very narrow, and it is narrow with respect to this question of conduct and ethics in two main respects: we can call them, if you like, negative and positive. The negative injunctions of the gospel with regard to conduct are perfectly familiar to us all: 'Thou *shalt not* kill.' 'Thou shalt not steal.' 'Thou shalt not commit adultery.' 'Thou shalt not take the Name of the Lord thy God in vain.' 'Avoid every appearance of evil.' If a thing is doubtful, it is wrong, and you must not do it. The gospel goes so far as to say that though a thing may be perfectly right for me, if it is a stumbling block to a weaker brother, I must not do it for his sake. Says someone, 'That is exactly why I have no use for such a gospel: it makes life a misery. You have to put on a black suit, and walk to church with your head down.' But have you realized that if every man and woman were as narrow as the gospel of Christ would have us be, there would be no more drunkenness, no need of Divorce Courts, no need for the League of Nations? Why? the world would be a paradise. It would be perfect, even as God Himself is perfect! The narrowness of the gospel – I speak with reverence – is the narrowness that is in God Himself. Oh, that we all became narrow, that we might enter in through this strait gate! 'Few there be that find it,' says our Lord. Yes! because it takes an exceptional man to say 'No' to temptation, and to restrain and control himself. It takes an exceptional man to deny himself in order to make things easier for others. On the broad way there is a great crowd! 'Many there be which go in thereat.' It does not take an exceptionally great man to sin. Any fool can sin, and every fool does sin. But that broad way leadeth to destruction. There is the narrowness of the gospel in its negative injunctions.

But I want to show you its narrowness in its positive injunctions. This, of course, is the great theme of the Sermon on the Mount. If you would really see the narrowness of the gospel you must come to the Sermon on the Mount. One of the great words of this generation is the word love. But if you really want to see the greatness of the word love you must narrow it down: you must focus it. You do not know what love really means until you love your enemies. The great task which is set before the Christian is to love ugly people until they are made beautiful. Another great word today is the word brotherhood. We believe today in doing good, and in helping others. But if you want to see how great that word really is you must narrow it down. You must bless them that curse you, and pray for them that despitefully use you. The task set before the Christian is to 'do good to them that hate you.' Another great word is the word happiness. There are those who say, 'I want to enjoy myself, and I have no use for religion. Why should I bury myself alive?' Again you have a great word, but you must narrow it down and focus it, if you would discover its real size. You know not what happiness means until you can 'rejoice in tribulation,' until you can be happy even in the midst of persecution. The task for the Christian is to be happy even when the clouds have gathered and the sun has ceased to shine, and everything has gone wrong.

There, then, we see something of the essential narrowness of the gospel. It is, in other words, this narrowness of the expert, or, if you like, the narrowness of the highest circle of achievement. You are all familiar with the saying that there is always plenty of room for a good man at the top. The higher the circle of achievement, the smaller will be the number found in it. For instance, there are many who can sing remarkably well, but very few Carusos; there are many who can play the violin amazingly well, but very few Kreislers: there are many who paint extraordinarily well, but comparatively few Royal Academicians. That, it seem to me, is the very point which our Lord makes in this text. 'Do not be content with living anyhow.' He says, in effect: 'Do not be content with living on the ordinary level of life. Come up to the top. Ascend the mount. Live life tremendously, live life as an expert. Live as I live, yea, come to the very summit. Be ye perfect, even as your Father which is in heaven is perfect.'

But, lastly, if you would see the narrowest and straightest point of all, you must confront the gospel at that point at which it tells you that salvation is only possible in and through one particular Person and especially in His death. There is the point at which perhaps the majority tend to object. 'I have agreed with you entirely, so far,' says someone, 'I liked your emphasis upon the soul, your emphasis upon personal decision, and your emphasis upon ethics and conduct. But when you tell me, now, that I can only be saved by believing that Christ died my death, I find it impossible to follow you. The conception is too narrow. I cannot understand it. It seems to me, to be almost immoral. I cannot accompany you any further.' What has the gospel to say to such a man? It does not argue with him. It challenges him. It turns to him and says something like this: 'If you can find God without going via Calvary, do so. If you can find liberation from your besetting sin without the power of the cross of Christ, carry on. If you can find peace and rest to your troubled conscience without believing in the death of the Son of God for you and for your sins, go ahead. If you can lie on your deathbed and think of facing a holy God without fear and without alarm, I really have nothing to say to you. But, if ever you should feel lost and miserable and wretched; if ever you

[277]

should feel that all your righteousness is but as filthy rags; if ever you are filled with terror and alarm as you think of God, and His holy Law; if ever you feel utterly helpless and hopeless, then turn back to Him, the Christ of the cross, with His arms outstretched, who still says: 'Look unto me and be saved, all ye ends of the earth.' It is there that the whole of humanity is focused. He is the representative of the whole of mankind. He died for all. But still more wonderful, according to Paul it is also true to say that, 'in Him dwelleth all the fulness of the Godhead bodily.' Complete man and complete God and all in one Person! God-Man! In Him, God and man are indissolubly linked, and through Him and in Him the way is opened from hell to heaven, from darkness to light, from despair to hope.

Let me show you, as I close, how perfectly this text, and all I have tried to say with respect to it, can be illustrated from the story of our Lord's earthly life and pilgrimage. Consider His birth and the self-emptying that it involved. Try to think of the narrowness and straitness of Bethlehem, when the Word was made flesh and eternity came into time — 'Strait is the gate.' Then think of Him in the wilderness at the commencement of His earthly ministry, tempted forty days and forty nights. Then watch the Scribes and Pharisees and Sadducees and Herodians, as they spread their net round about Him, and gradually draw it in—'Strait is the gate and narrow is the way.' Then look at Him in the Garden of Gethsemane – the very Son of God, by whom and through whom all things were created, confined to a garden surrounded by soldiers. And then, in a few hours, in the police court, with a soldier standing on each side. In the Garden, He could at least walk backwards and forwards along the path; now He is not allowed to move—'Strait is the gate, narrow is the way.' But still it is not finished – see Him on the cross nailed to the tree – the Son of God, the Creator of the world – fixed there, unable to move hand or foot. He dies. They take down the body and place it in a grave. Peer into that grave – can you see any light there? Do not the very sides seem to fall in and to collapse? – 'Strait is the gate, narrow is the way'. It leads to death, the grave, darkness, utter desolation.

And there we should have to end if we but believed what so frequently passes as gospel at the present time. But – blessed be the Name of God – the gospel goes on. It does mean Bethlehem, it does mean the wilderness and temptation, it does mean enemies and persecution, it does mean Gethsemane, trial, cross, death, yea and the grave. BUT – on the morning of the third day, behold, the resurrection! He bursts asunder the bands of death and rises triumphant o'er the grave! The darkness leads to dawn and to the light of endless day! 'Strait is the gate, narrow is the way – BUT – it leadeth unto life.'

If you accept the gospel and yield yourself to it, it will mean another birth for you; it will mean trial and temptation, it will mean persecution, it will mean the crucifixion and death of an 'old man' that is in you. BUT, it will lead to life which is life indeed, life more abundant, yea, the very life of God Himself.

'Enter ye in at the strait gate.' Come on to the narrow way!

21: *What Worldliness Forgets*

*

> *And as it was in the days of Noe, so shall it be also in the days of the Son of man. They did eat, they drank, they married wives, they were given in marriage, until the day that Noe entered into the ark, and the flood came, and destroyed them all. Likewise also as it was in the days of Lot; they did eat, they drank, they bought, they sold, they planted, they builded; but the same day that Lot went out of Sodom it rained fire and brimstone from heaven, and destroyed them all. Even thus shall it be in the day when the Son of man is revealed.* Luke 17 : 26–30[1]

We have in these words and in the corresponding account of them in Matthew 24 and Mark 13 what we may well term our Lord's view of history. Just before the end, almost under the very shadow of the cross, He gives His disciples this glimpse not only into His own and their own immediate future but also one flash of insight into ultimate history and the end of all things. It is generally agreed that in this discourse He blends a picture of the destruction of Jerusalem in AD 70 by the Romans, with the picture of the ultimate end of the world, suggesting as He does so that the former, in addition to being an actual fact of history, is also a picture and a prophecy of that which is yet to happen on a world-wide scale.

The subject is at one and the same time difficult and fascinating and, as a result, has become the subject of much controversy, not to say of much error also. The trouble has generally arisen because men have not been careful to observe the warnings uttered by our Lord Himself and also by the apostles – the warnings against being over-

[1]Aberavon, December 12, 1937.

concerned about 'the times and seasons' and the almost
morbid desire to be able to fix dates and to fit historical
events into the scriptural picture. Without desiring to
enter into the controversy at all, we would simply indicate
that the very general nature of the terms used, the
deliberate avoidance of any definite times or dates, the
refusal to answer the questions put to Him except in
enigmatical, allegorical language – all this surely must mean
that our Lord was concerned above all else to lay down
certain general principles rather than a specific detailed
programme. He was not concerned that men should
agitate their brains by trying to discover and to determine
when exactly the end should come. His desire, rather, was
that all men in all ages and generations should be ready for
it whenever it might come, and that that thought might be
the controlling and guiding principle of their lives.

But though Christ's statement of His world view of the
future course of history is couched in these general terms, it
is sufficiently definite and specific to enable us to enunciate
its leading principles and to contrast them with all other
views. Indeed it is as definite as this, that it entitles one to
say that in many ways and in many respects there is no
better test which can be placed upon a man's profession of
the Christian faith than just his attitude towards these
matters. I often feel that instead of asking men directly
what they think of Christ, and thereby far too frequently
giving them the opportunity of being blasphemous, and of
setting themselves up as judges who can express pompous
and arrogant opinions on matters which are eternally
beyond them, we should rather turn to them and ask a few
questions such as, 'What do you make of the world
situation in an ultimate sense? How does the present state
of the world and its people fit in with your whole view of life
and of man? Is your view of history one which caters for,
and is able to explain, the world as it is today? What in
your opinion will be the future story of this world?'
Anyone who answers such questions at all fully and
intelligently must reveal at once whether he is a Christian
in the New Testament sense of the word, or not. I wonder

[281]

what our individual answers would be to these questions. Shall I put them all together in one question? Here it is: How does the present world situation affect you? Does it depress you and make you feel hopeless? Or does it just confirm your view of life and of the world? Does it fill you with feelings of profound pessimism, or does it leave you in a mood of ultimate optimism, though you deplore what you see around and about you? Does the state of the world surprise and shock you, or is it more or less what you would have anticipated? Your answers to these questions proclaim exactly where and what you are in the light of the Christian gospel. You observe that I have presented you with only one of two alternatives each time. That is so because there is no possible third view. In the last analysis there are only two views of history – the view stated most perfectly perhaps by Hegel, and that of the New Testament. (I leave out of consideration, of course, those views which really have no system at all and believe in nothing but some vague fatalism and are utterly pessimistic).

And the real difference between the two views can be best expressed and understood if we consider what they have to say with regard to the whole question of progress. We shall confine ourselves solely to the three aspects of the question which are dealt with in our text and context.

The first aspect is the one which deals with the actual course of history, in a sense, from the mere standpoint of mechanics. The non-Christian view believes in a gradual and indeed an inevitable progress. It may sometimes describe the progress as being the result of the interaction of action and reaction, or of thesis and antithesis, but still it believes that there is within the world a principle at work which, slowly but surely, is leading steadily in the direction of an ultimate perfection. Every century, therefore, in a sense should mark an advance on that which went before it, and everything which has happened has, in some way or other, contributed to the general advance. The trend is upwards and the ultimate destiny or goal is perfection. Standing diametrically opposed to this is the New

Testament teaching as shown here. It teaches a system which is marked by crisis and judgment rather than by what, in another connection, has been termed 'the inevitability of gradualism'. The course of the world and its history is so much in the downward direction that it leads to events such as the Flood, the destruction of Sodom and Gomorrah, the destruction of Jerusalem and, ultimately, to the destruction of the world itself, all of which are expressive of the judgment of God upon sin and wrong-doing. And, for the more positive side, were it not for critical interventions into, and actual interruption of and interference with, the history of the world, that history would long since have come to an end. That is the first point of difference.

The second has reference to the question of the respective places of God and man in the process of history. According to the non-Christian view the really active agent is man. God is either a passive spectator, or else He is mainly concerned to encourage us and to direct us and to give us His help and His aid. It is man that really matters, and even when they talk of 'the divine spark in man' the real emphasis is upon the fact that man has the divine spark in him, rather than that the divine spark should be in man. This view believes in man, in his powers and ability, and history is what man does and what man is going to do. The Bible, on the other hand, is a record and account, essentially, of what God has done and what God is going to do. It does not brush man aside altogether, for after all God's action is not only upon man but often-times through man. But the emphasis is on God. God as Creator! God as Judge! God as Saviour! God as the one who manipulates history according to His own Sovereign will from the outside. History, to the Bible, therefore, is not so much what man has done as what God has done to and about man. And, as our Lord shows here, the big things are His coming, His dying and His coming again. That is the history that really matters, that is the only history that will matter. Man may do many things – but one thing really counts, the coming of the Son of Man in all the glory of His kingdom to usher in the end of all history.

The third respect in which we are anxious to compare these views is with regard to their view of the condition or the nature of man as it is affected by the process of history. To the non-Christian view there is nothing which is so striking in the process of history, and nothing in which it glories so much, as the way in which man has been steadily improving. There is nothing in which they delight so much as to compare primitive man with the man of today. The whole idea and assumption is that, as the centuries pass, man as a being is reaching higher and higher, and ever leaving behind him things which are unworthy, and ever stretching out towards a condition of entire perfection. As time passes, therefore, it must follow of necessity that the world becomes an increasingly better and nobler place and that those things which formerly used to disgrace mankind and its history just vanish and disappear altogether. Man, according to that view, becomes increasingly better and better.

Nowhere is the complete and utter denial and contradiction of that position stated more clearly and categorically than in these words uttered by our Lord Himself which we have taken as our text tonight. Listen to them again: 'As it was in the days of Noe, *so* shall it be also in the days of the Son of man'. And again, '*Likewise* also as it was in the days of Lot ... *even thus* shall it be in the day when the Son of man is revealed'. Do you appreciate the true significance of that? Our Lord goes back to the very dawn of history – not a mere few hundred years but right back almost to the beginning. And His astonishing, indeed astounding, statement is that at the very end of time, whenever that may be, men and women will still remain essentially what they were at the beginning. How we like to boast of the great advance of mankind even during the past one hundred years! According to our Lord, man is still essentially what he was four and five thousand years ago, and ever will remain the same. And it is here that we see most clearly that the real difference between the two views of history is the difference between a superficial and a deep

[284]

view. All kinds of changes and differences are certainly to be seen on the surface of man's life. He makes, and has made and will undoubtedly yet make many advances in the realm of secular knowledge and scientific discovery; he dresses differently, and culturally he may well be less uncouth and altogether more polished. But, in spite of all that, he remains in his essential nature, deep down in his being, precisely what he always has been, and sooner or later, in some shape or form, that fact will ever be revealing itself. Those who merely look at the surface of life and of the world, therefore, are always confident and optimistic about man and, when confronted by a situation like the present one, are left baffled and without an explanation. Those, on the other hand, who take the deep view, the Christian view, realize that there is nothing better to expect, and that while man's nature remains essentially the same, in some way or other it must continually give rise to the same manifestations of itself. But our Lord, here, is concerned to emphasize the root principle which gives rise to all the varied manifestations, the root principle which ultimately is responsible for all the ills of mankind. And that is what can be described most accurately by the word 'worldliness' or 'worldly-mindedness'. It is this attitude or state of mind and of heart which has characterized mankind from the beginning, which still characterizes it today, and which will continue to characterize it, that accounts for all its trials and its tragedies. Here is the cause of the ultimate doom of the world – the end of all things.

Have you realized all this? And have you realized that it is no mere question of theoretical interest, but one which concerns you vitally. According to our Lord there are only two groups of people – those who are in this condition of worldly-mindedness and those who are not. And their ultimate fate depends entirely upon that fact. The worldly will share the fate of the people before the flood, and the people of Sodom and Gomorrah. The others belong to the group containing Noe and his family, and Lot – the saved. To which group do you belong?

In order to assist you in arriving at an answer to the

question, I propose to consider with you some of the main characteristics of this condition as they are exposed and revealed in our text. Our Lord chooses as His examples the people before the flood and the people who inhabited the cities of the plain. An account of these people is given clearly in the book of Genesis and we are all familiar with it. Does not one thing strike you at once as being rather strange? Why is it that our Lord does not mention their wickedness, yes, their extreme sinfulness? He was well aware of all the facts and yet He chooses to emphasize just the aspect of worldliness and of worldly-mindedness without even mentioning the terrible list of foul and horrible things of which those people were guilty. Why is that? It is obviously done quite deliberately.

The answer is, of course, that our Lord, like the Bible everywhere, is concerned with causes and not with effects. The people before the flood, and those of Sodom, were guilty of many excesses and of many terrible actions. But the vital question is, why were they so guilty? What was it in them that ever made them do such things? The answer is, that it is all due to a particular state of mind – the state of mind called worldliness. How exactly and precisely that manifests itself does not really matter in an ultimate sense – what counts is the disposition. Now this is a vitally important distinction which is often forgotten but which ought to be quite familiar to us if only because we see it so often in other spheres and realms of life. Let me give a few illustrations. Some people express their joy by noise and boisterousness, others become silent when really happy. Some men in a state of intoxication are noisy and querulous, others are quiet and reasonably affable. But both are drunk. Some people are very demonstrative in the matter of their affections, their likes and dislikes. But we know full well that they have not of necessity a greater degree of love and affection in their hearts than those who are more reserved and stolid. And so on. Now the Bible, and our Lord here, teach that very principle. With our false view of man and of history we look merely upon the surface and are interested primarily in actions. Our Lord teaches that God looks upon the heart. Some men guilty of worldliness go to great extremes and become violent, but that is simply their particular way of expressing that which sometimes can express itself in exactly the opposite manner and at time be highly respectable as judged by human standards.

It is very important therefore that, as we come to consider whether we are in this condition of worldliness, we should do so in terms of what our Lord emphasizes as sin, and not what we regard as sin. According to Him this condition manifests itself in the following ways.

First of all, worldliness ignores the highest part of man's nature and lives only for that which is lowest.

Before the Flood we are told that 'they did eat, they drank, they married wives, they were given in marriage'. Likewise in the days of Lot, 'they did eat, they drank, they bought, they sold, they planted, they builded'. Now clearly all these are activities which are not only legitimate but really essential to life. There is nothing wrong in them in and of themselves, and as such they are quite innocent and harmless. Why are they singled out then? The answer to that is, in a sense, the whole story of the Bible, the whole story of man and his troubles. God made man according to a certain plan and pattern. He made man in His own image and endowed him with certain gifts and powers. He made him body, soul and spirit and desired that each of these parts of man's nature and make-up should be developed and find adequate expression. That man should eat and drink was something planned by God Himself, who gave man what we call the body, or the animal part of his nature. To that end God provided food and drink that man should be satisfied in that respect. God also desired that man should live a communal life and that he should enjoy the blessings and pleasures of creation with others. So God decreed and ordained marriage and the family and various other common activities and pursuits in life. He thereby catered for and provided for the soul of man. 'Eating and drinking, marrying and giving in marriage, buying and selling, planting and building'. Yes, these things are perfectly legitimate and it is nothing but a false and un-Christian asceticism that condemns them. Why then does our Lord single them out here and hold them forth as the kind of life that leads to disaster? You must, surely, see the answer. These things are all right in their proper place, but when they become the be-all and end-all of life they are in the wrong place. God made man body, soul and spirit and provided for each. Those who live only for the body and the soul, and entirely ignore the spirit, are leaving out of consideration God's highest and greatest gift to man, and living only for the lowest. That was the trouble with those ancient people. They gave themselves utterly and entirely to the things which our Lord catalogues. They had no other interest in life. That was all, that was everything – eating, drinking, marriage and the family, business and pleasure. Not a thought of the spirit, of their higher nature, no time given to the cultivation of God's highest gift to man.

I stated it as a general principle in my introduction that the Bible teaches that man's essential nature still remains the same. Do not these words prove that contention to the very hilt? Might not what is said of the people before the flood, and of the people of the cities of the plain, be said with equal accuracy of the men and women of today? Indeed, I can imagine no more perfect description of this present generation. It is unusually and exceptionally true of it and that in detail. Eating and drinking certainly play a larger part in the lives of the people than they have done for generations. Eating and drinking have become ends in themselves, and are frequently the main topic of conversation. Marrying and giving in marriage, yes, settling down in life and regarding creature comforts as being more important than anything else. Buying and selling, business and money-making in order to have still more comfort and pleasure! 'Planting' yes, and 'building'! What a perfect description of this present generation which lives for these things – comfort and enjoyment, wealth and pleasure. What a perfect account of life today in town and city, suburb and country. Is it not clear that men and women live for these things – their families and their homes, their wireless sets, their motor cars, their newspapers and their clubs, their pleasures, games and entertainments? These things, plus work or occupation, engage the whole of the average man's life, and work itself, is definitely regarded as an inevitable nuisance which robs us of so much of the time that we would prefer to spend in other ways. 'Eating and drinking, marrying and giving in marriage, buying and selling, planting and building' – what was true five thousand years ago is still true today. But what of you, my friend? How much of your time do you give to thought about your spirit, your higher nature? How much of your time do you give to its cultivation and its development? Are you satisfied merely with that life that caters only for the body and the soul or do you feel a sense of divine discontent? Are you dissatisfied with your life, are you struggling after something better and higher, and would you even sacrifice much food and drink, money and pleasure and all else for the sake of that higher life? Do you crave for just more and more of that worldly life and do you envy those who can afford to have it with greater freedom than yourself? Or do you long for something bigger and vaster, something spiritual, something eternal in its very essence? Have you seen through the unutterable smallness, shallowness and animal nature of the popular life of the world? Do you realize that God made you for something bigger and that it is an insult to Him to ignore His greatest gift to you? What utter folly to boast of our advances when nothing is so clear as the fact that the ambitions of all classes, rich and poor, educated and ignorant, are still the same as those of these ancient people – eating and drinking, marrying and giving in marriage, buying and selling, planting and building'.

The second characteristic of that type of life is that it ignores the next world and lives only for, and in terms of, this present world.

The graphic words that our Lord uses bring out this

point very clearly. They lived that kind of life 'until the day
that Noe entered into the ark, and the flood came and
destroyed them all'; right until the day that Lot went out of
Sodom. The very lilt of the words suggests this – 'eating
and drinking, marrying and giving in marriage'. Not only is
it essentially a low kind of life, it is also essentially lazy and
limited. But I would not over-emphasize that aspect, as
there is also in it an element of arrogant self-satisfaction
and self-sufficiency. We have but to read these ancient
accounts to see once more how little the world has changed
in that respect also. How easy it is to see those people
priding themselves on the life they lived. How wonderful
life seemed in Sodom! It had its smart set, its fashions and
its things to do, precisely as they are to be found today.
And most people wanted to go to the cities to see life,
precisely as they do today. The life of the shepherd was
despised; the great thing to do was 'to go to town', to walk
up and down the streets, to laugh and talk, to enjoy the
sights and have the pleasures. How happy and how carefree
it all seems! How thrilling, how wonderful! Never a
thought about anything, and especially never a thought
about any possible end to all this! Hand to mouth, from
day to day! But again I must be careful, because once more
the arrogant elements come in. For they all had the feeling,
really, that that kind of life was to be permanent. Hence the
planting and the buying and selling, and especially the
building. They were settling down to enjoy life and to
make it as permanent as they could. They never thought
about any life or any world save this. The only future that
ever gained their attention was a future which meant the
perpetuation of their present life. Need I point out the
exceptionally close and almost perfect analogy to the life of
today? Business and pleasure, work and play, my house, my
motor car and all those other things, why should this kind
of life not go on for ever? What is there to stop it, with all
our hire-purchase systems, our health schemes, and all
our wonderful modern advances? Why trouble to think
about the future? And especially, why think about the end
and the next world, when this world and this life are so

wonderful? Why take a rest and step out of the game now and again, and consider whither it is all leading? Why think, when thinking only gives rise to misgivings and tends to make us miserable and unhappy? Carry on! And they did carry on in the old world ... 'until the flood came and destroyed them all'.

Men and women are still thus carrying on. They are sure that there can be no more war, because we have advanced so much ... 'until' war actually breaks out. We are sure that as the result of modern science there can be no more pestilences and outbreaks of diseases ... 'until' the epidemic of typhoid fever is actually upon us. We are sure, and will remain sure, that there is no God and no after-life and judgment 'until' we find ourselves standing actually in His presence, or rather failing to stand and desiring to hide our faces from Him. What of you, my friend? How are you living? Do you ever envisage the end of your life on the face of this earth? Do you ever think of eternity beyond the grave? Do you ever try to prepare yourself for it and to make provision for it? No! I am not suggesting that you should retire out of life and spend a morbid, miserable life of introspection in a cell or a cave! By all means, eat and drink, marry and give in marriage, buy and sell, plant and build, and enjoy every good and every perfect gift that God in His infinite grace has given to us men and for our enjoyment – yes, do all that, but do not live for it, do not be absorbed by it, do not be mastered by it, above all, never live by it and for it. Realize that you have an immortal spirit within you, that you are but a passing stranger in this present world and that soon you will be in the next world and face to face with God. It is upon people who fail to realize all this that sudden calamity and swift destruction descend, leaving them utterly confounded. Do not be misled by the world and all its glamour, its 'lust of the flesh and the lust of the eyes, and the pride of life' for all this 'shall pass away' and you with it. 'The things that are seen are temporal, but the things that are not seen are eternal'. Can you thank God that that is so?

But after all what shows how utterly blind this worldly type of life is is the way in which *it ignores God and His gracious warnings and offers of deliverance.* Once more I would indicate that man's nature does not change. There is nothing which is quite so pathetic as the way in which men ignorantly imagine that godlessness and irreligion are something new and the particular glory of this enlightened twentieth century. The fact is, of course, that there is nothing which is quite so old. It has always been the cause of the downward trend in the history of mankind, always the cause of every critical intervention of God in judgment in some shape or other – the cause of the flood, the cause of the destruction of Sodom and Gomorrah, the cause of the destruction of Jerusalem in the Old Testament days and again in AD 70. And it will be the cause of the final judgment of all things when 'The Son of man will be revealed' in all His glory, and the end of all history and time will have arrived. Irreligion and godlessness should never cause a true Christian to be pessimistic or to be filled with doubt as to whether the gospel is true or not after all. For it has all been predicted. Was it not our Lord Himself in another place who, in the form of a question, says precisely what He says here. 'When the Son of man cometh, shall He find faith on the earth?' (Lk 18:8) By being godless and irreligious, men are not only continuing to be what they have always been but, further, they are verifying prophecy and fulfilling our Lord's predictions.

But I do not desire to dwell on that aspect, but rather to call your attention to the tragedy of it all. Men, in rejecting God, only spite themselves. In ignoring His warnings and His offers they only ensure their own utter misery and damnation. For in spite of all that we have seen to be so true of man, God has not turned His back upon him. Had human history been nothing but the story of man and of man's effort alone, it would have degenerated to perdition and putrefaction long ago. But, blessed be the Name of God, such is not the case! In spite of all the sin and arrogance of man, God has not ceased to love and God has not ceased to be active. He has looked upon earth and seen

[292]

its pity and its sorrow and its inevitable end. He has warned man. He sent Noah and instructed him to preach repentance and righteousness to the people, to call them to give up their sins and turn to God lest destruction come upon them. He instructed Noah to build his ark and thereby warn the people. Later, with the cities of the plain, he used the man whom Peter describes as 'just Lot' to preach to the people, to turn them in a like manner, and to plead with them to reform and turn to God before it was too late. God did all that, and He continued to do so right through the Old Testament dispensation through His law, His prophets and in many other ways. They all pleaded with the people to flee from the wrath to come and to turn to God. But finally He sent His only begotten Son, Jesus of Nazareth, the One who spoke the words we have been considering together. He not only warned and preached righteousness and called to repentance – He did infinitely more. Noah could only build an ark and urge repentance, Lot could go no further. But here is One who makes a way out. He not only exposes the sin, but atones for it by bearing its punishment. He talks here about 'suffering many things and being rejected of that generation'. And it happened to Him. He was rejected, He was despised, He was crucified and killed. But by that very death He was preaching pardon and forgiveness for all who believe in Him. Noah could only preach righteousness and show His belief in God by building the ark, Lot could go no further. But here is One who pleads the merit of His blood, here is One who says, not 'Save yourselves' but, 'I have died to save you'.

We have all sinned against God, we all merit punishment. We have forgotten Him, ignored Him, disregarded His way of life and tried to please ourselves. All that merits punishment and will most certainly be punished. A time is coming when Christ will return to judge the world and all its people. He Himself has given the warning. But He Himself also has provided the way of escape, the way of salvation. He offers free pardon, however deep and great our sin, a new beginning and a new life. Those who ignore and reject all this, and live simply for this world and its life, can expect nothing and deserve nothing but doom. But those who accept can and will look forward to the day of His coming. For when He comes they shall see Him; more, they shall be made like unto Him and they shall live and reign with Him for evermore. In which of the two companies will you be? Decide now by listening to Him and giving yourself to Him. Amen.